By the Students and Staff
of Georgia-Cumberland Academy

TEACH Services, Inc.
PUBLISHING
www.TEACHServices.com • (800) 367-1844

World rights reserved. This book or any portion thereof may not be copied or reproduced in any form or manner whatever, except as provided by law, without the written permission of the publisher, except by a reviewer who may quote brief passages in a review.

The author assumes full responsibility for the accuracy of all facts and quotations as cited in this book. The opinions expressed in this book are the author's personal views and interpretations, and do not necessarily reflect those of the publisher.

This book is provided with the understanding that the publisher is not engaged in giving spiritual, legal, medical, or other professional advice. If authoritative advice is needed, the reader should seek the counsel of a competent professional.

Copyright © 2015 TEACH Services, Inc.
ISBN-13: 978-1-4796-0644-3 (Paperback)
Library of Congress Control Number: 2015919928

New International Version (NIV): Holy Bible, New International Version®, NIV® Copyright ©1973, 1978, 1984, 2011 by Biblica, Inc.® Used by permission. All rights reserved worldwide.
New American Standard Bible (NASB): Copyright © 1960, 1962, 1963, 1968, 1971, 1972, 1973, 1975, 1977, 1995 by The Lockman Foundation
English Standard Version (ESV): The Holy Bible, English Standard Version Copyright © 2001 by Crossway Bibles, a publishing ministry of Good News Publishers.
New Living Translation (NLT): Holy Bible. New Living Translation copyright© 1996, 2004, 2007, 2013 by Tyndale House Foundation. Used by permission of Tyndale House Publishers Inc., Carol Stream, Illinois 60188. All rights reserved.
Good News Translation (GNT): Copyright © 1992 by American Bible Society
New King James Version (NKJV): Scripture taken from the New King James Version®. Copyright © 1982 by Thomas Nelson. Used by permission. All rights reserved.
Easy-to-Read Version (ERV): Copyright © 2006 by Bible League International
The Voice (VOICE): The Voice Bible Copyright © 2012 Thomas Nelson, Inc. The Voice™ translation © 2012 Ecclesia Bible Society All rights reserved.
New English Translation (NET): NET Bible® copyright ©1996-2006 by Biblical Studies Press, L.L.C. http://netbible.com All rights reserved.
World English Bible (WEB): by Public Domain. The name "World English Bible" is trademarked.
GOD'S WORD Translation (GW): Copyright © 1995 by God's Word to the Nations. Used by permission of Baker Publishing Group
Holman Christian Standard Bible (HCSB): Copyright © 1999, 2000, 2002, 2003, 2009 by Holman Bible Publishers, Nashville Tennessee. All rights reserved.
King James Version (KJV) by Public Domain
The Message (MSG): Copyright © 1993, 1994, 1995, 1996, 2000, 2001, 2002 by Eugene H. Peterson
Living Bible (TLB): The Living Bible copyright © 1971 by Tyndale House Foundation. Used by permission of Tyndale House Publishers Inc., Carol Stream, Illinois 60188. All rights reserved.
New Century Version (NCV): The Holy Bible, New Century Version®. Copyright © 2005 by Thomas Nelson, Inc.
The Clear Word: Copyright ©2003 by Jack J. Blanco. All rights reserved

Published by

www.TEACHServices.com • (800) 367 1844

Acknowledgements

Parents in Support of GCA (PSGCA) is an organization that supports the students, staff and families of Georgia-Cumberland Academy (GCA). We elected to spearhead GCA's first devotional book, believing that it will be an inspiration to our students.

There are numerous people who were involved in the development of *To Know, To Love, To Serve*. Without their participation this book would not exist, and they deserve recognition for the time and talents they shared.

The GCA English department, consisting of Kimberly Carr, Nick Sigler, Patricia Muriel and Dori Boggess, took valuable time in their classes to teach our students how to write their devotionals.

Nancy Gerard incorporated staff and alumni participation, and was an integral part of the project from its inception to publication.

The wonderful GCA support staff helped in a variety of ways. Randy Kelch kept us connected with the technology needed. Jim Lewellen created a way to place online book orders on the GCA home page. Deborah Theus and Susan Jenkins assisted in the business office as we dealt with book sales. Patti Speer helped us stay in touch with the parents.

McKenzie Martin and Jes Rosales, our student editors, put in long hours editing many of the submissions.

Kalie Kelch wrote the text for the back cover. Her administrative assistance was also invaluable in several stages of the book.

The cover design was a result of Nick Sigler's input. Photos were taken by Skylar Jacobs and Laura Dancek.

The copy editing team of Greg Hudson, Josh Woods, Nancy Gerard, Shannon Scott, and Doris Starkey were an enormous help, dedicating many hours of work in a short period of time to make the project a success.

Sue and Timothy Hullquist, owners of TEACH Services, Inc. were wonderful to work with as publishers, and were consistently reassuring and helpful throughout the entire process.

The members of the PSGCA leadership team helped with sales and distribution: Donna and Tony Baumann, Ed Dancek, Melinda and Todd Goodman, Noelle and Deryl Holland, Chichi and Chuck Onyeije, Shannon and Derin Scott, and Marsharee and Todd Wilkens.

More than anyone else, we want to thank the authors who contributed to this book. Your testimonies will add to our readers' understanding of what it means to know, to love, and to serve. We are grateful for your wiliness to courageously share.

— Laura Dancek
Leader, Parents in Support of GCA

Foreword

Every once in a while you read something that strikes you. Some call those moments an epiphany. For whatever reason, your past, your temperament, your hopes, and your fears come up against a statement or a story, and it grabs you. At times the story or the thoughts you read might cause you to make a major decision in your life.

When I was a young teenager, I was struggling to understand what it means to live as a Christian. I did not feel that I was accepted by God. It took almost no time of self-reflection for me to confirm that I certainly didn't act like a good Christian or Adventist. Others spoke of feelings of acceptance, love, and joy in their spiritual lives. My spiritual life had all of the excitement and meaning of a dirty sock.

I read my Bible. I didn't enjoy it. I listened to sermons in church. They mostly scared or bored me. The reality was – I was basing whether or not God accepted me upon how I felt. My human emotions, which changed by the minute, were my measure of whether following Jesus made any sense.

In my attempt to figure it out, I started reading the book *Steps to Christ*. All of a sudden, on page 51, I read the words that Ellen White wrote over 80 years earlier—words that seemed to be written especially for me: "Do not wait to feel that you are made whole, but say, "I believe it; it is so, not because I feel it, but because God has promised."

Those words have carried me through many dark times in my Christian walk when I didn't feel like, or act like, the Adventist I professed to be. Words or stories can change our lives. God can use the words and thoughts of this devotional book to help you in ways you can't imagine.

The words of Scripture, the words of pastors and teachers, and the words of friends can help all of us better understand God's love for us. The mission of Georgia-Cumberland Academy begins with this concept—"To know Jesus as Savior and friend." We come to know someone by talking, listening and reading. "To love God and the people He brings into our lives." As we come to know Jesus, our love for Him grows. And as a result of that growth of love, we will want to "Serve the needs of society and the church."

So don't put this book down—read it. Put off other stuff that is less important, and read the words, thoughts and experiences of the students of GCA that are captured in this book. Perhaps there is something in this book that will change your life.

— Gregory A. Gerard, Ed.D.
Principal, Georgia-Cumberland Academy

Above All Else
To Serve

You shall fear the Lord your God. You shall serve him and hold fast to him, and by his name you shall swear.
(Deuteronomy 10:20, ESV)

As we near the end of time, we will be greatly tested. Our faith will be tested at the cost of our salvation. It may not come in the way of having to stand in front of thousands at gunpoint to proclaim your faith. It may come in the form of an unbelieving friend asking you to go to the movies Friday night or Sabbath afternoon. Whatever the case, we must hold fast and serve God above all other desires.

I find confrontation very awkward. I will try to avoid it all costs, but there is a time when you need to step up and voice your belief.

One day while I was talking to a friend, the subject of our beliefs and religion came up. He is homosexual and found it hard to accept the Seventh-day Adventist message, because he didn't want to admit that what he was doing was a sin according to the Bible. I love this friend and didn't want to say anything that might be too personal and hinder our friendship. I had to decide: "Do I stand up for what I believe in, or do I just let it go so as to not risk my friendship?"

I was reminded of a text in the Bible where Jesus told His disciples a parable. Christ was showing us that if we couldn't be trusted in small things, how could we be trusted in the bigger things? So I decided I had to voice my belief concerning his homosexuality. I'm not going to say it was easy and that his response was that of accepting, but with Christ's help I was able to stand up for Him, and that's all that mattered. "I have said these things to you, that in me you may have peace. In the world you will have tribulation. But take heart; I have overcome the world (John 16:33, ESV)

— Javiera Alquinta, Class of 2018

Staying Constant
To Know

Seek the LORD and his strength; seek his face continually.
(1 Chronicles 16:11, KJV).

Do you ever have those moments? Like, those moments where you feel the Holy Spirit is working in you? That moment when all your worries vanish and you feel so content with God that nothing really bothers you because Jesus is the answer to all of life's problems? The name of that feeling is called being on a spiritual high and for most people it comes by surprise making you feel on top of the world with God. Then, after that amazing time of just feeling right next to God everything goes back to normal and the feeling of fulfillment disappears. Eventually, the moment leaves you but gives you the longing desire to again reach the same level of contentment.

"What goes up must come down," said Sir Isaac Newton. Our relationship with God will never stay at the highest point. Trying to keep it there will only be harder because eventually it will just collapse. Of course, not doing anything at all will lead us to separation from Him. So what should we do if keeping it high all the time isn't the answer? Stay constant. We need to learn to have a constant connection with God. For example, when you first meet someone you can't just say he or she is your new friend. You actually have to spend time with that person and make an effort to get to know them better. God is the same way. We have to make an effort to seek Him and get to know Him for ourselves. No one can show you the perfect way to walk with God. It's a personal experience that needs to grow on a daily basis. Finding new ways to make your relationship with God exciting is a way of helping you want to learn more about Him. God will be with you in the times you don't feel Him and even in the times you feel Him the most. He wants us to know Him better so when those highs come to an end we are able to get back on track and keep constant with God.

— Gabriela Alvarez, Class of 2018

Knowing God
To Know

Fear not, for I am with you; be not dismayed, for I am your God; I will strengthen you, I will help you, I will uphold you with my righteous right hand. (Isaiah 41:10, ESV)

When I was young, about ten, my family and I took a vacation to Puerto Rico. One of my favorite places was a natural waterslide. It was a cool, slanted waterfall with a natural slide look, perfect for sliding down. I rode down it at least a hundred times. After that, there was a beautiful swimming hole, right near a small waterfall. This waterfall was about 7 feet tall. I, in my ambitious 10-year-old mind, decided that I was going to jump off the waterfall. As I got close to the waterfall, I began to feel a suction towards it, but I paid no attention to it, because the water wasn't over my head; I could walk. Eventually, the water got really deep, and pretty soon I lost my footing and slipped. Now the water was over my head and I was getting sucked into the waterfall. I freaked out, and sent a short, anxious prayer: "God, save me!" Just as I was about to get sucked under water, my foot caught on a rock and I was able to use it to push myself out of the suction of the waterfall and get back to the safety of the swimming hole.

Before I even went on the trip to Puerto Rico, God knew that I was going to ask Him to save me. He was there with me the entire time. He knew that when I needed Him the most, He was going to save me. God is always with us, and He wants us to ask Him into our lives. He will always help us in any way that we need Him to. All we have to do is ask. There is no reason you should ever be afraid to ask God help you.

Pray and ask God to help you with the small things and the big things. Don't leave anything out; let Him involve Himself with every aspect of your life.

— Dylan Anderson, Class of 2017

Letting Go
To Love

And he said to him, "You shall love the Lord your God with all your heart and with all your soul and with all your mind. (Matthew 22:37, ESV)

To love God is to know Him. I had a wonderful experience at Cohutta Springs. I met some amazing people who really showed me who God is. I have never met nicer people. I had a lot of anger and hate inside me; not against people, just against God. I had always heard God loves you!!! But because of some things that had happened in my life, I didn't see that God loved me. And then it really clicked.

I could never let go of my bad feelings until one night as we were all talking in a group I stood up talked about it. I felt as if when I was talking about it God was just pulling it out of me, and it didn't go back in. All of a sudden I felt better and this peace came over me. I heard that nothing bad comes from God. Only good comes from God. I was only there for a week and I really believe that I fell in love with God. His power is amazing. He showed me that I could let go of all of that baggage that I was holding on to and all the hate that I had inside.

It's like when Peter saw Jesus walking on the water and he got out and started walking towards Jesus. When he got distracted and lost faith, he started to sink. Then Jesus came and scooped him up. That was me. I saw God in other people, but not completely. I semi-believed. I was sinking deeper and deeper until that night when Jesus came and scooped me up. I am safe and I feel as if I am walking on the water with Jesus.

"Anyone who does not love does not know God, because God is love." (1 John 4:8, ESV)

— Rain Anderson, Class of 2018

Nashipae
To Serve

My brethren, count it all joy when you fall into various trials, knowing that the testing of your faith produces patience. But let patience have its perfect work, that you may be perfect and complete, lacking nothing. (James 1:2-4, NKJV)

Not long after arriving in Narok for a practicum with World Vision Kenya, my friend and colleague Brian bestowed upon me a Maasai name. He told me I should be called Nashipae (pronounced naw-sheep-eye), and so thrilled at the prospect of being invited into such a lovely and intriguing culture as the Maasai, it didn't even occur to me to ask if the name had a particular meaning. I was just happy to be doing valuable work in Africa while earning my master's in community development. It wasn't until weeks later when I first visited a small Maasai village to perform trainings, and proudly introduced myself as Nashipae to the listening crowd, that the name was met with smiles and laughter.

"Do you know what that name means?" the translator asked me, smiling broadly.

"Ummm, well, no," I admitted.

"It means joyful one."

This wasn't the last time I would have it translated for me. Each English-speaking Maasai that I confronted from that point forward was eager to explain my name to me. I was told on numerous occasions that this name was well-suited.

"Your name fits you exactly," Isaac said after a training one day.

"Who gave you your name? They chose well." Robinson commented.

I was proud of my name. I loved introducing myself to my Maasai neighbors and friends as Nashipae, waiting for the translation to come, and smiling at the response.

But I have to admit that it wasn't a name that was always easy to live with. While I had fallen deeply in love with Kenya, the Rift Valley, and the Maasai people, not every moment of the journey was a joy-filled one. In many ways, it was the hardest summer of my life, made even harder by the distance from my family and friends. My heart took a serious beating, and I spent hours praying the same prayers for emotional healing, and for the courage and patience to truly trust God with my life and future.

Healing from heartbreak is never easy, and I had to do so while feeling disconnected from everything that felt normal and comfortable.

Yet, I am joy-filled. I embody a name that I think was given to me not only by Brian; I think God had a hand in my christening. He knew that though I might be struggling, I would also be filled with His incredible and engulfing peace. He knew that I might need a friendly reminder of the fruits of the spirit He is growing in me. He knew that I never would fully be able to turn off my smile towards the children who call to me on the street, running forward with outstretched hands ready to greet me with anticipation. He knew that no matter how difficult my day had been, that the moment I arrived in the village to work with the community I would immediately forget myself and my troubles and become absorbed in the honest and inspiring story of those I was working with.

It isn't always easy living up to the legacy that God has called us to. I have fallen short probably hundreds of times this summer alone when I chose to allow my own sorrow to overshadow the joy He has given to me. And yet, I have been told to count it all joy when I fall into various trials, knowing that the testing of my faith produces patience. Let patience have its work, so that I might be perfect and complete, lacking nothing. (James 1:2–4)

And now, as I adjust back to life, missing the place where I have so clearly seen God working in me and around me, I am excited to see how God guides me through every stage. I am counting it all joy.

I am Nashipae.

— Jordan Arellano, Class of 2009

High Flying
To Know

And we know that all things work together for good to those who love God, to those who are the called according to His purpose.
(Romans 8:28, NKJV)

It all started when I received the email notification that my flight from Kenya to Ethiopia had been changed to leave about 30 minutes after the original schedule. I had been living in East Africa for the last four months, studying for my master's in global community development, and I had fallen in love with Kenya. I was ready to be at home with my family and friends, but I also knew that I was leaving behind a memorable summer and some treasured friendships. Africa, as I discovered after my year as a student missionary in Chad, could be infectious. And I hoped I would be back again soon.

However, at the moment I received that email, a little twinge of fear took root in my heart, because now my layover in Ethiopia would be about forty-five minutes. As any traveler knows, anything can happen in 45 minutes and a brief delay could mean that my direct flight from Addis Ababa to Los Angeles would be a faint memory, not to mention the potential luggage malfunctions that could occur. But even after receiving the worrying email, I chose to not worry and trust that God would get me home in His time. So when I arrived at the Jomo Kenyatta airport on the evening of August 19, I was excited, slightly sad to be saying goodbye, but overall thrilled at the prospect of soon being in California to visit some of my dearest friends. Not only that, but this was to be my official first solo international travel. I have traveled internationally on several occasions with legs of the journey that were solo, but this was to be the first complete solo route.

I was extremely content with the friendly woman at the Ethiopian counter who put priority tags on my luggage, which reassured me that if I were to reach Ethiopia in time, my luggage would follow me all the way to L.A. I met and chatted with an extremely friendly Ethiopian gentleman who I discovered is a microfinance expert, an area of development that I know little about, but am very interested in. I recorded some of my last memories from Kenya and read my book. Finally, I boarded the flight in good spirits, and lovingly bid Kenya goodbye as the wheels lifted off the runway.

I was seated next to a sweet older Kenyan woman. We didn't speak much. I'm slightly ashamed to admit that I'm not always the friendliest traveler, often preferring to keep to myself, absorbed in a book or my own thoughts. But my cheerfulness on this flight encouraged me to even compliment my neighbor on her pretty scarf, and we briefly discussed the general coldness of planes.

I noticed, however, that as the short flight progressed, I slowly grew more and more nervous that I wouldn't be able to make it to my next flight, or my luggage would be lost. Or both. Or I would be alone and stranded in Ethiopia. Each time these thoughts would pop up, I would try to banish them with a prayer of trust, but they kept recurring, especially after I realized my layover was much closer to twenty minutes than forty-five. After what seemed like the slowest landing and exiting ever, we found ourselves all standing on the tarmac. Just standing. No bus or transport in sight. I looked under the plane, and to my relief, glimpsed my own suitcase set aside. Those priority stickers work wonders. But I was now more nervous for myself than my luggage.

At long last, the shuttle appeared, and I ended up standing next to a woman who was just as frantic as I was to board her flight to Hong Kong in twenty minutes. But who should appear on my other side but the sweet, old woman who had been my chatting buddy on the plane. In the probably five (but felt like thirty) minutes that it took to reach the terminal, I discovered that my little friend was also on her way to Los Angeles. I wish I could draw a picture to show you the look of pure delight that passed over her face when she discovered that I, an almost complete stranger, would be on her flight to LA. You can't fake joy like that. And my heart first rose with the sweet gesture, then plummeted as realization dawned on me. This incredibly sweet, old woman was in the same fix that I was. Her flight would also begin boarding in a few minutes, with the same distance of terminal to dash across that I did. As I looked at her, I felt like she might even need a wheelchair, a thought that she verbalized once we were inside.

"What on earth am I going to do with her?" I thought desperately to myself. In those intervening moments of decision we were briefly separated going up the escalator with what felt like a thousand other people. But by the time I reached the top, I had made my decision. We were in this together. Do or die, we were going to try to make it to our flight together. I briefly waited for her to reach the top of the escalator, asked if it was OK if I carried her carry-on suitcase (its wheels were broken, so it demanded full weight bearing) and we started off. For a woman who had just mentioned wanting a wheelchair, she was insanely fast. We darted through the crowd, me with my enormous backpack and her little suitcase clutched in my hands, her with her beautiful scarf and warm smile.

It's hard to describe my thoughts as I ran through the Addis Ababa airport at 11:00 p.m., extremely late for my flight, with an old Kenyan woman in tow. They were probably something close to this:

"How did this situation happen?"

"This is probably what Jesus would do, but I don't feel too saint-like at the moment."

"I thought I was on my first solo adventure!"

"This is honestly too hilarious and memorable to question whether it's a good idea or not."

And just like that, my thoughts were silenced as we reached the security line right in front of our gate. We could see the crowd of people lined up, ready to begin boarding. We had most certainly made it in time.

It wasn't until this point that we were really able to make each other's acquaintance. Her name is Julia, and she is going to LA to visit her son who lives there, and she will be there for an unforeseen amount of time. We discovered that our seats on the apparently enormous transcontinental flight were very close, and she exclaimed on several occasions, "It was all part of God's plan!"

As my heart rate slowed, and I was flooded with relief that we had actually made it to our flight, I was able to smile back at her just as broadly as she smiled at me and say, "It certainly was God's plan, wasn't it?"

— Jordan Arellano, Class of 2009

The Blessing
To Serve

For I was hungry and you gave me food, I was thirsty and you gave me drink, I was a stranger and you welcomed me, I was naked and you clothed me, I was sick and you visited me, I was in prison and you came to me. Then the righteous will answer him, saying, "Lord, when did we see you hungry and feed you, or thirsty and give you drink? And when did we see you a stranger and welcome you, or naked and clothe you? And when did we see you sick or in prison and visit you?" And the King will answer them, "Truly, I say to you, as you did it to one of the least of these my brothers, you did it to me." (Matthew 25:35–40, ESV)

As I type, I am still covered in sweat and dirt—the meager remains of what I've touched, smelled, and seen today. I couldn't wait to write it out. I didn't want to forget, though I'm not sure that I could if I tried. As a twenty-one-year-old student missionary in Bere, Tchad, I've experienced more in the last few months then I ever imagined. I have seen starving children and dirty hospital floors. I've tasted rice every single day. I've felt my head pounding and stomach clenching from malaria-induced fevers. I've heard French greetings, babies crying, and roosters crowing alongside the call to prayer at 4:00 a.m. announcing the new day. But of all the senses, today it was the smells that most captured my attention. I can still faintly discern bleach and soap that linger on my hands, and as I breathe them, my mind goes back over the last few hours.

I don't even know her name. It is likely in Nandjere, the local language, which I couldn't pronounce anyway so I didn't bother trying. My adoptive missionary mom, Tammy Parker, is a friend of hers. She used to come over to Tammy's house often to ask for food. She looks like she is ninety years old, but she is probably closer to seventy. Life is hard in Chad, and even more so in a remote village like Bere, so people age quickly and die young. She lives in a small dark hut much like my own, but unlike hers, mine doesn't look as if it hasn't been cleaned for as long as she's been alive. She hasn't been able to come to Tammy's house for a long time since her cataracts have almost blinded her and she can scarcely walk anymore. As in most cultures (not American, though) elders are regarded here with extreme respect and are cared for in the homes of their children—another good reason to have ten or twelve kids, I suppose. This woman, however, has been forgotten. Sure, she has a hut within her family compound, but they don't bother feeding her, washing her or her clothes, or even helping her move outside of the hut. Tammy comes by occasionally to give her food, but it doesn't last long.

Today Tammy felt inspired to help her. Her daughter Brichelle and I were so excited at the prospect, that we ended our tutoring session early and walked just outside of the hospital compound to where she lives. The only way I can think to describe her hut is that it was not fit for an animal. In America someone could be fined or imprisoned for keeping their dog in that sort of condition. We caught the rank smell of urine left on the floor because she was unable walk. The bed was made of sticks with a straw mat placed on top. When you touched the dingy mosquito net, puffs of dust would float out into the air. The corner of the room was the depository for random spare parts of everything you can imagine. Fetid water stood in pots. The "blanket" that she used to sleep on was brown, but there was no guessing as to its original color.

We started right away. Tammy and Naomi (the beautiful Tchadian translator who is a dear friend) helped her slowly shuffle over to a straw mat under a tree. The only people home were what I assumed to be grand- or great-grandkids. They shuffled about, drew in the dirt, and played games that looked something like jacks with rocks. As soon as we had her outside, we commenced to take everything else out, too. We disassembled the bed, piling up the sticks and bricks outside. We moved the few pots, mosquito nets, and other assorted trash that had piled up over years of neglect. When they started sweeping it was like a small dust storm brewing and billowing outside of the hut.

Next, Brichelle and I started with the mosquito nets. We slowly pulled up a gasoline container, that had the top cut off and a rope tied to it, out of the well again, and again, and again. My back ached, but it was the first time I'd felt so alive since I'd been here. We poured in a small amount of bleach with the nets in a bucket and let them soak. Then we rinsed it over and over until the water didn't become mud each time. Finally, we took the big block of soap that people use for washing *everything* (clothes, food, dishes, themselves), and scrubbed until the nets were almost white again. We did the same for the so-called blanket and some clothes. We soon rejoined Naomi in the hut where she had rinsed the cement floor with bleach water. It almost resembled a habitable place now, at least for Tchadian standards, and I was once again reminded of why I don't *completely* hate cleaning—seeing the change from dirty to clean is very rewarding.

Tammy sent Mundung over with some bricks that we were going to use to prop up her bed. Naomi reassembled the bed with a bit of effort, and carefully laid out each stick so that it would lie mostly flat. After placing the straw mat on top of the sticks, Naomi pulled out the clean sheet and pillow that Tammy had sent. They were so white I almost couldn't believe it. We replaced the usable items, retied the mosquito nets, and then came the most interesting part—the bath. Brichelle and I didn't help because we didn't want to invade her privacy, but Naomi would shout over the short wall of the bathing room the interesting things that were happening. When she soaped the white curly head, she could see tons of black bugs running for cover. She was thin—very, very thin.

Naomi dressed her in some new clothes that Tammy had provided. I almost laughed at the bright green Iowa shirt that she now sported, which clashed horribly with the African pattern skirt wrapped around her thin waist. She shuffled slowly back into her hut, and as she lay down on the clean white sheets she began whispering a blessing over us which Naomi translated. She prayed that God would always watch over us and give us a good life and that we would know of all the wonderful things God has accomplished through us. How could this woman, who had almost nothing, pray for God to bless us? I have everything in the world that I could want. She has literally nothing, including love and companionship. Yet she was so grateful that she tried to bless us with the very things she did not possess. Tears were sliding down her wrinkled brown face, and I choked back some tears of my own.

And so now I sit, the sweat drying on my back and forehead, and feeling like I've been a part of something so much bigger than myself. Today I thought I was going to be a blessing, but instead I am the one who has been blessed.

— Jordan Arellano, Class of 2009

Why Worship?
To Love

Though I speak with the tongues of men and of angels, but have not love, I have become sounding brass or a clanging cymbal.
(1 Corinthians 13:1, NKJV)

There has been much conflict over worship styles during my lifetime. Whether discussing the use of drama, percussion instruments, prerecorded music, guitars, video displays, sound effects—you name it—there are usually people available to weigh in on each end of the spectrum. If we go back far enough, we can find a time when there was conflict over the appropriateness of an organ and harmonized music in church. Those who are most passionate in these conflicts assume that there is a best way to worship, a *best* way to please God with our church service, and that we are to aim at getting as close as we can to this idealized formula in our worship planning.

For a moment, though, let's step back from the fray and ask, "Why worship at all?" In doing so, an immediate response is made to this question by a worship zealot from the right end of the worship spectrum, saying that God tells us to worship Him, and we have to do it right. If we might take one more step backwards, we might respectfully ask God directly, "Why?" I believe that God's response would be something like this:

"The reason is not *because I said so*. Moreover, it's not because I need your approval and praise to maintain My self-esteem. It has to do with the way I engineered your brain. Whenever you hold up another person in admiration, you gradually begin acting and thinking like that person—for good or for bad. This is why it's so important to keep good company. You become like the people you hang around. Since worship is the highest form of admiration, I'm counting on this process to change your thinking to be more like Mine. For it to work, though, you must freely choose. That's why it's somewhat meaningless to order others to worship Me, like old King Nebuchadnezzar did by having people worship him. By beholding Me, you will be changed into being like Me."

God's prompting us to worship Him is for the healing of our broken minds, not because He somehow needs an ensemble of His creatures incessantly chanting His praises. In the person of Jesus, God made it clear that He is humble and unassuming beyond comprehension—considering He's the architect of the universe and the biophysicist who engineered the human mind.

There's even more, though. If we are genuinely drawn to express admiration for God, not only will it begin to change us, but it will also inspire us to express genuine appreciation to those He brings into our lives. The expression of gratitude becomes contagious within our sphere of influence.

With all this in mind, how valuable is praise when it is forced or mindlessly given? Under these conditions, it's not much different than "a resounding gong or a clanging cymbal."

Father, through the revelation given us about You in the words, life, and death of Jesus, may our admiration for You blossom, prompting us to express praise for Your character through our ongoing dialog with You. May we also find ways of expressing admiration of the good we see in those around us. Amen.

— Larry Ashcraft, Class of 1977

If You Have Seen Me ...
To Know

If you have seen me, you have seen the Father. (John 14:9, CEV)

Jesus spoke these words almost 2,000 years ago, but we have yet to fully accept them as true. It's understandable as to why. We humans worship violence—from our movies, to our sports, to our electronic games. To us, might makes right, and we can't imagine might without violence. When Jesus walked among humans, He left no hints of being a violent person. Sometimes people cite the cleansing of the temple as an exception, but the fact that children were singing His praises right after this event excludes the possibility. The whip Jesus fashioned was to motivate the livestock to exit, not to hit people. Since Jesus gave no evidence of violence, many are forced to conclude that the Father can't be exactly like Him, for popular Christian theology requires a violent God. Mark Driscoll, former pastor of the Mars Hill mega church in Seattle, once said, "I cannot worship a guy I can beat up." And so it is with much of the rest of Christianity. We simply can't have the Father be non-violent like Jesus is.

Why is this? Why are we so inclined to cast the Father as violent? It has to do with forgiveness, or lack thereof. We Christians can usually manage to forgive an unrepentant person who has wronged us, but only as we rest in the thought of God eventually making this person pay for the wrong. Our whole sense of justice is supported by this assumption. If God weren't going to "get them" someday, then forgiveness would be out of reach for many, hence the need for a violent God.

Even popular blueprints of salvation invoke a god of violence. God has been offended by humans breaking His law, so Christ died to pay the price for the offense. Then we turn 180 degrees and call this payoff God's forgiveness, full and free. It's no wonder we have difficulty genuinely forgiving those who have wronged us. By beholding this kind of a god, we have changed into something similar.

To take the phrase, "sin pays its wage—death," at face value is far too simplistic for many. We must conscript God to pay out sin's wage, to violently meter an appropriate amount of punishment on our oppressors to satisfy *us*. Without this display of violence, we feel that justice hasn't been served.

How did we get into such a rut? How did we start seeing God as being violent like us? We've had much help from the father of lies, who realizes that if we truly know the Father as Jesus revealed Him to be, then he's lost the war for our souls. Lucky for us, though, God came and lived among us to show us exactly what He's like. Immanuel, God with us, made it so clear that violence is not one of His character attributes. God isn't the way His enemies have made Him out to be. He's exactly as Jesus revealed Him to be.

Father, heal our twisted views of You. Heal our violent tendencies. Help us view all the Bible stories through the lens of Jesus. May our characters be transformed by realizing that You are just like Him. Amen.

— Larry Ashcraft, Class of 1977

Be Still
To Love

Be still, and know that I am God; I will be exalted among the nations, I will be exalted in the earth! (Psalm 46:10, NKJV)

High school offers a lot of stress during the average four years of high school. A student will spend at least twenty-five all-nighters and over 1,000 hours studying for tests or finals.

It was during this time that I experienced one of the most spiritually altering points in my life. It was towards the end of my junior year, and I was desperately trying to pull my grades up because of my lack of trying during my freshman and sophomore years.

Relief came on our junior trip. It helped me take a step back and relax and it gave me a break from school. When I returned to school I found myself overwhelmed by school, gymnastics, and other extra-curricular activities. Before this point in my life I wasn't that close to God. Not that I didn't believe in Him, I just didn't talk to Him much. During my gymnastics show I did what I hadn't in a long time —I prayed for God to help me. He did and I had a good show. This shows me that no matter what, God is there and if you take the time to be still and know He is God, He will come and be there to help.

— Patrick Auge, Class of 2016

Lame Excuses
To Know

The fear of man lays a snare, but whoever trusts in the LORD is safe. (Proverbs 29:25, ESV)

I am a four-year senior at GCA and have loved my experience and enjoyed every moment of my time here. To be honest, though, my first two years were not as good as my last two. Some would have called me a hermit or a loner. I would stay in my room and not do anything. Don't get me wrong, I wasn't like the person who didn't know how to walk straight, let alone throw a football around. I liked sports and I would occasionally go play a game of soccer or football but I was more afraid of being judged or made fun of when I did. So instead I would stay in my room and do nothing.

Towards the end of my sophomore year my world history teacher/gymnastics coach approached me and asked me if I wanted to go to gymnastics practice that night. I had been in gymnastics in elementary school and really didn't want to do it again, so I refused and went back to my room and stayed there. Over that summer while I was working I saw him again, and he suggested that I try out for gymnastics when I got back to GCA. I again refused and said that I didn't want to. The summer came to an end and school started again. When I got back to GCA he asked me again if I wanted to come to tryouts that night and I said no. I gave the lame excuse of "I don't want to get injured" and wrote it off. We talked some more, and he suggested I go anyway. I did and I enjoyed myself, and for the first time in my high school career I felt like I belonged somewhere. I showed up the rest of the week, and by the end of the week, found myself truly wanting to make the team. I stayed up till three in the morning waiting for the roster and when it came out the next day I found myself on the team. Gymnastics has been the number one best decision that I have made during my time at GCA I found myself becoming the person I really wanted to be my first two years and am enjoying myself more than I could have ever dreamed my sophomore year.

I think of this as being like heaven. God keeps encouraging us to go and we keep coming up with lame excuses, such as, well I have friends here, or I like "some" sins, or could I just do this first. But when we actually talk to Him and "try out," we find that we belong there. By the end of our trying God out, we find ourselves waiting and wishing for Him to come back so that we can join Him in heaven where we truly belong. All it takes is for us to trust in Him.

— Patrick Auge, Class of 2016

Dependence on God
To Love

And we know that in all things God works for the good of those who love him, who have been called according to his purpose.
(Romans 8:28, NIV)

My parents divorced when I was three years old and moved several states away from each other. I don't remember them ever being together, but growing up I never really realized that my family was different. Then, in the seventh grade the stress of rarely seeing my mom and having to go between parents for holidays really started to bother me. I often wondered if their divorce was my fault, if I caused too much stress on their relationship and they felt the need to end it. I turned to self-harm and stopped eating as a way to block out those feelings. When I was physically hurting and wasting away, I couldn't worry about my home life. During these times I lost touch with God. Honestly, I don't remember if I ever had a relationship with Him, but I know that part of my life butchered whatever was left of it.

I would often wonder where my God was, because I could not see Him working in my life. But as I grow older I realize it's because I wasn't actually looking for Him. Not once did I cry out for His help, or ask for His guidance. I only thought of what I could do to improve my situation. I thought if He wanted me to have a better life, He would have provided it. But it is important to realize that God allows us to have bad experiences because it helps us grow and learn to lean on Him. It's our choice in those times to either ask Him for help or to blame Him. I chose to blame and ignore my Savior, and I have suffered for that choice. However, if we choose to ask God to help us through tough situations, if we lean on Him when we feel like there's no one else, then He will be our greatest rock. God is willing to help us no matter what we have done; all we have to do is ask. God can take any pain you have experienced or are experiencing and make something good come from it.

— Gabby Avendano, Class of 2015

Curious About Lip Balm
To Know

For all have sinned and fall short of the glory of God, and all are justified freely by his grace through the redemption that came by Christ Jesus. (Romans 3:23–24, NIV)

One time when I was seven, my parents, siblings, and I all went to a store. When we were ready to pay at the front, I saw a really cool lip balm that I liked. The curious side of me wanted to get it and put it on. Well, of course, as a curious little seven-year-old, I *had* to put it on, even though I was told many times never to open something new at a store. My parents finally noticed and they got upset. They sent me to the car with my mom until my dad got out of the store. I thought that opening the lip balm would be cool; that smelling it, and trying it on, wouldn't really do anything because I had seen many people doing it before. My parents didn't like what I had done so they punished me and sent me to the car.

Sometimes we just think to ourselves, "Oh, but they won't notice," or "It's okay, no one is watching you, go ahead, take it." That is what our enemy, Satan, wants. He wants us to fall into the trap of sinning. People who have a close connection with God have an easier time overcoming it.

Everyone sins or does something bad. Even though it is little, it is still a sin. We are being tempted by God's enemy, but if we ask God every morning to help us when we are about to sin, He will. If we are ever in a situation, like opening something at a store, stop wherever you are, send up a little prayer, and ask God to help you make the right decision. If you get to know God better, it is even better for you because you will have that special connection.

— Merlyn Balboa, Class of 2019

Doubting the Savior
To Know

The Lord is a refuge for the oppressed, a stronghold in times of trouble. Those who know your name trust in you, for you, LORD, have never forsaken those who seek you. Sing the praises of the Lord, enthroned in Zion; proclaim among the nations what he has done. (Psalm 9:9–11, NIV).

Coming to Georgia-Cumberland Academy had to be one of the most trying experiences in my life. My family was going through a lot of financial struggles that were affecting us in every aspect of our lives. Many times I found myself doubting the power of God even though I had read many Bible stories because I grew up in a Christian household. I hadn't had many experiences of seeing God do miracles in the present day, so I was very surprised when I saw the hand of God moving and handling every issue that came up. The money for my tuition came from places that I didn't know existed. The transportation came through so that we could have a ride up to GCA for orientation. Yet there was one more hurdle my family had to cross—we had no place to live. My family moved to Calhoun, Georgia, the very day school was to begin. One can imagine the stress and anxiety that we were put through. As soon as the day was over God had given my family a home ten minutes from GCA, and a vehicle.

Each time I doubted God, I had to remember that He would never leave me hanging. All that I had to do was hold onto Him and He would take care of all my problems.

There are times in life that we have doubts and we forget that there is a God who loves and cares for us. Sometimes we feel as if we have to handle everything on our own, and that can be very overwhelming. There is a reason the Bible has many texts about trusting in God. As humans going through day to day, we become stressed and feel alone. Constantly, we remind ourselves that we have a God that is there for us to protect us through difficulties in life. This will help us cope and be okay even when times are hard.

— Zemira Barnett, Class of 2016

God Is There
To Know

If I go up to the heavens, you are there; if I make my bed in the depths, you are there. If I rise on the wings of the dawn, if I settle on the far side of the sea, even there your hand will guide me, your right hand will hold me fast. (Psalm 139:8–10, NIV)

This summer I worked at the GCA business office. On my way to work one morning I was involved in a car accident. Someone didn't see me and hit the back left side of my car, right behind where I was sitting. I was by myself so I had no idea what to do. Somehow I remembered this one time my mom got into a slight fender bender and I remembered what she did. She had told the person to follow her to the nearest parking lot, so I did just that. Fortunately, the person who had hit me was very kind.

I knew I needed to call my parents, but just my luck, neither of them answered. I called my grandparents hoping and praying that they would answer the phone. They did and I explained everything. In the middle of that phone call my dad called me, and both of my parents made their way to where I was. A policeman came, filed the report, the car got fixed and everything was fine.

After the car accident, I immediately broke down, because I thought that I had disappointed my parents even though the accident wasn't my fault. I had just gotten the car at the beginning of this year, and I felt really bad about wrecking it. I wasn't injured and neither was the person who hit me, but I was emotionally injured. My dad assured me that all my parents cared about was me, and that I was all right. They said the car didn't matter as long as I was safe.

This really made me love God even more. He kept me safe when I was in trouble. I know He sent an angel to be right by my side in the car to make sure nothing happened to me. I also grew closer to my parents in this experience, and I think God knew that was something I needed. This whole experience led me to really get to know God and to know how He really does work in mysterious ways. He helped me get through the emotional damage and realize that everything really does happen for a reason.

If you're ever going through a time in your life where it seems as if God just isn't there and you don't know why He's letting horrible things happen to you, just pray. God is there and soon He will let you know. Just have faith that He will lead you through anything you're experiencing and that it will soon pass.

— Alexis Baumann, Class of 2017

Family Inspiration
To Serve

Future generations will serve him; they will speak of the Lord to the coming generation. (Psalm 22:30, GNT)

My family has been serving the Lord for two generations on both sides of my family. My mother's father served as a conference administrator for twenty-six years, and his wife worked as an executive secretary for twenty years. As a teacher, my mother has always been working in the Seventh-day Adventist church, as well as being a musician and trust services worker. As far as my mom's side is concerned, there is a lot of involvement in our conferences.

My dad and his mother have been in the ministry for a combined total of thirty-three years. When my grandmother worked in the Georgia-Cumberland Conference, she worked in the treasury department for twenty-three years. My dad, as well as my grandma, has also worked in the ministry since 1998. Not to be biased, but he is the best pastor that I've ever heard. He speaks with a passion that only God can give. I think that people can relate to him through the stories that he tells of his childhood. Instead of just reciting the Bible stories, which would still be acceptable, he tells these stories so that people can *see* the main character of the story instead of just imagining them.

My parents, my brother, and I are all musical. The pianists in the family are my mom, my dad and myself. Ever since they were children, my mom and dad have been playing piano. My dad has told me many times how he practiced for many hours during college. I take more after my dad than my mom in my piano playing, but not by very much. Mom has a classical base, or, in other words, she is classically trained. Mom reads notes more than she hears songs. I, like my dad, play more by ear. Dad is very advanced when it comes to ear training. He knows multitudes of chords on the piano. He also plays guitar by ear. The ear training that I have is advanced, and I'm slowly, but surely, learning how to read notes as my mom does.

With all this inspiration to go into the ministry of the Seventh-day Adventist Church, I hope and pray to spread the Word of the Lord to the future generations of tomorrow. They are the most important ones who need to know about the Lord and His purpose. My parents and grandparents are constantly encouraging me in the right direction for the Lord.

— Nathan Begley, Class of 2019

Fitting In?
To Serve

Yet what we suffer now is nothing compared to the glory he will reveal to us later. (Romans 8:18, NLT)

Fitting in is all a kid, teen, or even an adult wants. I know that people will say or do anything to be a part of the crowd. While my family and I were on a cruise, I would always hang out in the teen room. One night one of the girls I met and I went and sat down with a group of friends that knew each other from outside the cruise. We were all chatting and laughing when the girl randomly brought up that she was a Christian.

In an instant the whole mood shifted. They all started bashing on the girl, saying people who believed in God were stupid. The girl started to get extremely uncomfortable. My heart was racing a thousand beats per second, when one of the guys eyed me. He asked me what I thought about God and Christians. I immediately started panicking inside. I had a choice. Fit in with the crowd, or be ridiculed.

Instantly, all eyes were on me. I said the most microscopic prayer in my heart for God to give me strength. I took a deep breath, and simply said, "I'm a Christian, and I believe in God." I wanted to disappear because I knew what was coming. But the guy said something I never thought I would hear. He said, "You're going to admit you're a Christian after all we have said about them? Wow!" He was in disbelief that I was willing to intentionally put myself out there after I knew what everyone around me thought. After that there was a sense of respect, and that's when the conversation ended.

I didn't know if they were going to yell at me for being one of God's "stupid" followers, ignore me the rest of the trip, or treat me like a piece of garbage. But I had the choice whether to stand up for what I believe in, or conform to this sinful world. Take it from a teenager who is struggling every day with what she believes. Standing firm in your faith is not easy, and might not always end on a high note, but "what we suffer now is nothing compared to the glory he will reveal to us later" (Rom. 8:18, NLT).

— Ally Bergherm, Class of 2017

Thankfulness?
To Know

And we know that in all things God works for the good of those who love him. (Romans 8:28, NIV)

I just now passed a church marquee with the message, "Thank God no matter what happens." Really?! I could not disagree with anything more strongly. Thank God for 9/11? Thank God for my neighbor's child who died because she was struck by a bullet from a stupid drive-by shooter? Thank God because my friend's wife died from breast cancer? Really? That is just plain stupid. It makes God out to be a monster. Don't preachers think about what they say?

I know that Romans 8:28 says all things work together for good for those who love the Lord. Fine. That means our loving heavenly Father is able to pick up the tragic pieces of our disasters and help us. But I do not have to be thankful the tragedy occurred. He didn't do it. He isn't any happier than we are that it happened. What I am thankful for is that He is there for us when bad things happen.

Sometimes I am afraid we get so syrupy with our faith we are afraid to be angry when rotten things occur. Loving God doesn't mean we have to go around being thankful for all the things that happen as if He is doing them. He is not. Bad things happen in this world. Okay? We have a loving Father who knows how to give good gifts to His children and is just as miserable and broken as we when our children, grandchildren and neighbors are hurt.

Please, I beg you. Do not be thankful no matter what happens. Be angry that there is an enemy in the land. Be thankful that no matter what happens, we can be more than conquers through Christ (Rom. 8). In I Thessalonians 5:18 Paul tells us to be thankful in all circumstances. That means be thankful in all circumstances that we have a God to help us.

— Roger Bothwell, Former Staff

Our God is a Bulldog
To Know

Be alert and of sober mind. Your enemy the devil prowls around like a roaring lion looking for someone to devour.
(1 Peter 5:8, NIV)

Mark Twain said, "It's not the size of the dog in the fight, it's the size of the fight in the dog." If you haven't seen it yet go to YouTube and search for bulldog vs. bears. There you will see Jules, a twenty-pound bulldog, chase two large bears out of its California yard.

When I was a little guy someone really frightened me with I Peter 5:8 which says, "Be alert and of sober mind. Your enemy the devil prowls around like a roaring lion looking for someone to devour." I thought it would be hopeless to do battle with him. I knew he was a fallen angel but now he was described as a roaring lion. What could I do when he showed up?

We need to be careful when we talk to little people. It was years before I discovered Romans 8:31–32 (NIV), "If God is for us, who can be against us? He who did not spare his own Son, but gave him up for us all—how will he not also, along with him, graciously give us all things?" and verse 37, "In all these things we are more than conquerors through him who loved us. For I am convinced that neither death nor life, neither angels nor demons, … will be able to separate us from the love of God that is in Christ Jesus our Lord."

While it would be foolish to be cocky in this battle for our souls, "If you think you are standing firm, be careful that you don't fall!" (I Cor. 10:12, NIV), it is not necessary to be afraid. "Don't be afraid!" Elisha told him. "For there are more on our side than on theirs!" (2 Kings 6:16, NLT).

So let God be our bulldog. Satan is no match for us when God is on our side.

— Roger Bothwell, Former Staff

Skid Marks
To Love

Then He said to her, "Your sins are forgiven." (Luke 7:48, NKJV)

Skid marks were all that was left. A tow truck had taken away the car, and a crew had cleaned up all the shards of broken glass. As time goes by, rain and snow and traffic will wear away the black stains. Not all skid marks are the remnants of an accident. Sometimes they are just the opposite. Skid marks on the end of a runway mean many flights had safe landings.

Life leaves skid marks on people. We are marked by life's tragic events. Accidents, death, disappointments and failed goals mark us, and, like the disappearing skid marks on the highway, time has a way of helping our emotional past to slowly fade. But it does take time even for the bold who act as if they are recovered. It is one of the reasons we advise people who have lost a dearly loved spouse not to make any major decisions for at least a year. No matter how seasoned, we are not immune.

Jesus forgives sins in an instant. It often takes much longer for us to forgive ourselves. We rue our mistakes and harbor wrongs that we have done. Jesus forgives, but the skid marks remain and it takes time. Forgiveness is a two-way event. As we forgive others so must we forgive ourselves seventy times seven. We wonder how we could have been so stupid. Well, we are. It's part of being a human—a major part. But just as surely as the black stains disappear on the highway so they will fade for us. Living the abundant life promised to us by Jesus is acknowledging our humanity and forgiving ourselves. Hopefully, some of your skid marks are and will be the remnants of safe landings.

— Roger Bothwell, Former Staff

Avian Ado
To Love

Do not be anxious about anything, but in everything by prayer and petition with thanksgiving let your requests be made known to God. (Philippians 4:6, NIV)

It was such a beautiful day I decided to sit on the patio and read. Our patio also has bird feeders that we faithfully keep well-stocked. But the birds did not appreciate my presence. A catbird, newly back from the south, sparrows, and chickadees took it upon themselves to scold me for "violating" their space. It was difficult focusing on the text of my book because of the avian ado. I finally gave up and came back inside. Strange they never scold me when I am filling their feeders.

I think this story illustrates itself. God feeds us. "Give us this day our daily bread." But there are times we really don't want Him bothering us. We have lives to lead. We want to do it ourselves. We use the power of choice that He has given us to forge our own path. Forget the "He leads me in paths of righteousness." We are so like the birds. Keep the food coming and then go away.

Often times when I have officiated at a wedding I have made a perfunctory appearance at the reception and then disappeared. I noted that my presence was stifling the party. I have also listened to people complain when times grew difficult, but never heard those same people being thankful when times were good. Being thankful is such a mentally healthy thing to be. When we are thankful we are aware of the good things that we have or are happening. When we are thankful it is difficult to be pessimistic, which is an illness.

— Roger Bothwell, Former Staff

Mr. Flattoad
To Love

For God so loved the world that he gave his one and only Son, that whoever believes in him shall not perish but have eternal life.
(John 3:16, NIV)

There is a flat toad on the street in front of my home. I checked our begonia basket to see if it is "our" toad. All summer we have had a toad hide in our begonia basket each day. In the evening it jumps out to forage for whatever. It wasn't in the basket this afternoon. Could Mr. Flattoad be ours?

I am concerned and remembered something Jesus said about His Father and birds. "Are not two sparrows sold for a penny? Yet not one of them will fall to the ground outside your Father's care" (Matt. 10:29, NIV). Did God care about the toad? Would He care about it more if it were "our" toad? Does loving someone add value to him or her?

Several years ago I had a graveside service for someone. I mean "someone" because we did not know his name. We were burying him in the anonymous section of the cemetery. It was a very plain section off to the back edge of the cemetery. There were no flowers or shrubs, only numbers. The only people there were the undertaker, me, and two gravediggers who were waiting for me to finish. Did he have less value because there wasn't anyone there that cared? You might ask, "Didn't you care?" Sorta. I needed to because no one else did. I wondered if he had a child or grandchildren somewhere? Would they care if they knew?

If loving someone gives added value, then he had a lot of value because the most important Being in the universe cared. Just in case you have ever wondered about your worth, just ask what price was paid for you. For God so loved the world that He gave His only son for you. Talk about added value. You are something wonderful.

— Roger Bothwell, Former Staff

Ministry Working
To Serve

If anyone serves Me, let him follow Me; and where I am, there My servant will be also. If anyone serves Me, him My Father will honor. (John 12:26, NKJV)

If there is one thing GCA opened my eyes to, it's serving others. I remember when I fell in love with medical missionary work. It was on the spring break mission trip to Guatemala my senior year. I got to help in the medical clinic there and was amazed at what a reward I got from serving others. Throughout college as I pursued my nursing degree I always had the desire to devote some of my time to medical mission work.

Soon after graduating college I took the biggest leap of faith I've ever taken. I left home to volunteer with ADRA for eight months working on a riverboat in the Bolivian Amazon region as a nurse. Not only did I get to serve God there, but I learned to know and love Him in a deeper way. I got to do some incredible things, such as help deliver a baby, live among the natives, work at a small town hospital, care for hurting people, form new friendships, learn a new language, and much more.

By getting away from the fast-paced American lifestyle, I broke my habit of being "me-dependent" and I learned to be "God-dependent." Truly, it was the hardest lesson of my life and one that I pray each of you can discover for yourseves.

I'm sure we have all struggled with handing our burdens to God. It's not easy to leave decisions up to Someone we cannot see. That's where faith comes in. With each problem I faced during my time in Bolivia I was blown away by God's evident replies to my prayers. The verse stating, "ask and you shall receive" became real. Prayers were not always answered the way I wanted, but in looking back I could always see why God would say yes, no, or wait patiently.

The scariest place to be is where we don't feel we need God, and that we can handle situations alone. Upon returning home to America I prayed a dangerous prayer. I asked God to forever place situations in my life that would make me feel my need for Him. He never once left me unfulfilled.

Service brings us out of a self-centered mindset and focuses us on others and on God. I challenge you to find a way to serve God in your life. Serving God helped me know Him, love Him, and trust him more. I thank GCA for sparking my love for service.

— Courtney Brackbill, Class of 2010

A Life of Love
To Love

Dear children, let us not love with words or tongue but with actions and in truth. (1 John 3:18, NIV)

My dad used to ask me if I ever wanted to talk to my grandpa. Sometimes I would say yes, sometimes I would say no, but when I said yes my dad would call him and it was always fun to talk to him.

Love is a big part of my life. Yes, I love God, I love music, I love wakeboarding, I love my friends and family, but when I love a person I truly care for them and I look out for them. God's love isn't rude or self-seeking. His love isn't easily angered and doesn't keep record of wrongs. When He loves you He won't give up on you. That's how everyone's love is supposed to be. We're human and we're not perfect, but we still need to try to keep our love for God and others pure. I, as a human, understand that it's hard to always love your neighbor or anyone because we're sinful and people get on our nerves sometimes. We honestly just can't stand certain people, but we still need to treat them with care and respect. Even if they don't treat you that way, because no matter what, you need to treat others how you wish to be treated.

— Meredith Brackbill, Class of 2019

Never-Ending Source
To Know

And my God will meet all your needs according to the riches of his glory in Christ Jesus. (Philippians 4:19, NIV)

Prayer is a powerful tool that God gave us to communicate with Him. When I was younger, I was taught that whenever a prayer is lifted up, God is nigh and will answer. If I would just simply utter the name "Jesus," He would move mountains. I always believed in those words but never fully understood them.

While in elementary school, and living near Lawrenceville, I attended Carman Adventist School. It was about a forty-five minute to an hour or more drive, depending on traffic. For a period of time while attending school, my father was not working and money was tight. On one particular day, we didn't even have enough money to put gas in the car. However, my dad's old truck had a little over 'E' left in the gas tank. As I stated before, we lived a ways from school and would need more gas to cover that distance, but instead of worrying we prayed. We fervently asked the Lord to bless the truck and to get us safely there. After praying, we piled into the vehicle and headed for school. During the entire trip we cautiously watched the gas gauge as we traveled, and not once did the needle move. Upon returning home, my dad exclaimed that it wasn't until he pulled into the garage that the truck completely shut off.

God showed me His presence that day as I recall this miracle. This is one of the first times that I felt and knew my God on a more personal level. How frequently have I gone about my day without praying once! It is so easy to forget about God, even when we don't intentionally mean to. Prayer is not a luxury or an option. It is a necessity in order to build a relationship with God. God is expectantly waiting for your connection, so don't hesitate to call on Him.

God knows your needs; He is just waiting for you to remember.

— Ashley Brandon, Class of 2016

Getting Through the Night
To Know

I will exalt you, LORD, for you lifted me out of the depths and did not let my enemies gloat over me. LORD my God, I called to you for help, and you healed me. You, LORD, brought me up from the realm of the dead; you spared me from going down to the pit. Sing the praises of the LORD, you his faithful people; praise his holy name. For his anger lasts only a moment, but his favor lasts a lifetime; weeping may stay for the night, but rejoicing comes in the morning. (Psalm 30: 1-5, NIV)

When I was in eighth grade, one of my friends committed suicide. He had been struggling with anger issues for quite some time, and when I look back at it, I see all he wanted was attention. He just wanted some help. At the time, I didn't think I would get over his death. For months, every time I closed my eyes, I saw his face. Every time I passed his mom in the hallway at school, I could see the pain radiating from her face. Looking back, I see the change that I have gone through since then. Now, it is a distant memory and I have found peace.

Pain and suffering are unfortunately very common in this world. Everyone experiences their own struggles, some more than others, and we never can truly know what someone is going through. Luckily, God knows, and He never leaves us to defend ourselves. He stands with us, comforts us, and because of that, we know that one day everything will be ok. God is a loving God, and a God that is not going to leave us to suffer. It may not seem like things will turn out OK at first, or even a while after, because pain is not something that goes away overnight. It is a healing process. God is here to heal the scars that are left on us. It is a slow process, and it may seem that the sadness will never end, but I promise you, joy will come in the morning.

— Claire Brewer, Class of 2016

The Still Breeze
To Know

Be still and know that I am God. (Psalm 46:10, NIV)

It was my first year at summer camp, and we were all sitting at the fire bowl for church. I was not really listening to the speaker. I was too occupied thinking about what was happening later on that day. As I was sitting there, a cool breeze came blowing through the fire bowl. I don't know if you have ever been to camp in the South, Georgia in particular, but it is hot. So when this breeze came through it made me stop and pay attention.

This is how I feel God speaks to us as humans. He comes in and catches our attention. Just like the wind stopped me from thinking about myself, and pay attention, God's voice brings us away from ourselves and focuses our attention on Him. Like the breeze, it is not always a big, in-your-face voice from the sky. It is usually a small stirring you can barely feel.

The problem is that we usually do not stop and think of God on a daily basis. Like the breeze at camp, however, we do not have to do it on our own. I did not focus really hard and there was the breeze. The breeze came and got my attention. God does not expect us to always consciously think of Him, but when we need Him, He will be there.

— Robby Bridges, Class of 2016

And Know I Am
To Know

He says, "Be still, and know that I am God; I will be exalted among the nations, I will be exalted in the earth."
(Psalm 46:10, NIV)

During my junior class trip I had a chance to get closer to many of my friends. Many of them I had not talked with much that year because I was not seeing them as much. We stopped for Sabbath lunch at the Portland Head Light, and many of us decided to cook out on the grills at the park. We purchased burgers the day before, and started to grill them. It was rather chilly that day, and we were not dressed for the cold Maine temperature. We were dressed for the warmer Georgia spring. Since we were cold, we all gathered around the charcoal grill. Because it was cold we did not feel like leaving the fire, so we spent about two hours together. It was then I realized that even though we had not spoken as much as we used to, we were still friends.

It is the same way with God. We do not always spend as much time with Him as we do at other times, but He is still our God. Just as my friends and I were still friends. My friendships were rekindled, and so our relationship with God can be renewed. Just as with my friends and me, we have to spend time together to keep a relationship going. To do this we have to be still. God tells us this in the above verse.

Being still is how we get to know God. We need to know God so He can work through us. The text said that God will be exalted among the nations, and in the earth. He wants to do this through us but we have to know Him first. Knowing is the first step to everything else in a relationship. After you *know* someone you can then learn to *love* them and later to *serve* them.

— Robby Bridges, Class of 2016

Lessons from Water
To Serve

For since the creation of the world His invisible attributes are clearly seen, being understood by the things that are made, even His eternal power and Godhead. (Romans 1:20, NKJV)

As someone with scientific training, I am privileged to be able to see God's character in the world He created. I see His love of order in the elegance and subtlety of the laws of physics and chemistry. I am awed by His creative genius when I consider that the genetic code—the rules by which cells convert information encoded in DNA or RNA sequences into the amino acid sequences that make up proteins—is the same for all living organisms on earth! I can even see a model of God's throne room in the structure of the atom.

One of my favorite lessons in nature is water, a simple substance that we use every day. Water illustrates the idea behind the Trinity in a way that makes sense to me and to my students. In nature, water occurs in three forms: solid (ice), liquid (water), and gas (steam). Ice, water, and steam all have different properties and behaviors. Ice is cold and hard, steam is hot and builds up pressure, water is wet and flows. However, they are all the same substance, an atom of oxygen bonded to two atoms of hydrogen, or H_2O.

Similarly, God the Father, God the Son, and God the Holy Spirit relate to us in different ways and seem to do different things. God the Father is the Creator, the Sovereign, and the Sustainer of the universe. He is Lord and King over all. At times I see Him as infinitely remote and incomprehensible. Jesus is similar to God the Father in His creative power, but to me He seems so much more approachable because I can relate to Him in His experience in human form. God the Holy Spirit is hard for me to describe, but I have seen His work in my life and others' lives. In some ways He is the easiest for me to relate to because of His constant presence in my mind and heart.

Yet in spite of the different appearances and actions of God the Father, the Son, and the Holy Spirit, they are all fully God! The mystery of the Trinity confused me (and many others) for years before I understood the simple lesson God left for us in water.

— Marty Briggs, Science Teacher

How People Should View Us
To Know

By this all people will know that you are my disciples, if you have love for one another. (John 13:35, ESV)

People see Christians as people who have rules and doctrines. They see Christianity as a set of rules that you have to follow, and if you're not perfect and follow everything that the Bible says, then you'll be sent to hell. This is not how the world should view us.

The world should view us as a loving, caring community who follows a God who isn't controlling, who isn't all rules and regulations. He's a God who cares, a God who loves us no matter what, through all our mistakes, all our bad times, and all our hurt. He is a God who sees us as a blank canvas, a lump of clay, or a piece of wood, all waiting to be made into something. He doesn't see us as a black board full of sins and impurities. He sees our hearts, and what we can become if we allow Him to work in us.

And as such we must go out and spread the word—the word that our God is a loving God. They must not know us by our doctrines, they must know us by our love!

Since God has so graciously gifted us with the gift of forgiveness, shouldn't we pass this gift along to others? I would be wrong to not pass His love and grace to others. So my challenge to you is to sit down by yourself and think of all of those who have wronged you, all those people that have hurt you, and all those people that have betrayed you. I challenge you to just let it all go. Forgive them as the Lord has forgiven you. Remember, "They must know us not by our doctrines, but by our love."

— Michael Brogden, Class of 2019

Serving God Is Serving Others
To Serve

Each of you should use whatever gift you have received to serve others, as faithful stewards of God's grace in its various forms. (1 Peter 4:10, NIV)

One of the most admirable traits a person can have is compassion and love toward others. God actively demonstrated this during Jesus' time on Earth. The joy others received from His work and teachings was irreplaceable. One of the greatest ways to bring happiness to God is by being like Jesus to others. One of God's greatest delights is when His heavenly love is bestowed through His followers into others' lives.

In the past, I had the opportunity of helping at a local homeless shelter. At my school, families collected everyday necessities and organized them into packages and bags. Then, my mom and I went to the shelter to deliver them. When we were at the front desk filling out information for the deliveries, recipients of the donations walked by. The look in their eyes contained so much excitement. Later, the manager of the shelter expressed how much they appreciated our gifts. Even though this wasn't an outstanding deed, so many people benefited from it. Through us, others were blessed and in turn, I was too. Afterwards, I felt so happy that I could help them. I will never forget that experience.

Serving others is not hard. God works in amazing ways. His ways can involve lots of planning and preparation or they can simply be a compliment. Little, encouraging actions can make someone's day, and in some cases, be the start of a stream of positivity. One of the characteristics of service is variety. Lots of people spread God's word in many different ways, such as mission trips or community service. Even though my deed wasn't life changing, it was extremely rewarding. An important part of serving others is being sincere. How can someone fully receive God's love when it is half-heartedly presented? I believe that these opportunities will not only change the recipient's life, but the benefactor's. This shouldn't be a challenge. Instead, serving others should be a joy.

When we do things to positively impact others, God rejoices. Our mission as followers of Him is to spread His word so others can know and receive His goodness. As a disciple of Christ, I know I must serve Him all my life. In order to do this, I must serve others.

— Juliet Bromme, Class of 2018

Military Check
To Know

The LORD doesn't see things the way you see them. People judge by outward appearance, but the LORD looks at the heart.
(1 Samuel 16:7, NLT)

Military check is when your dorm room is very thoroughly checked for cleanliness. Military check was coming up, so my roommate and I decided to start cleaning. When we first started, the task seemed impossible. There was dust, dirt, and other gross things on everything. As we cleaned, I wondered why we had to have room check. Later that night in dorm chapel the dean said that the reason for room check, especially military, was to make sure the dorm doesn't get pests such as cockroaches or mice. That made sense to me.

So we went back to our room and wiped down everything we could see, vacuumed the floor multiple times, and organized all our stuff. Cleaning took a long time and made me think, wouldn't it be easier to just throw everything out of sight so the room appeared clean? I thought about this for a while, but since I'd been told that military was super strict, I decided to actually clean. But the temptation to just throw everything somewhere hidden to just make the room appear clean was always there.

I think the same kind of temptation is there with our relationships, especially with God. The temptation is to try to hide our sins instead of confessing them or overcoming them. God doesn't just see the outside; in fact, He's focused on the inside. You can't hide your sins from God. Even if other people can't see them, God can. But if you confess and ask forgiveness for your sins God will help you. It's like your heart is your dorm room and it's too dirty to clean, so you just stuff everything into hidden places. Even though you tried hiding your sins, God will see them and you will fail room check. But imagine having a professional come in and make your room spotless and perfectly organized. I believe that's what God will do if you accept Him into your heart and let Him help you with your sins.

Just know that having God help you clean out your heart is the best thing to do to get ready for the real room check, the second coming. Let me leave you with this question: is your heart ready for room check?

— Jacob Brown, Class of 2019

God Will Fight for You
To Know

The Lord will fight for you; you need only to be still.
(Exodus 14:14, NIV)

Throughout the course of my high school journey, I can definitely say that my junior year was the hardest. Don't get me wrong, I had a lot of good, fun times, but bad times quickly followed. Spiritually, I was struggling a lot. My life seemed like it was getting worse and worse, and there was no light at the end of the tunnel. My best friend got kicked out, people were saying things to me that killed me, and I felt like God was anywhere but near me. Those aren't even the really bad things either, they are just scratches on the surface. My family life wasn't going well, and I started believing all the bad things the devil was feeding into my mind. I thought life wasn't worth living. And sometimes I still struggle with that. I get caught up in everything that is going on in my life and lose sight of what is really important. And what really is important isn't my grades. To be honest, I know that I shouldn't say that, because school is very important. When I had to choose between my mental health and my grades, and let me tell you it was hard to choose, I chose my mental health almost every time. The devil really began tempting me and I could see him at work more and more in my life, and I hated that.

That year the verse Exodus 14:14 really stuck out to me. It tells of how God will fight for us, and He will never stop fighting for us. We just have to take a step back and realize that we can't keep fighting Him. We have to be still. And trust me, I know that is hard, because life throws waves and billows at you just to try and knock you down. Remember this though, God created those waves, not to hurt you, but to test your faith. And if He created them, I'm more than positive that He can control them.

— Rebecca Brown, Class of 2016

Getting to Know God
To Know

Thus says the LORD: "Let not the wise man boast in his wisdom, let not the mighty man boast in his might, let not the rich man boast in his riches, but let him who boasts boast in this, that he understands and knows me, that I am the LORD who practices steadfast love, justice, and righteousness in the earth. For in these things I delight, declares the LORD." (Jeremiah 9:23–24, ESV)

What does it mean to know God? Many people struggle with coming to know God, myself included. The whole concept of God in itself can be a little overwhelming. How can we come to know this all-powerful, all-knowing God?

The best way to begin to get to know God is to read the Bible. After all, what better way to get to know God than reading His Word? As you read the Bible, He will speak to you through the words that are written. The more you read His Word, the more you will get to know Him. Set some time aside each day specifically for reading the Bible. Once you do this, you will truly notice a transformation in your life by incorporating God in it.

Prayer also goes hand in hand with reading the Bible. It's good to communicate both ways. In prayer, we can ask God for understanding and to grow closer in our relationship with him. We can also lay our problems and worries at His feet, as well as praise Him for the great things He has blessed us with in life.

Getting to know God can be difficult at first; it's hard to get to know something you can't even see. But once you take the time to develop your relationship with Him, you won't regret it. Having God in your life will be the best thing that has ever happened to you.

— Alex Bucher, Class of 2017

The Greatest of These Is Love
To Love

And now these three remain: Faith, hope, and love. But the greatest of these is love. (1 Corinthians 13:13, NIV)

Back in my day, by this I mean eighth grade, I wasn't loving at all. Actually, I was aggravated at everything and everyone. Because I was angry all the time, I got in trouble all the time, even though the reasons for my discipline were quite petty. I was constantly angry, with a bad attitude, I set myself up, and if I had been *loving* instead of angry my entire eighth grade year could have actually been a great year. I think this is why 1 Corinthians 13:13 exists, to show us that if we are loving, our whole lives can be changed.

This verse is important to remember because it tells us that faith, hope, and love are the three most important aspects of Christianity and life. We as people and Christians need to demonstrate all of these actions, but the most important is love. Love is the perfect description of God. Everything that is good is love. Love is everything the Bible teaches us to do. "Love thy neighbor as thy self," "turn the other cheek," "treat others how you would treat yourself," all of these are simply saying to love each other. If everybody loved each other the world would be a completely different place—no Hitler, no ISIS, no Osama bin Laden—everything would be at peace. Even though achieving world peace is nearly impossible, you can still make a difference wherever you are. So next time something happens that might frustrate you, think of how the situation will change for the good if you are loving, and then put those thoughts into action.

— Kevin Burgess, Class of 2019

God Watches Out for Us
To Love

And we know that God causes everything to work together for the good of those who love God and are called according to his purpose for them. (Romans 8:28, NLT)

There once was a man living in England during the time of Queen Mary. He was a Protestant preacher with his own church and a strong belief in God. The preacher had been warned many times that if he didn't stop teaching the people about God and his own belief in God, he would die.

One day while he was giving a sermon, there was a loud pounding on the door and they heard a soldier say, "In the name of the queen open this door." The door was slowly opened and soldiers marched in and grabbed the preacher and dragged him back to their horses. The congregation cried out to the preacher but he told them not to worry, God would be with him.

The soldiers took him to a horse, told him to mount up, and then started to ride toward the place where he would die. That night when they stopped at an inn, the preacher's horse reared up knocking the preacher off the horse, leaving the horse and man injured. Angry as the soldiers were, they knew that they would not be able to travel until both were back to full health. The soldiers stayed at the inn until the preacher and his horse were healed. It could have been weeks, it could have been months, but by the time the soldiers were ready to travel a letter came in saying that Queen Mary was no longer on the throne. Shocked but grateful, the preacher returned to his church with his life intact.

This story reminds me that because the man believed in God and loved Him, God worked things out for him. It reminded me that God protects His children. It shows God's love and mercy and that He is always on our side.

— Kristin Burgess, Class of 2019

Was Jesus a Hippie?
To Love

But the greatest of these is love. (1 Corinthians 13:13, NIV)

hip·pie ['hipē]
NOUN—(especially in the 1960s) a person of unconventional appearance, typically having long hair and wearing beads, associated with a subculture involving a rejection of conventional values

One love refers to the universal love and respect expressed by all people for all people, all things for all things.

> Except for the selfish human heart nothing lives just for itself. Every tree and shrub and leaf pours forth oxygen, without which neither people nor animals could live; and people and animals, in turn, support the life of tree and shrub and leaf. The ocean receives streams from every land, but it takes only to give back. The mists rising from it fall in showers to water the earth, so that plants may grow and bud. (White, *Humble Hero*, p. 7)

> Yes, how many years can some people exist
> Before they're allowed to be free?
> Yes, how many times can a man turn his head
> Pretending he just doesn't see?
> — Hippie Anthem "Blowin' in the Wind."[1]

A dusty Man walks up to a well. His hair is long and unkempt. He has a crowd of people who follow Him everywhere. He is known to go by Himself for long periods of time and talk to His "Father." He sits down and asks a sketchy woman from the bad side of town for some water.

A dusty Man walks up to the famous preachers. He tells them they are like empty, white washed tombs. He tells them they are a den of vipers. He tells them that all their rules are irrelevant.

A dusty Man gives a speech on a mountain. He says that the meek and the mild are heaven's child. That the peaceful souls and the pure in heart are guaranteed to have a part of a kingdom not on earth. He says people should be like salt, that hating is the same as killing, that looking lustfully is the same as committing adultery.

A dusty Man sits down to eat with the lowest of society. The cheaters, the thieves, the whores.

A dusty Man advises His followers to carry nothing with them but a walking stick.

A dusty Man washes the feet of the ones He loves.

A dusty Man dies for the ones who kill Him.

But before that, a brilliant God scrawls His love across the universe, in the form of a planet called Earth.

A brilliant God creates a world where everything is meant to work together with love and harmony.

---

1 Songwriters: BOB DYLAN Blowin' In The Wind lyrics © BOB DYLAN MUSIC CO; http://www.lyricsfreak.com/b/bob+dylan/blowin+in+the+wind_20021159.html (accessed November 10, 2015)

A brilliant God saves a worthless race, because it was not worthless to Him.

A brilliant God frees His people.

A brilliant God does not turn His head and pretend not to see.

A brilliant God, a dusty Man—one and the same—shows a violent earth the real meaning of one love.

So if we are striving to be like Jesus, and Jesus was unconventional to some extent, as some hippies were, what does that mean, and what does that look like?

First, it means we reject conventional values, instead striving for values that are in accordance with our heavenly Father.

Second, it means we are called to love and respect everyone, despite their families, income, race, age, or where they live. We are also called to stand up for our fellow man.

Lastly, we need to live in harmony with, and protect our earth just as God assigned us to do in Genesis (when He made man stewards of the earth). This could be in the form of recycling, using Earth-friendly products, or biking somewhere instead of driving.

— Kylie Burgess, Class of 2017

"Send Me!"
To Serve

Here I am. Send me! (Isaiah 6:8, NIV)

I remember the day that my parents sat my brother and I down and told us that we were going to move to the other side of the Atlantic Ocean. I also remember thinking, *Okay, well, let me know when you're coming back to visit!* As a 9-year-old, it wasn't the most exciting news to hear. To leave my family, my closest friends, my culture behind seemed like such a hard thing to do. A few months later, we were engaging ourselves in the new culture until it became our new home.

My junior year of high school, my parents, once again, sat us down and as stubborn as I can be, I thought, *Oh no. There's no way I'm moving again. I have one more year of high school left! How much could my life change in just one year?* Well, God was already working on that because after a long tearful conversation with my parents, I found myself saying what Isaiah said: "Here I am, Lord. Send me."

Earlier in chapter 6, Isaiah is realizing how powerless he is next to God. We can relate to how Isaiah felt when we think about how far we are from being like Christ, who was unaffected by sin, but God knows that. Jesus told us to go out and minister to all the nations, and to put our attitude and our differences aside to let God send us to where He wants us to go. It's hard to let God take control because we all like stability in our lives. Just like me, we want to stay in our comfort zone, but God encourages us to let Him guide us.

Isaiah was more than willing to serve the Lord. When he asked God for how long He wanted Isaiah to witness to other nations, God told him forever. Just like Isaiah, we should allow God to work in us so that we can be a blessing to others and glorify Him forever. Moving was the best decision I have made yet, and just like God was able to use me, He can use all of us. If we allow God to use us as a vessel for Him, we will be able to see the wonderful things that He has in store for us.

— Laia Burgos, Class of 2015

Never Forsaken
To Know

A man who has friends must himself be friendly, but there is a friend who sticks closer than a brother. (Proverbs 18:24, NKJV)

I had about five friends when I was in the fifth grade. We sometimes played basketball together at recess, ate together, and shared our hot Cheetos that we laid out on the table for all of us to enjoy. We spoke of everything: girls, sports, school, and television. We were sometimes even nice enough to share our answers. But there was one friend that I trusted more than anyone, Reynaldy. He had been my first and closest friend since I came to America. He helped me learn English, played soccer with me, and came over to my house all the time.

One day in recess, we all decided to play a game of catch, but instead of using our hands, we used our feet. We were terrible. Every one or two touches, the ball would roll away or fly out of the circle. My friend Sammy passed me the ball, and I made the mistake of kicking the ball as hard as I could. They all sprinted back inside as the ball flew through the window of a classroom and shattered the glass. Thankfully, there weren't any students or teachers inside. Soon enough, they were outside, frantically searching for who was responsible for the broken glass. All my friends told the teacher that they weren't involved in the shattered glass. All except Reynaldy. He told the teacher that it had been an accident that we were all involved in, and that he and I were both responsible for the damage. There were consequences that had to be paid, but there was also a lesson that I would never forget: even though all my so-called friends had left me at a time when I needed them, I had one that stood by my side.

The good news I want to give to you today is this: God will be that true and faithful friend when no one else will. He has never forsaken us, and He never will.

— Marcos Burgos, Class of 2017

Gods Children
To Serve

For even the Son of Man did not come to be served, but to serve, and to give his life as a ransom for many. (Mark 10:45, NKJV)

During my first year at GCA I had the opportunity to go on the school's annual mission trip. They decided to go to Nicaragua to build two churches for the local Adventists there. After talking with my parents about it I decided to go, and the experiences I had there really brought me closer to God. It was my first mission trip and I didn't really know what to expect. Being in the third world country was not something new to me but I still wasn't sure what kind of conditions we would be under when we got there.

When I got there the first thing that struck me was the extreme heat. Right outside the airport in Managua there was a guy handing out free water bottles that really showed me the kindness of the local people. The place we stayed at was like a three story open hotel. It was honestly better than I expected even though we had to suffer through cold showers every day.

Building the churches was strenuous work and I will never forget our school and the locals coming together to help bring their small tight-knit community a church. The experience that really will have a lasting impact on me was on Friday night when my friend invited me to come to the local church for their vespers program. During the program we students were going to help entertain the kids in their Sabbath School room. The kids were just overjoyed when they saw us. We sang songs with them, played games with them, and even with a language barrier it still was an experience that I will never forget. There is truly nothing else like seeing children with smiles on their faces praising God in song. God calls us to serve those in need because all people on earth are God's children.

— Andrew Burke, Class of 2017

Christ Gives Me Strength
To Know

I can do all things through Christ who strengthens me.
(Philippians 4:13, NKJV)

Philippians 4:13 is a very important verse to me. This verse says that I can do anything with Christ by my side. If I'm going through difficulties in my life, this verse really comforts me telling me that nothing is too hard for God to handle.

I can recall many times throughout my life where God has taken care of me. One particular experience comes to mind. I was born with a cataract in my right eye. My parents received a call from a family member who was doing some research about my cataract. They had found the top pediatric ophthalmologist in the country who could remove my cataract, and save my vision. The surgery took place just two weeks after I was born in an attempt to save my right eye from going blind. Although I don't remember this trial, I'm sure that God was there with me. By the grace of God, today my right eye's vision isn't the best but, with my glasses, I can see.

My parents told me that before my surgery I was not allowed to eat for eight hours, and as a baby of just two weeks old, God kept me from going hungry. This passage has proven to me time and time again that with God's help anything is possible, and I am a witness of that today. God blessed me with a great team of ophthalmologists and anesthesiologists to help me during my delicate surgery. The surgery was a huge success, but for the first eight years of my life I had to wear eye patches to strengthen my right eye. God has been very faithful and kind to me, and with Him I truly believe anything is possible.

— Daniel Burke, Class of 2019

Rushing over Me
To Know

Cast all your anxiety on him because he cares for you.
(1 Peter 5:7, NIV)

The water rushed over me. I couldn't breathe as I was pulled into the depths of the ocean by a strong current. I felt helpless; words were unable to escape from my mouth. I thought my life was about to end. All the sudden, two strong arms rescued me from beneath the water. I looked up and saw my grandfather's face, red from the amount of energy he had expended to reach me. No lifeguards were on duty in the waters of Destin, Florida, so my non-swimmer grandfather came to rescue me from my distress.

God works in mysterious ways. He rescues us from the deep abyss, from our troubles, and from worldly deceptions. We don't have to worry about earthly trials and tribulations if we fully rely on God. As we grow to know, love, and serve Him, He casts away our cares. Love the Lord, for He is your rock. The only thing He asks of us is to pray and accept Him. He has the power to overcome any hardships in your life. Never doubt the abilities of God; He is almighty. Today, take time out of your day to pray and ask for His help in the problems. Don't call Him only during times of need, but every day read your Bible and speak to Him. He loves you and He wants to hear from you.

Dear Lord,

Please guide me today in Your ways. Allow me to do Your will and not my own. Help me to feel Your presence and to not worry about the troubles of this world. Help me to know You better. Amen.

— Katie Buxton, Class of 2016

My Best Friend
To Know

Greater love has no one than this: to lay down one's life for one's friends. (John 15:13, NIV)

How many times have you said to someone, "Nobody knows or understands me like my best friend"? Or "I would do anything for my best friend. That's my ride or die!" I'm sure you've said it many times throughout your lifetime. If you're anything like me, not only have you said it many times, but also you've probably said it about a few different people. Don't get me wrong, nobody is expected to keep the same best friend from childhood through adulthood. Why? Because people change, your family may relocate for your parents' new job, or you may relocate for school. The fact of the matter is, things happen and not one mortal being remains the same throughout their lifetime.

As a chaplain living in the girl's dorm, I've seen many cases of the above statement. Girls who were once best friends before GCA or their freshman year are not the closest of friends their senior year if they're even still friends at all. While that may seem terrible, it's the truth. But there is one friend that will never fail you, leave you, or forsake you. The Bible says He's a loyal friend (Proverbs 18:24); He's an all-knowing friend (Jer. 1:5); and most importantly, He's our "ride or die" friend (Rom. 5:8). If you haven't already, make Jesus your BFF today and He'll be the one friend you'll *never* have to replace.

— Rachaun Amber Callender,
"Chaplain Amber,"
Former Staff

Stronger Than Death
To Know

I can do all things through Christ who strengthens me.
(Philippians 4:13, NKJV)

It was my sophomore year here at GCA. On this one particular morning I received a phone call from my mom, saying that my dad's best friend was having heart problems, and was sent to the emergency room. At that moment I was a little scared, but kept telling myself, *he is going to be ok. He is going to push through it.*

A week later, about two weeks before Christmas break, I received another call right when I had gotten off work. It was my mom again, but this time her voice was a little shaky. I knew what she was going to say, but I didn't want to hear it. Then the words that I hoped I would never hear came out of her mouth. He had passed earlier that morning. I felt weak, tired, and drained of all energy. This was a man I saw as family, like an uncle. He had given me words of encouragement when I didn't want to come to GCA. Then to hear that he was gone, and that I had never gotten to see him before he passed, was devastating. I was almost sick, but later when talking to my dad, he reminded me of one of the last conversations Mr. Henry had with me before I left for school. He told me there was a reason that I was sent to GCA.

He said, "I know God has a reason for you to be there, but it is your job to let Him in and allow Him to work through you. Even though you may feel weak and outnumbered, I know that you are strong enough to push through it. I've seen you do it before. But remember our God is stronger to help you overcome anything."

That's when it hit me, he was right. If I just let God take control and remember to do everything that I do for the glory of God, He will make me strong enough to overcome any obstacle, weakness or sadness. It all reminded me of the memory verse my seventh and eighth grade teacher used to tell us. Philippians 4:13—"I can do all things through Christ who gives me strength." This is a text we should all remember, because we sometimes forget that nothing is too big for our God.

— Ashlan Calvin, Class of 2016

The Love of GOD
To Love

Love is patient, love is kind. It does not envy, it does not boast, it is not proud. It does not dishonor others, it is not self-seeking, it is not easily angered, it keeps no record of wrongs.
(1 Corinthians 13:4, NIV)

When I was fourteen I was a troubled student, a terrible son, and a fake friend. I was constantly fighting with myself and many around me. I felt so alone, and totally out of everything from grades to sports to my success at home, and spiritually detached. I was constantly fighting with my parents, and I didn't feel any personal attachment to them. I was told about God constantly and His love for people, but I didn't really want to hear it anymore nor did I believe it. I felt as if God had abandoned me, and that many others abandoned me. I started to be extremely disrespectful, and I wanted to do things my way.

Like most teenagers I wanted to find myself, and I turned to many different things to find that love and contentment. I tried many things from video games to intoxicating myself. I started to get into much legal trouble. I tried to change my life around in many different ways on my own, but it never worked out for me.

My pride, entitlement, and loneliness, were at the point of no turning back when I talked to a counselor named Ciera. She was a guest speaker at a local community service group, and we talked for a while. I told her about what I was facing, and she took the time to listen. For the first time it seemed I was able to talk to someone that actually cared, and she introduced me to God in a different perspective. She told me about a God who gave everything He had, and what He did so that we could be with Him. She also told me that God wasn't into punishing people constantly if they mess up and showing that as a real friend He would never leave us.

I then found out for myself over time that God is love. He constantly shows it to us though we honestly do not deserve it nor are worthy to receive it. (John 3:16, NKJV) says, " For GOD so LOVED the world, that He gave His only begotten Son that whoever believes in Him should not perish but have everlasting life." God cares for us by constantly giving us grace and allowing us to start over with Him on our side. Each day just remember that you have a friend closer than a brother that cares for you and is willing to help and show you love if you just let Him in. So give in. You may never know what miraculous changes may happen.

— Pedro Campbell, Class of 2019

Imitation
To Know

Whoever claims to live in him must live as Jesus did.
1 John 2:6, NIV

When the word *imitation* is spoken, the thought of acting like someone comes to mind. As a child I recall times when my friends and I had adventurous moments of imitating people. Usually when one imitates someone it is to mock or make fun of them, which was the case for my friends and myself. Other times, however, imitating someone can be for good. There are many role models which one could imitate, maybe someone in your family or perhaps a person with a leadership position. The catch-phrase of imitating God also comes to mind. What exactly is imitation? Imitation is striving to simulate or to copy someone else's behavior or actions. You may hear many people say we must imitate Jesus and strive to be more like Him. How exactly do we imitate Jesus?

First of all, we must know who Jesus is. If I were trying to imitate one of my favorite actors, I would have to spend some time understanding the way he talks, the way he dresses, the way he communicates with people, the way that he carries himself. In the same matter if we are to imitate Jesus, we must spend quality time to learn about Him and understand who He truly is. How can we learn about Him? There are many ways; one of the best is through study of the Bible. The Bible gives us clear detail about the character of Jesus. Another route to take is prayer and listening to what He has to say, and being attentive to that still, small voice.

Second, we cannot do it alone. Never should we think that imitating the character of Jesus will come from our own strength. However, it is up to us whether we ask God to help us or not. We should not think of it as an impossible task either because Philippians 4:13 states that we can do all things through Christ who gives us the strength.

Third, it's a daily process. We must take it step by step and analyze what we are learning. For example, in the realm of soccer when you go out to play for the first time after your first practice you won't have everything perfected; rather, it's a process that takes time and dedication. In the same way after a devotional for the very first time we should not expect to understand and to know God. View it as a daily process that will improve as time goes by.

By knowing God, we are able to imitate him. 1 John 2:6 says, "Whoever claims to live in him must live as Jesus did." To know, to love, to serve" should be our motto. If we strive to imitate Jesus, we will know more of Him. This is the beginning of a journey towards becoming more like him.

— Eduardo Campos, Class of 2017

Miracle in Juliaca
To Serve

For the angel of the LORD is a guard; he surrounds and defends all who fear him. (Psalm 34:7, NLT)

Five years ago I had the opportunity to go on a mission trip to Peru. While I was there the government of Peru sold the silver mining rights to Canada. The villagers were not happy and were rioting in Cuzco. So we headed to Juliaca, which was a long way from the rioting. We stayed in the area for a few days and rented a bus to take us anywhere we needed to go. But on the way back to the airport, we found out from a tollbooth operator that the rioters had moved from Cuzco to Juliaca, and that they had created a roadblock between us and the airport.

They were letting people walk through, but they would throw rocks at any vehicles that tried to drive around. We gathered together in the bus and prayed for protection. Then we kept driving towards the airport. When we got to the roadblock, we pulled off the road to assess the situation. Vehicles were parked along the side of the road, and people were streaming out of them. Some of them were carrying luggage, others were empty handed. There were rocks in the road about the size of bowling balls and they looked like someone had thrown them there.

As we were looking at this, we also noticed the Adventist university across the road. We had stopped there earlier in the week and one of our translators had gotten the president's business card. So we called him and asked him what we should do. He told us he was going to escort us onto campus and that we could figure it out there. Once we got on campus he told us that the only way to the airport was through a village. The only problem with this plan was that the rioters lived in that village. But we prayed for protection and continued on. We all got down in the back of the bus, so if they started throwing rocks they wouldn't hit us. My dad could see between the seats and as we went through the village, no one paid attention to us, not even the dogs barked. "Dear Jesus, thank you for taking care of us. Please give us the courage to talk to others about you. Amen"

— Savannah Cantrell, Class of 2018

Showing God's Perfect Love
To Love

Love is patient, love is kind. It does not envy, it does not boast, it is not proud. It does not dishonor others, it is not self-seeking, it is not easily angered, it keeps no record of wrongs. Love does not delight in evil but rejoices with the truth. It always protects, always trusts, always hopes, always perseveres.
(1 Corinthians 13:4–7, NIV)

When I was a little girl, I always dreamed about falling in love. I mean, what little girl doesn't? To me, love meant that you had to like the person or that you had to have intimate feelings for them. I didn't realize that love could be just smiling at someone and showing them that you care. Oftentimes, people take love, or the word "love," for granted. It's used so freely that it seems as if it's something we should be saying, even if we don't mean it; it seems to be insincere.

But what we don't realize is that God's love is sincere. When He says He loves us, we know that He means it and that He cares for us. If we're struggling and we need reassurance, we can count on Him because He will guide us and protect us.

Love does not always mean that you have to be intimate with that person. It could just be a simple gesture like letting them know that you're there for them if they need it. There is a difference between loving someone and being in love with someone. Many times, people get those two mixed up.

If you ever see someone who's struggling or having a bad day, just smile at them or even talk to them. Let them know that you care; let them know that you love them. Love doesn't have to mean that you have to have feelings for that person. It can also mean showing that person that you're trustworthy, patient, and kind.

So before you judge someone and pass him or her by, think about how they're feeling. Maybe they're having a bad day. All they really need is for someone to show them a little love. Show them how God has loved us so they, too, can pass it on. Letting them know that they have an amazing Creator who loves them could change someone's life.

— Olivia Carlson, Class of 2019

To Know the Savior
To Know

And the God of peace will crush Satan under your feet shortly.
(Romans 16:20, NJKV)

One day I took my dog outside before I left the house. She ran around our truck out of sight. I moved so that I could see her again, and I was horrified. My little puppy was happily licking the back of a large, black snake. I called over to her, "Daisy, Daisy, DAISY!" waiting for her to recognize me trying to help, but she didn't listen. Instead, she turned so that she was looking right at me, licking the snake. Stunned, I thought of what to do to pull her away from it. Quickly, I ran up and snatched her and put her back inside the house.

Back out to battle the snake, I thought of a way to kill it. All at once, I jumped in the truck, started it, and slammed it into drive. Back and forth I ran over the snake, until it was completely dead.

Just like I saved my puppy from the snake, similarly, Jesus walks along with us until we run out of sight. Then He watches as we lick the slick back of sin. While we're busy with sin, God our Father calls out to us to recognize Him and come back to Him in safety. Stubborn as we can be, sometimes we hear His calls and instead of returning to Him, we listen as we continue down the same evil path not wanting to know Him. As we make stupid mistakes, God is putting in action ways to pull us back towards Him. But as soon as we allow Him to take us, He is ready to save us from evil and kill the snake.

So, as we live we will be tempted with many things. These things will look so good to us, but they're not. They are temptations of Satan waiting to be given into by us stupid, sinful, humans. Like the snake that he is, Satan waits until we are hooked then he bites us. But if we remember to listen and recognize God's voice, He is always there, waiting for us to turn to Him. He's calling our name waiting for us to listen and come to Him so He can save us from Satan.

— Hannah Carr, Class of 2017

Nothing to Fear
To Serve

For I am the LORD your God who takes hold of your right hand and says to you, Do not fear; I will help you. (Isaiah 41:13, NIV)

 This is a testimony of one of my family's close friends. He was on his way back home with his family from preaching at one of his churches. On their way back home, their car drove into some oil that was left on the road from a previous accident. He struggled to keep the car on the road, but ended up falling from a 300-foot-high cliff. The car rolled down the hill and was completely crushed. The police rushed to the accident and to their surprise, when they got there, the family was fine. They didn't have a single scratch on them. The pastor, his wife, and their two young children were inside the crushed car without a single scratch.

 After they got out of the car, the police walked up to the pastor and showed him the cliff, the surroundings, and all of the memorial crosses and said, "Do you see all these memorial crosses? It is a miracle that you and your family are alive. I don't know what God you believe in but He protected you and your family."

 This story really speaks to me because we can see how God works in our lives. He protected the pastor and his family. The pastor had a good relationship with God. He completely trusted Him and enjoyed spreading God's love to other people. God protected their family from the car accident, and He will protect you, too. He will be there with you no matter what, wherever you go. You just need to give your life to him and put everything in His hands.

— Kehilan Castillo, Class of 2018

The Big Step
To Love

Now faith is confidence in what we hope for and assurance about what we do not see. (Hebrews 11:1, NIV)

As once described by Martin Luther King Jr., "Faith is taking the first step even when you don't see the whole staircase." Sometimes being afraid can stop us from having a valuable and exceptional relationship with God. A lot of the time it's just hard to fully trust God. Trust me, I know. It can be intimidating to rely completely on someone else instead of yourself without knowing the outcome. Faith is to believe in what you don't see, but how is that possible? I once heard that faith is based on being consistent. The more consistent you are with God, the more you get to know Him and see who He really is. Faith is the outcome of a relationship. The deeper, and more natural and consistent you are, the deeper, and more natural and consistent that faith will become. By getting to know Him as a friend and having that relationship with God, it becomes easier to trust Him and believe in His word. Faith is trust. Faith is to love Him even if you've never seen Him. I trust God with the little things.

For example, losing my key card. I know sometimes it may sound dumb and even foolish to ask for little things but God listens to us no matter what. All we have to do is ask. Be consistent with God, get to know Him one-on-one, on a more personal level. Look for Him and don't be scared. It doesn't matter who you are or what you've been through, He is there just waiting for you to ask for His help. Once you do that, just trust Him. Have faith in who He is and show your love towards Him.

— Kehiry Castillo, Class of 2016

The Nursing Home
To Serve

For I was hungry and you gave me something to eat, I was thirsty and you gave me something to drink, I was a stranger and you invited me in. (Matthew 25:35, NIV)

When I was a freshman I honestly believed I had the worst job ever. I was assigned to one of the local nursing homes in Calhoun. At first I hated the job. I dreaded going to work every day and I was always one of the first kids back on the bus.

After a while I was transferred to a different nursing home. My new boss was nice and I thought she was really funny. While I was working there I observed her work while she interacted with the residents. She made those residents happy when she walked around and talked with them or did an activity that they liked to do. My boss told me that the reason she loved her job was because she could help others in need and bring a smile to their faces.

I tried to remember and use that mentality when I went to work as I would help someone eat, get them a drink, help them put a sweater on, or whatever would be required of me. After a while I started loving my job. I couldn't wait until work every day because I knew that I could do something with the residents I was assigned that we both liked to do. They would always tell me that they loved me and were always glad to see me come in and sad to see me leave.

Just as Christ went out into the world to be a servant for God, teaching the world of God's love and mercy, we need to be servants for God. When we go out there and put a smile on someone's face to brighten their day or help another person with their homework, projects, work, or whatever we are called to do, we just need to remember to serve God by serving others and in return, God will bless you.

Reflect: How can I serve others?

Prayer: God, use me to be your servant ...

— Alexis Castro, Class of 2018

Man on the Road
To Serve

For even the Son of Man did not come to be served, but to serve, and to give his life as a ransom for many. (Mark 10:45, NIV)

When driving along the road, you sometimes see someone sitting on the side of the road that might be homeless or in need of something. Think about what you do when you see that person or family. Do you lock your car doors, thinking there is a strange man out there? Do you hope the light turns green before they have a chance to see you? You wouldn't want to feel guilty. I'm sure many of us have done some of those things before.

However, that is not showing Christian love and being a good servant of God. Many of us are selfish in our thinking when it comes to that. We think someone else will do it. Well, if everyone thought that, then who would do it?

Lots of times people think they are too busy to stop and help someone they see. That is just being arrogant. Turning up our noses and looking the other way is not what God planned for us. We should be serving selflessly and for the glory of God every day. To serve God the way we should, we need to be willing to go outside our comfort zone. Sometimes that means we should do something we don't want to do.

When you see some guy standing on the side of the road, go up to him. Give him money, clothes, food, a friendly hello. Going out of your way for someone is one of the ways God calls us to serve. As Christians, we should know how to serve others. Jesus was the perfect example of being a humble servant whenever he could. Our goal as Christians is to be like Jesus and one way we can do that is through serving others.

— Briana Castro, Class of 2018

The Prodigal Son
To Know

So he got up and went to his father. But while he was still a long way off, his father saw him and was filled with compassion for him; he ran to his son, threw his arms around him and kissed him. (Luke 15:20, NIV)

As an eleven-year-old girl, I was a little more rebellious than expected. This caused my parents to discipline me more rigorously. One afternoon my parents and I had an argument, and I was being very disrespectful. They quickly punished me and prohibited me from doing what I loved the most, playing with my friends. So at that very moment I decided to make the wrong decision, thinking I was doing the best for myself. I willingly ran away from home.

I quickly gathered the few belongings I possessed and packed them in my small pink suitcase. I went down the street to my friend's house and stayed with her for only an hour. After contemplating how difficult life would be without the help of my parents, I quickly went back home. Ashamed and scared I thought I wouldn't be accepted back. I knocked on the door and stepped in the house.

My mom hugged me and said, "I love you, don't do it again," with great grief. I hugged her back tightly.

The prodigal son was a son who loved his father greatly, but wanted to go on his own adventure and live his life. His father didn't want him to leave, but he allowed his son to decide and learn from his mistakes. The son left to live a sinful life, but when he realized what it meant to be away from home, he recognized his faults and wanted to return. He was scared and ashamed, but his father received him with a huge smile and prepared a feast to celebrate his return. I left just like the son left, but at the end I returned and was accepted just like the prodigal son.

So many times we believe that we won't be forgiven and accepted back because of the mistakes we've made but that's not true. Just like my parents and the prodigal son's father forgave, so will God. We need to learn to forgive. God loves us all so much that no matter what, He will always be waiting outside the doors with His wonderful arms stretched wide open, waiting for us to come back and celebrate with Him.

— Jojo Castro, Class of 2016

Forgiveness Is Love
To Love

For if you forgive other people when they sin against you, your heavenly Father will also forgive you. But if you do not forgive others their sins, your Father will not forgive your sins.
(Matthew 6:14–15, NIV)

It was a summer afternoon when my family and a couple of family friends decide to go to the lake. I was only eleven years old. This day was the most memorable day because it changed my life in an undesirable way. I clearly remember getting abused in the lake by a close family friend that I innocently trusted. After the incident I refused to tell anyone about it, even my mother.

Years passed but I still had so many flash backs about the situation. I was so traumatized and hurt by it. The hate I had for him kept growing bigger and deeper. I wished so many bad things upon him and held no mercy for him. I was full of hate and anger. I finally reached the point that I could no longer keep it to myself because I was so frustrated and enraged, not only at him and myself, but also at God. I told my mom what had happened. She talked to me and prayed with me. It seemed like it was useless. I didn't want to speak to God because He allowed something like this happen to me.

Honestly, I thought this hate for him would never go away. It took me a while to realize that the only way I could be happy and forget about it was to forgive him and love him. This had to be one of the hardest things in my life. Slowly, with God's help and me allowing Him to enter my heart and change it, I finally felt less hateful about it all. Now, at seventeen, I feel more at peace. When I think about the situation I don't feel that same hatred anymore. I just feel forgiveness.

You may be having a beautiful day when all of a sudden something hits you and changes your life forever. You never expect it, and you are probably asking God why it happened to you, but that's what the devil desires. He wants you to hate and not forgive others. The only way you can forgive and be happy yourself is through God's help. Always keep God in your heart and love others even when they hurt you. Forgiveness leads to love.

— Jojo Castro, Class of 2016

Supernatural Salvation
To Know

And hope does not put us to shame, because God's love has been poured out into our hearts through the Holy Spirit, who has been given to us. (Romans 5:5, NIV)

    I don't know how any of you were brought up, but I grew up in a Seventh-day Adventist home going to church. There was always a pressure I felt because the people at church were so adamant to tell me to tell others about Jesus. And that freaked me out because when you start going door to door talking about Jesus you usually get one of these reactions: One is they love it, it's an answer to prayer, or they can hate it, and some people just find it really annoying.

    That's just how it is with God—they love Him or hate Him. Sometimes we are tempted to blame ourselves when we get adverse reactions about God. "What did I do wrong? How can I change?" We believe a lie that God needs us, but it's quite the opposite. God doesn't need us at all. It says in Acts 17 that Jesus isn't served by human hands as if He needed anything.

    It's a blow to my pride, but its good news because sometimes we get the wrong idea of God that we as a people complete God. And we don't. God's already complete. The point is that whatever we say to people about God, it doesn't matter how they take it because we don't save people, God does. We shouldn't be offended when we get turned down.

    So when we are at our lowest point in life, it gives us great hope because whatever people say, it's up to God. We need to stop taking the supernatural out of salvation—it's always supernatural, always. Romans 5:5 (NIV) says, "Hope does not put us to shame, because God's love has been poured out into our hearts through the Holy Spirit, who has been given to us." That's supernatural, and it's awesome to know we experience that. So in the end, when talking to someone about Jesus, we can say, "I can't save you, but I know a Savior who can."

— Parker Center, Class of 2015

Compassion from a Mom
To Love

Love is patient, love is kind. It does not envy, it does not boast, it is not proud. It does not dishonor others, it is not self-seeking, it is not easily angered, it keeps no record of wrongs. Love does not delight in evil but rejoices with the truth. It always protects, always trusts, always hopes, always perseveres.
(1 Corinthians 13: 4–7 NIV)

When you truly think about it, this is what love is to all, whether someone is religious or not. If you told them this statement, they would most likely agree. When I was in the third grade, a new kid came to my school. We became friends almost instantly, and truthfully it was all because of our favorite video game. When I went to his house for the first time, his mom treated me like her own child.

Before his mom had even met me, she treated me like her own. She opened her home to me and I could tell she truly cared about me. To this very day I call her Mom and she calls me her son. She is always there to help me and is very understanding when she needs to be. Another thing is that she always puts others first. I don't think I can remember a time when she put herself ahead of others or told someone they were wrong unless she truly had a good reason.

In the same way, my mom shows this kind of care to my best friend. As a mom she treats him as well as she does me. She is always there to help him when he needs it. When she can, she does her best to try to make every time he comes over even more special than the last. She always seems to have something planned, and even when she doesn't, she can come up with it on the spot. This is the kind of love that I think is meant in 1 Corinthians 3:4–7, and by God in heaven who loves us as His own children no matter what we have done.

— Colton Chancey, Class of 2018

Grim Consequence
To Know

Eye for eye, tooth for tooth, hand for hand, foot for foot, burn for burn, wound for wound, bruise for bruise.
(Exodus 21:24–25, NIV)

Monofilament line peeled off the spool. My weighted hook and worm soared. But they did not make it all the way to the coffee river beyond. I attribute this shortcoming to my diminutive stature and strength at the time. A little Deric noticed his line was caught in something near the shore. I padded down the bank, leaving church friends and family behind. My eyes focused on a sapling with a wormless hook wrapped around it. I seized the sapling with tiny hands, desperately attempting to shake my hook free of its captor.

A sharp pain jolted my whole right arm. I lifted my right hand to reveal one half of the hook in open air and the other half buried in my index finger. Dumbfounded, I shrieked for my parents' aid. The burly arms of my father hefted me as I stared at the gored finger. Tears dripped from my jaw, and blood ran down the length of my elevated arm and into my shirt.

We were truly in the wilderness. A day and night into our canoe camp trip had put the group of thirty far from civilization and roads. Scared, I heard but did not listen to the adults talking about what to do with me. Finally, my dad solemnly approached me with a pair of rusty pliers.

"The barb is deep in your finger, I must drive it around the bone and through the other side."

The words struck me with fear. I knew this had to be done. My dad picked me up and set me on a bench. Tears rolled down his cheeks as well as mine. The pliers gripped the hook. Pain was all I knew for five seconds, then, nothing. A throb faded to an ache, then a scab, then a scar, then a memory.

Sometimes we get ourselves into horrible situations. We become so helpless that all we can do is scream. God is always there to save us from our mistakes. Our Father hates to see us in pain but will never hesitate to do what is needed to save us, even if it requires pain on His and our part. When you struggle, never forget that there is a God who will carry you and cut your burdens free.

— Deric Cheshire, Class of 2017

Subtle Ways
To Know

Many are the afflictions of the righteous, but the LORD delivers him out of them all. (Psalm 34:19, NKJV)

This day was a normal day like any other. I was driving back to school from eating lunch at home and I really wasn't expecting anything interesting to happen. There is a four-way stop a mile from my house. Normally, I will admit, I don't do a complete stop. Usually, I'll slow down really slow and roll through. However, this time, I felt a decently strong notion not to roll through and to completely stop. So, this time, I decided to completely stop and as soon as my car stopped, another one flew through and really surprised me. I was so surprised and thankful that I listened to that notion and came to a complete stop. Otherwise, I would've been hit and it would not have been a good rest of the day.

Looking back on it, I realize that there is no way that God wasn't a huge part of it. I clearly felt something abnormal that caused me to stop. However, it wasn't strong. God will send signals and little things to tell you just to keep you safe sometimes. Not all of them are going to be giant or huge things that will be superobvious. Just always be on the lookout for these, because God sometimes has subtle ways. He is just so loving like that.

There is a text that I found in the Bible that pertains to this. This text is found in Psalm 34:19: "Many are the afflictions of the righteous, but the LORD delivers him out of them all." This shows that if you are righteous God will protect you. This was one of David's songs singing to King Saul to support him. I think anyone would have found comfort in this kind of a saying and I know I did. Hopefully you will too, and will be on the lookout for God's subtle and protective ways.

— James Chin, Class of 2016

Fun Service
To Serve

God is not unjust; he will not forget your work and the love you have shown him as you have helped his people and continue to help them. (Hebrews 6:10, NIV)

When it comes to looking for fun things to do on spring break, serving others for a week generally isn't the first thing that comes to mind. However, the blessings are worth it. During my sophomore year I decided to join my school's annual mission trip to Central America.

I had never been on a mission trip before, so I wanted to go, but I wasn't sure whether or not it was worth it. I knew it would be fun, but there would be tons of work and the cost isn't small, either. I really had no idea what to expect. So I prayed quite a bit about it. At first it was just asking Him whether I should go. I then decided to ask for some sort of sign. The next day when I woke up I just felt it, words can't really explain it, but I just felt that I absolutely had to go on this trip. I had waited until the last second to sign up for sure. On the last day, I talked to the supervisor and said I was sure about going on this trip. The time came and we left for the mission trip.

I don't think any other trip has blessed me as much as this trip did. Serving others really does benefit you. The list of good things I got out of it goes on and on. I learned to trust God in every way and in everything. Seeing how grateful everyone was after we finished blessed everyone. Not only did my relationship with God grow stronger and more real, but my friendships also became more real as we learned how to build and serve others together. In the end, the trip ended up being more than worth it. I see myself going on another one soon. If you have the chance, take it. If you have any doubts about going on a mission trip, pray to God and in the end it will always be worth it. The blessings and memories will last a lifetime.

— James Chin, Class of 2016

To Lose Ourselves
To Serve

Therefore, I urge you, brothers and sisters, in view of God's mercy, to offer your bodies as a living sacrifice, holy and pleasing to God—this is your true and proper worship. (Romans 12: 1, NIV)

Service: the action of helping or doing work for someone. That was the dictionary definition of service, but is that all what serving is, just doing the work? Reading that definition made me feel indifferent. But as I dug in deeper into service I learned that it wasn't just the actions. I go to GCA, and they have many opportunities to serve others in community service and mission trips.

I went on a mission trip to Panama in 2015 with GCA, and going there really changed the way I looked at service. As I went they had different areas that you could help people in different ways. They had the construction site, the school, pew construction, and the medical area. I spent most of my time at the construction site and it was really hard work. We had to dig sand and gravel, pour cement, carry buckets of brick and gravel, and we had to do that all in ninety-degree weather.

I began thinking, *this is a lot of hard work for a church I'm not even going to attend*, but then I began to look around and to focus on things other than myself. I also realized that I was here for a purpose for others and not myself, and that we were there to show a good example. When the next day of work came around, I noticed that I had more motivation to get the things done, because I realized that the people here needed a church—some place that they could call a sanctuary to God. At the end of the day I felt more fulfilled and happier in what I did. Not only did I recognize that it made me feel more fulfilled but I also recognized that I was also serving God through that, and, in a sense, worshiping Him.

So serving is more than just the action when you do it wholeheartedly. Not only will you help others, but in turn you give yourself the feeling of fulfillment. Even many wise philosophers say that only a life lived in the service of others is worth living. So recognize that serving is an act of worship to God, helps you mentally, and also helps the people around you. So go out and lose yourself in service to others and in turn you will gain much more.

— Mei Chin, Class of 2018

Give Him Time
To Love

The one who does not love does not know God, for God is love.
(1 John 4:8, NIV)

As a kid I always wondered why I couldn't see God. I didn't quite understand who He truly was. At the time God to me was just someone my parents believed in, and because they did I had to as well. When I started school I was teased for a variety of reasons. I was told that I was not going to get anywhere in my life by teachers and students alike, and other stuff of that nature. This carried on for eight years, from kindergarten to the seventh grade. I was confused as to what I had done to attract this negative attention.

I remembered my parents always telling me that God would never leave me and was available 24/7 for all my problems. I started to take religion more seriously my third grade year where other students constantly harassed me. I started to pray all the time, day in and day out. There seemed to be no response from God. I used to ask myself, *is God really real? Does He care about me and my problems? Why is He not answering me?* These are questions I used to ask myself on a daily basis.

One day I was sitting outside praying about my current situation like I had been doing for several years now, praying for change to come to the people that where treating me and other students sub-standardly. The next day when I went to school, I learned who God really was. Those same people that had treated me as if I was an inferior, came over and apologized to me and not just to me, but also to everyone that they had wronged. A few of the kids started to get to know me better and I developed friendships with most of them. After all those years God had indeed answered my prayers. I got baptized that same year. To know who God really is you should stay as persistent as you can in prayer and most importantly never give up on Him, because He will never give up on you.

— Nate Chu, Class of 2017

Speak to the Earth
To Know

But ask the beasts, and they will teach you; the birds of the heavens, and they will tell you; speak to the earth, and it will instruct you; and the fish of the sea will declare to you. Who among all these does not know that the hand of the Lord has done this? In his hand is the life of every living thing and the breath of all mankind. (Job 12:7–10, ESV)

More than ever, mankind is flourishing with new inventions and technology. Every aspect of our daily lives is brewing with worldly obligations and distractions. I have come to find myself, under the pressure of time, constantly subject to the lack of it. With this realization, I have also come to find that I must make time. Take it from the dedication I devote to the things of this world and give it fully to God. However, have you ever sat down to dedicate your time to God, and been almost completely unable to clear your mind of all the clutter it maintains? This is when I believe that it is important to step out of our daily element and make time with God surrounded by His glorious handiwork.

"Speak to the earth." Last year I went on a weeklong backpacking trip for science class to Cumberland Island. It consisted of hours of long hiking trails, research, documentation, and discovery. But what I remember most from that trip is not how tired I became or how much fun I had with my classmates. What I remember most vividly is the feeling of quietness which overcame both my ears and my mind.

My teacher actually forbade us from engaging in any form of conversation that had to do with things like, social media, technology or even upcoming homework. It was complete seclusion from my daily element of life. Each morning we would sit around the campfire and have worship after which we would find a spot and take personal journal time. Later during hikes, he would separate us within five minutes of each other, so that we walked alone in the forest. There was complete and perfect silence surrounding me, interrupted only by my own thoughts and the soft hum of wildlife.

It was in those moments that I truly felt the closest to my Creator. Surrounded by the magnificent work of His hands, separated from the creations of man, my mind could not help but to be clear, dwelling on His omnipotent beauty. Become familiar with the earth, and in the recognition of the wondrous things He has created, you will grow in knowledge of Him and His love for you.

— Desiree Clemons, Class of 2018

Reward of Service
To Serve

And now, Israel, what does the LORD your God require of you, but to fear the LORD your God, to walk in all his ways, to love him, to serve the LORD your God with all your heart and with all your soul. (Deuteronomy 10:12, ESV)

My freshman year during spring break I went to Panama for a mission trip. We got to our motel really late, and then we unloaded the buses of all of our baggage. We had to walk up a hill to get all of it to where we were going to sleep.

That night after a long day, we all went to sleep. The next morning, we ate breakfast and went straight to work, all of us signed up to split up to different places like the school, pew building, construction, etc., but before we split up we went up to the construction site which was on the top of a very big hill. When we got up there, we talked about what was going to happen while we were there. Then we prayed over the construction of the church and everything else that was going on in the schools and other churches.

At the end of the first week, we had church at a lady's house where the people of that area have been holding church services for a very long time. At this moment there were a lot of people that were already thanking us for what we were doing. I never knew I could hear the words "thank you" so many times. We finished most of the church and they held their first church service. I met a lot of people over the mission trip, and both the adults and the kids were thankful for what we were doing.

God wants us to serve in all we do. He wants us to serve Him and others. When you serve, it makes God happy and you never know how much someone appreciates what you are doing for them.

— Kiera Coker, Class of 2018

Hide and Seek
To Know

You will seek me and find me when you seek me with all your heart. (Jeremiah 29:13, NIV)

In my senior year of high school, two of my best friends, Kenta and Landon, and I would play an awesome game. This game was like hide and seek but with a little twist. Kenta, didn't want to play. Landon and I would sneak into Kenta's room while he was out and hide. Our hiding spots changed from behind the door, under his sink cabinet, or anywhere else we could contort our bodies. We went to great pains to get into his room unseen, sometimes waiting periods as long as forty minutes for him to arrive, while knowing that the boredom would be greatly rewarded.

Kenta would enter his room with the same loud entrance, scuffing his feet and slamming the door behind him. Landon and I would wait patiently for him to get close, and then when he was in range we would jump from our spots startling Kenta, while we enjoyed the awkward expressions that graced his features.

Kenta soon became paranoid by our game. He would enter his room calling our names, and checking everywhere he thought we could hide. Sometimes we were where he looked, and other times we were in places he thought we couldn't get. But the majority of the time we were in our own rooms.

Unfortunately, many people see God the same way, they think He is waiting to catch them sinning and smite them down. But God is loving and will always protect you, He will never forsake you, nor forget you.

— Joey Collier, Class of 2014

Completely Still
To Know

Be still and know that I am God! (Psalm 46:10, NLT)

It was almost a normal Friday vespers concert in the amphitheater, but on the way to my seat, my shoe broke. Sandals aren't great shoes to be wearing while walking through the woods and should be avoided, but of course I didn't think about that. After one shoe was broken, I decided I was going to take off the other one, too. Bare feet and the woods don't go together. The whole scenario reminded me of Moses and the burning bush in Exodus 3 when God said, "Take off your sandals, for you are standing on holy ground."

As the sun went down, and Sabbath made its way in, the atmosphere became more reverent. In closing, the band played the song "Holy Spirit" and I could feel a presence making Itself known as we invited the Holy Spirit to come be with us. The people who knew the song sang it along with the band and those who didn't listened.

Afterglow, the optional extra service after vespers, was the most powerful part of that program. Nobody was forced to be there, and it was only the people who wanted to be there who stayed. A fire was burning brightly in the middle of the tightly knit group. Everyone began to spread out and invited the outliers into the circle of praise. When we started, I was standing between my friends, but soon I had a different friend on one side and a stranger on the other.

The music got progressively louder as everyone sang. Nobody cared what they sounded like because they were caught up trying to praise God through music. With my eyes closed I sang along too, until I stopped singing so that I could just listen. I stood completely still with my feet bare, my arm around a person I didn't know, and listened. I was surrounded by trees and beautiful people who, at that moment wanted nothing more than to sing as loudly as they could to praise the God of heaven. With my eyes still closed I could feel God closer than He had ever been. In that moment, I knew that God was real and He was there.

— Kyra Collins, Class of 2017

Selfless Service
To Serve

For what we proclaim is not ourselves, but Jesus Christ as Lord,
with ourselves as your servants for Jesus' sake.
(2 Corinthians 4:5, ESV)

One day I went with my dad to volunteer for Habitat for Humanity. At first it didn't seem like the most exciting thing to do, it was hot and most of it was hard work, but each time we went the excitement grew. The house was being built for a mother with three children. When the walls and roof were finished, she went to see the progress. She was full of excitement and started to plan the house. The next step completed was the sheetrock, kitchen cabinets, and bathroom fixtures. I wanted them to hurry so she could finally have her home. When the house was completed, Habitat for Humanity had a small ceremony to hand her the keys to her new house. She was happily crying and full of thanks. She started to touch objects in the house like they were a precious gift.

When I think back on this, I realize this is the same way our relationship with God should be. The Bible says He knew us before we were born, which means the walls and roof of my life are planned if I choose to accept Him and allow God to lead my life. I believe this can be made easier if we put self aside and serve others in any small way we can. God will provide those opportunities that not only build character but also give a chance to share what God can do for others through us. The most important advice that I can give you is to pray every morning that God will provide a moment that day to do a simple deed that may help someone see Christ through you.

— Abby Couron, Class of 2019

Just Move
To Serve

Nor is he served by human hands, as though he needed anything, since he himself gives to all mankind life and breath and everything. (Acts 17:25, ESV)

As the final notes faded into silence we stood there frozen, waiting for the lights to shut off. My praise band, "Undivided," had just finished its final performance together. I remember walking off that stage feeling nothing but joy. We were only on stage for a few short moments, but in those moments we were able to lose our focus on ourselves and remember what serving God was really about, that it didn't matter whether or not God used us. What mattered was that God moved.

Two years earlier, my band was huddled together back stage ready to close out GCA's Week of Prayer. We went through our ritual of standing in a circle and taking turns praying. "God," we begged, "use us." Every time we played on stage we'd gather together like this and ask God to use us. We went on stage and played our set. That night I left the stage feeling unsatisfied. I was concerned about the missed notes and how the band the night before had played that song better than we did. I went home frustrated, and started to listen to some music on YouTube. Somehow, I came across a video called "Get Smaller" by the band Tenth Avenue North. In the video the lead singer Mike Donehey talks about what is really means to be used by God and the humility that it brings. As I was watching this video something Mike said spoke right to my heart. "The shows that are often the best for our careers are often the most dangerous for our hearts. The temptation to want to be used by God can often become an idol and savior to our hearts."

That night I realized that I had it all wrong. Even though I had been praying, "God, use me. Use our band," what I really was praying was, "God use our band, more than any other band here. Use *our* sets. Use *our* songs. Use *our* talks." After that night I stopped praying, "God, use me." Instead, I started praying, "God, please, just move."

It's incredible how freeing that prayer made me feel. Instead of worrying about ourselves, we can now celebrate God just moving. Isn't that what really matters? God doesn't need us. Acts 17: 25 says, "Nor is he served by human hands, as though he needed anything, since he himself gives to all mankind life and breath and everything."

So when we serve, whether it is on stage, in a classroom, in your own home, let us not forget that everything we do is a gift. All that we have, all that we are, *all* is a gift. Serving is not about us, it's about us being an extension of His hand. So let's stop praying that God would use us, and just pray that God would move. Pray that He would use anyone and everyone to bring about His purposes. It may not feed your ego, but the joy you receive celebrating His work, will feed your soul.

— Aubri Dancek, Class of 2017

Mountaintop Experience
To Know

Now faith is the assurance of things hoped for, the conviction of things not seen. (Hebrews 11:1, ESV)

I lift up my eyes to the mountains—where does my help come from? My help comes from the LORD, the Maker of heaven and earth. (Psalm 121:1–2, NIV)

During my first year at Southern Adventist University, I went on my general biology class's Great Smoky Mountains camping trip. On Sabbath, I chose to go on a hike called Chimney Tops. It was probably the most fun I've had in a long time ... until we got to the pinnacle.

At the top of our trail, there was a steep rock outcropping that led to a small plateau where the view was said to breathtaking. At first, I had no intention of going up. I am not a fan of heights, and if you fell, you were gone. After a while, I figured that I had made it this far and would at least go part way up so that I could say I was on the rock. My friend and I started up but stopped for frequent breaks until we reached the most challenging part of the climb—a smooth-faced rock with not many places to support oneself. I wouldn't be going any further, or so I thought.

My friend was determined to get to the top. I knew I was physically capable of getting there, but my head was turning in circles, and my gut was tightening. As she started up, I decided that I might as well go the rest of the way with her. As I neared the top, I thought, *Once I see the view, it will all be worth it*. However, on reaching the point, I felt intense fear. The top was a scary place to be. As people posed for pictures, I clung to a rock and kept my eyes down, avoiding looking out to the beautiful mountains around me. I wondered why I had come. I had been promised something wonderful, but I didn't get to see it.

Then I realized I still had to get down. I began to panic. No one could make the journey for me. The only way down was for me to force my body to move. I was terrified as I inched down the rocky terrain. It was only by God's grace, good shoes, and encouraging friends that I made it down without a scratch. As I reached the bottom, I was grinning ear to ear, and that's when I realized: this was the true pinnacle, at least of my journey.

Sometimes, the mountaintop is not a place of victory. Life is not fair in that way. Often times, we work hard towards a goal with the end in mind. But sadly, when we reach it, some of us are left feeling like it was purposeless. Sometimes at the top of the mountain, where we should be able to see everything clearly, we are the most confused. It is here we are left screaming, "God, why did this happen? I thought You led me here. What do I do now? I don't see Your hand." It can be discouraging to see others experiencing the victory at the top of the mountain. Their success makes us feel irritated, wondering what we did wrong. We have to make a choice: we can stay at the top and remain angry and confused forever, or we can choose to continue the journey.

Those who continue on are those who know the meaning of faith.

Faith is not based on feelings. In order to reach our full potential, we have to follow God's leading even when it doesn't feel right. We sometimes get the false idea that following God means never feeling fear and uncertainty, but I think it means just the opposite. Following God means taking the path less travelled. Following God means hard work. Following God means climbing a mountain just to find desolation. Following God means that sometimes only at the end of your journey will you see the beauty of the mountain.

— Chelsea Dancek, Class of 2014

The Giant
To Love

So David triumphed over the Philistine with a sling and a stone; without a sword in his hand he struck down the Philistine and killed him. (1 Samuel 17:50, NIV)

During one football practice I was constantly running sprints and plays. On our team there was a huge lineman who towered over everyone. He intimidated all the smaller kids in school. While we were running sprints, he was teasing another student walking down the field to class. While I was watching, he started beating him up. I thought to myself, *this is not right and someone needs to put a stop to this*. Finally, I was fed up with him being mean to others. Although I was 200 pounds lighter, I was going to take on this 300-pound giant, however, I knew that I had the grace of God by my side.

I walked up to him and said, "Hey, put that kid down!" He dropped the kid and walks towards me.

The guy said to me, "What are you going do about it"

I told the man that he was not doing the right thing. I told him just to walk off and leave us alone and he did. I knew that moment that God had helped me talk this boy out of doing something mean again.

David was going to face the 300-pound giant just like me. Without a sword in his hand, instead he carried a rock and sling. He knew he had the grace of God with him just as He was with me. God was leading David's hand while he was slinging the rock. In comparison God was with me when I talked the guy out of hurting the other boy.

God will always be there when you need Him. No matter if you're scared or lonely and even if you just need a friend. David learned this when he killed Goliath and saved all the Israelites. I learned this when I saw the bully had been defeated. Hopefully, I saved all the kids he might bully in the future. Whenever you need God, just pray and He will answer your prayer. He loves you and is always there even though it may not feel like it at times, and you should love Him as well.

— Payton Daniel, Class of 2019

The Power of Love
To Love

If I speak in the tongues of men or of angels, but do not have love, I am only a resounding gong or a clanging cymbal. If I have the gift of prophecy and can fathom all mysteries and all knowledge, and if I have a faith that can move mountains, but do not have love, I am nothing. If I give all I possess to the poor and give over my body to hardship that I may boast, but do not have love, I gain nothing (1 Corinthians 13:1-3, NIV)

God wants us to give our hearts out to others. God helps us through life by showing His love to us. Love is so amazing. It is what motivated the Father to send His only Son to die for us. Without love, there would have been no salvation for mankind. Not only would we be without love, but without the redemption that was given by love. There would also be no faith and no hope. It is foundational for every other good thing in our lives. Only God will satisfy a heart.

David is a good example. He was a man after God's own heart. That's the way we were created to be. This is the spirit of what it means to love God and to be satisfied in Him. When we love God, we will follow and obey all of His commands and believe in all His Word. Love is also thanking Him for all His gifts, and enjoying all He is. It is this enjoyment of God that glorifies Him. Exodus 20:6 says, "But showing love to a thousand generations of those who love me and keep my commandments."

— Filippe Da Silva, Class of 2018

Confession
To Love

If we confess our sins, He is faithful and righteous to forgive us our sins and to cleanse us from all unrighteousness.
(1 John 1:9, NASB)

Over the summer, people will do yard work to keep their yards looking nice. One of the tasks is power washing. Power washing is a task that involves spraying the concrete with water at high pressure. If you pour a bucket of water before you spray the concrete, you think it doesn't look dirty, but if you spray it with high-pressure water, you can see a big difference. Think of the dark side of the concrete as sin, and when you pour water on it, it stays and doesn't look good, but if you spray with high-pressure water, it's like you are being forgiven for your sins.

In 1 John 1:9 it says, "If we confess our sins, He is faithful and righteous to forgive us our sins and to cleanse us from all unrighteousness." *If we confess*—it is like the high-pressure water. God is like the gardener, and we are the concrete. All our sins have built up in us and we can't get them off alone. The wand is forgiveness and the water is God's love.

If we don't confess for our sins, on the outside it would look just fine, but if we add a little water, then we can see all the sins we need to confess. If we ask God to forgive us, then we can be clean from our sins.

— Josh Davis, Class of 2016

The Envelope
To Know

For with God nothing will be impossible. (Luke 1:37, NKJV)

It was the summer before my junior year of high school. Plans had been made, and I had my school year mapped out, or so I thought. It was a Friday when I received a text from my mother that brought me to tears. It was looking like GCA would not be an option due to finances. GCA was my home and I could not imagine having to leave. I was across the country with my grandparents at the time and we started praying. I sent texts to my close friends, and I knew people all over the country were praying. The very next day after church, an envelope was handed to my grandparents. Enclosed in the envelope was a check. God had answered our cry for help and had brought support. To this day, I don't know who that church member was. All I know is that God used them.

It was at that moment in my life that I learned to know who God is. God is a God of miracles, a God who listens, and a God who answers prayers. He is a God that is a close, a personal God. It was that summer that I learned how much He loves me. Sometimes the situations in our daily lives seem too big to handle. That is simply because they are too big for us to handle on our own. Only when we come to know God, will we realize that God is bigger than all of our situations, and He will carry us through. All we have to do is call on Him.

As you go through your day, remind yourself that *nothing* is impossible with God. No situation is too big. Whatever problems might come up God is just a prayer away. He has greater things in mind and longs to be close to you. Come to know and trust your Heavenly Father.

— Michaela Davis, Class of 2016

God's Love
To Love

No temptation has overtaken you that is not common to man. God is faithful, and he will not let you be tempted beyond your ability, but with the temptation he will also provide the way of escape, that you may be able to endure it.
(1 Corinthians 10:13, ESV)

Today many Christians struggle with their faith. The thing is that Christians are known for believing in God. So why do Christians struggle with their faith? Well, just like anything you believe in, if you cannot see it then you have to have some sort of faith. The problem is not that people do not believe that God is real or not. The problem is continuing to trust in Him and to rely on Him.

As a Christian you need to exercise your faith by trying to get to know God. The problem I am going to address is the misconception of the phrase, "Give your all to God." From my understanding people lose their faith every day because they claim God is never there for them. They may say they tried to give everything to God, but they never heard Him speak to them. People might say that God failed them or He is a liar. After people go through those issues they struggle to continue their relationship with God. For some reason they cannot see the full extent of how that relationship works.

How can anyone ever learn something they do not know the answer to? The solution is simple; ask someone who you think might have the answer. If you claim that you looked hard for the answer, but never could find it, did you ever go to anyone other than yourself? Trust me, I struggled with this concept for my whole life. In fact, I finally found my answer after years of searching. I went through the phases and I know your pain. I just hope that if you are reading this, and you have had any of these questions or thoughts, that you will find a new beginning with the answer I give.

"Giving your all to God." The answer to this is what I call a cooperative relationship. Once you claim that you want to give everything to God, then you need to do your part. God will definitely help you no matter what and will always be there for you. The only thing you have to do is try. You must ask God to live in your life and allow Him to take control. Once you do this, then you must continue to surrender your life to God. The truth is that there will always be that one thing that holds you back, and you will not overcome it by yourself. But with God's help you can overcome any temptation.

You cannot expect that these things will just disappear. They will continue to come back, even twenty years from now. With God though, these temptations will lessen. Your problem may occur twice a week. That's when you pray about it and ask God to take it away, but your part is to pray again the next time it comes up. If you continue down that path, that problem may not occur for two weeks. Then the next time it happens, you have to pray even harder. All of a sudden, your problem is not happening for months, then maybe years, then maybe even longer.

God will help you through your problems, but you must do your part. It is a cooperative relationship. Ask God to be in your life and let Him lead in your life. After that, you will need to maintain your daily walk with Him for the rest of your life. This may be hard to hear, or maybe it is the most amazing realization you have had for years. Hopefully you can get something out of this, and it will help change your life.

This is the perfect example of how much God loves you. He has been there for you and will continue to be there for you. No matter what mistakes you make, or how many times you walk away, He will always accept you back. This is a big struggle that every person goes through, it just shows how much God loves every one. 1 Corinthians 10:13 says, "No temptation has overtaken you that is not common to man. God is faithful, and he will not let you be tempted beyond your ability, but with the temptation he will also provide the way of escape, that you may be able to endure it."

— Dylan Day, Class of 2017

Little Temptation
To Know

When the woman saw that the tree was good for food, and that it was a delight to the eyes, and that the tree was desirable to make one wise, she took from its fruit and ate; and she gave also to her husband with her, and he ate. (Genesis 3:6, NASB)

"Silence at last," I sighed. Wait a minute, why was it so quiet? Quiet only means one thing trouble. Then I heard the rustle of the kitchen trash. I jumped up rapidly, throwing my magazine on the floor and ran into the kitchen looking for my baby sister, Kassandra.

My suspicions were proven correct when I found her small frame covered in melted strawberry ice cream in the center of the kitchen floor. The trashcan next to her was completely tipped over and half on top of her. Her hair was covered in sticky, pink ooze and her tiny arms were completely hidden under the mess. She paused and stared into my upset face innocently. She knew that she wasn't supposed to be in the trash.

I took a deep breath and strolled over to start clean up duty. This was the second time this happened this week. First I had to clean up the floor, and then I had to give her a bath to wash it out of her hair. I was a little upset but she was just a baby. It was easy to just laugh it off and smile at her messy face.

This story reminds me of the Bible story when Eve ate the forbidden fruit. Eve ate the fruit even though she knew she was not allowed too. She saw that it looked good, which is exactly what Kassandra did. We have all been guilty of sin at some point in our lives. Sin can look very tempting and sometimes it will taste delicious, but inside we will know that it won't turn out well in the end. God will give us strength if we just ask Him for some help to destroy our temptation.

— Katie DeArk, Class of 2016

God in First Place
To Love

Whoever does not love does not know God, because God is love.
(1 John 4:8, NIV)

Love is a very important part of our lives. Every day we experience and show love, or do we? It seems to come in many ways. It could be love for an item, love for a person, love in doing something, etc. But is that really love? Think about it. Put God in your position. Would He have love for watching movies, playing games, or using phones? Do we really want to love distractions and entertainment instead of loving God? Are we going to set aside God's love for things of this world or are we going to set aside this world to love God?

I know a lot of people who get wrapped up in this world. They seem like normal people. They go to church, do their work in school, pray, and believe in God, but they don't really love God. They put other things in first place. Games, entertainment, friends, and family are put in before God. They seek worldly things instead of God. God gave his only Son to die for us. He showed the highest level of love this world has ever seen. He demonstrated salvation, grace, mercy, and love through this sacrifice. We were given eternal life. All we have to do is accept it by loving God. There are many ways to love God. Showing kindness to others, helping others, and being an example of God is showing love. We can also show God's love to others by bringing them to God. That is the love God is looking for. Are you willing to show this love to others?

— Brandon DeSouza, Class of 2019

Christians for Love
To Love

Your love for one another will prove to the world that you are my disciples. (John 13:35 NLT)

The world is watching how Christians love others. It is the world's right to judge our faith by the amount we love other people. We prove our faith in Jesus, not by how well we keep rules, but by the love that we give. Our love for one another is like a mirror reflecting God's love allowing the world to witness the power of lives transformed. In John 13:35 Jesus is saying, love one another and I will show the world that you belong to Me.

The best thing we can do to reach the world for Jesus is to love each other. If the world cannot see God's love modeled within our own Christian community, they will not be attracted to our faith. The world is desperate for love and to belong. The world is watching us, and they are looking to see if we are of one mind, with the same love, the same purpose, and if we are focusing on the interest of others more than our own (Philippians 2:2–4). The world will make a decision about whether they want to be a part of our community based on what they witness.

It seems in our world today that Christians are known more for what we are against rather than what we are for. This doesn't mean that that we should do away with God's laws or we should stop standing for what we believe. What this means is that our love needs to shine brighter—we need to let our light shine so that others will see the good (Matt. 5:16). We are meant be points of love and light shining into the darkness of the world lighting the way to Jesus. Our love needs to be a beacon drawing the world to Christ.

We make a statement about God by the way we love one another. It can be a positive statement or a negative statement. The world will form their opinion about Christ based on how we get along with each other—how we love each other. Christians are meant to be the salt (Matt. 5:13) that increases the thirst of the world for the Living Water—Jesus. We can be what the world needs us to be, but we have to love our fellow Christians first.

The world wants to know if Jesus' love for them is true. John 13:25 tells us that our love for one another will prove to the world that we are His disciples. The old saying, "actions speak louder than words" rings true—people may forget what we say, but they rarely forget what we do. The world is watching to see how we love one another. Our love is the evidence on which the world will base what they think about God's love. Will the world be drawn to Christ because of our love?

— Melanie DiBiase, Teacher

The Office
To Know

Gold there is, and rubies in abundance, but lips that speak knowledge are a rare jewel. (Proverbs 20:15, NIV)

There I was, in the principal's office for the fourth, maybe fifth time, that year. As usual, my principal asked me, "Why are you here?" I obviously wasn't in the mood to answer. I was sitting in the place where the troubled students sat. I wasn't a "trouble" student. Or so I thought. I was your average student, just trying to get through middle school, so I could get to high school with all of my friends. I don't think I ever realized that I wasn't the person that I thought I was. I thought I knew that I was a good kid, the one that no one would ever expect to get into trouble. But that's just the thing. I thought I knew, just like I thought I knew I was right when I disrespected my teacher, and was sent to the office.

I remember walking down the hallway, on my way to tell the principal how right I was. I had so much pride in my step, because I knew I was right. When I got to the office, I told the principal how I knew I was right. How I knew the teacher was wrong. After my rant was over, he explained how the teacher was right, and why I was written up. We think we know it all, but we need to realize that we know nothing, without God. Because that knowledge we think we have, is rarer then gold, rubies, and jewels.

The Bible tells us, "The fear of the Lord is the beginning of wisdom, and the knowledge of the Holy is understanding" (Prov. 9:10). Our knowledge comes from God. So, if we want it, we need to put our life in His hands. He will lead us in the right direction, and help us out of the mess we have created. With the knowledge of God, your life will be lived abundantly. And God will provide. Just like He did for Abraham, Noah, Moses, David, and YOU.

— Allen Dixon, Class of 2018

When Times Are Tough
To Know

Yet you, LORD, are our Father. We are the clay, you are the potter; we are all the work of your hand. (Isaiah 64:8, NIV)

Have you ever felt like your whole world was crumbling down around you and that God was distant from your problems? For me this question became very real at the beginning of my GCA experience my junior year. Coming to GCA, like other students, was a choice I made on my own. After praying about it all summer, I was sure that it was God's plan for me to be here. On the first day of school I was ecstatic about living in the dorm and the new experiences ahead in my life. The first few weeks of school, however, hit me hard. Being completely run down by all my new responsibilities, I felt destroyed and broken. The various expectations overwhelmed me. I had few friends, stress was overtaking me, classes were extremely difficult and hard to keep up with, and my world at GCA was not just crumbling down, but making me feel like I was not following God's plan.

But how can this be? I thought to myself. *After praying so hard and being so sure that God was leading me here, how can things be going so badly?* Later, after receiving reassurance from God through a letter from one of my previous teachers, I was sure that God wanted me here and that things would get better.

This is a lot like a metaphor I read recently. It conveyed that God is like a potter, He molds each of our lives according to His will. Sometimes the clay is not moist enough or is not molding properly, in which case the potter has to mend and pound it back to a simple pile of clay. If the clay had feelings, this process would hurt and the clay would feel neglected. This is a lot like what I was feeling. Despite my feelings, God was with me through every minute of my first few struggling weeks. In fact, He was closer to me then than when my life was going perfectly well. He was remolding my life when I thought He had forgotten about me.

God is molding each of us. We are His clay and beautiful masterpieces. When we go through hard times, He is not distant from us at all, but rather has His hands completely surrounding us. As He molds, He sees only the greatness that we will become, not the broken negligence of our pasts.

— Sadie Dixon, Class of 2016

Do You Know Happiness?
To Know

But I have trusted in thy mercy; my heart shall rejoice in thy salvation. I will sing unto the LORD, because he hath dealt bountifully with me. (Psalm 13:5–6, KJV)

I'm a typical Adventist, two loving parents, three older siblings, active in the church, never gone to a public school, always private, read my Sabbath School lesson, always give offering, yeah typical Adventist. In my childhood the only thing tragic thing that ever happened was breaking my collarbone. Even then I was happy with my broken bone! I got a lot of attention from my family.

One thing I have heard multiple times is how unnaturally happy I am, especially in the mornings. For some odd reason I am able to keep a happy, positive attitude in any situation, and it can come in handy for most situations. For any bad situation my response is always, "Could be worse!" When I began to get older and experience high school I noticed that being extremely happy doesn't get you very far. Apparently you have to be sad and miserable all the time to get the full high school experience. I never grasped that concept and continued to be happy and cheery all the time.

When my sister was in ninth grade she went into a surgery to get half of her brain removed for her seizures, had a stroke and went into a coma. Seeing my sister lifeless and not being able to move was hard, but I still stayed happy. When my grandparents passed away, and I was broken inside, hearing other people brag about their awesome grandparents was difficult, but I stayed happy. When I felt that the weight of the world was on my shoulders because my grades were not the greatest and my parents kept saying, "Be more like your brothers." It hurt because I felt like I wasn't good enough, even then I was still happy.

Why am I still happy? Because I know the pain won't last forever. Happiness doesn't mean you never get upset, just that when you do get upset and frustrated you don't have to stay there. Knowing the Lord helps you learn that there still is happiness in the midst of anger and helplessness. When David was in the wilderness running from King Saul he wrote many of his Psalms. Psalm 13 is a perfect example.

How long wilt thou forget me, O LORD? Forever? How long wilt thou hide thy face from me? How long shall I take counsel in my soul, having sorrow in my heart daily? How long shall mine enemy be exalted over me? Consider and hear me, O LORD my God: lighten mine eyes, lest I sleep the sleep of death; Lest mine enemy say, I have prevailed against him; and those that trouble me rejoice when I am moved. But I have trusted in thy mercy; my heart shall rejoice in thy salvation. I will sing unto the LORD, because he hath dealt bountifully with me. (Psalm 13:1–6)

Each Psalm tells the story of David in his broken state still happily praising God. He loved God so much that the bad things that happened seemed to contribute to a greater good. David spent time with God and got to know Him on a personal level. God created our emotions and knows them like the back of His hand. We will get upset, downright angry in fact, but never stay that way. God provides our emotions to help us heal after bad things happen. When you come to know God more your life seems to become brighter and brighter. Knowing God means you know happiness.
— Janelle Lyn Dobson (Nell-e), Class of 2016

The Deepest Darkest Hole
To Know

Jesus looked at them and said, "With man this is impossible, but with God all things are possible." (Matthew 19:26, NIV)

So there I was in the middle of the goalie box waiting for him to kick the ball. All eyes were on me. I was uncontrollably nervous, but trying my best to be calm. A person on my team had touched the ball with his hands. The referee called a penalty kick. I remember looking at everyone on my team to see what each one thought about the call the ref had made. They were speechless and in complete shock because the ref made the right call, so there was nothing we could have done. Next thing I did was pray. Yes, I prayed because I wanted God to help me stop this shot. The rival team had not yet scored against me, so you can imagine there was a bit of fear for that to change. The ref blew the whistle, the player kicked the ball and I dived to the right, all at the same time. I blocked the shot!

Matthew 19:26 says that Jesus looked at them and said, "With man this is impossible, but with God all things are possible." Now when it says that this is impossible, doesn't mean just penalty kicks but everything in life. I don't know if I would have blocked the penalty if I didn't ask God for help. Why did he help me block it instead of having the rival team score? I don't know but I thank Him that he did help me.

Sometimes we might be in the deepest darkest hole in our lives, and we don't even have a clue on what to do. God is always there for us, even when all of our "friends" aren't there. If you want your business to succeed, put God in control of your business and have Him first before all else. Not just in your business but in your life too. We also have to do our part in all of this. Just because He can do everything, doesn't mean you don't get to do anything. God wants you to want Him. So we can ask Him to help us in anything, and He will help us because He loves us. So if we put God first in our lives, then we can do things that we never even thought we could ever do.

— Irvin Dominguez, Class of 2016

Jesus Loves You
To Love

For God so loved the world that he gave his one and only Son, that whoever believes in him shall not perish but have eternal life.
(John 3:16, NIV)

When I was about three years old, my mother put my baby sister next to me on the bed. We were watching cartoons and having a lot fun. My mother told me to not let anything bad happen to my sister. So I said "Okay." My mother then went to the kitchen to check on the food that she was cooking. All of a sudden, she heard a loud, high-pitched yell. She quickly dropped everything she was doing and came sprinting towards us. When she entered the room, she saw me lying on my stomach on the side of the bed holding my little sisters hand. She was dangling off the side of the bed!

Sometimes you might be feeling like you're falling deep into sin, and sometimes you feel like you can't stop falling into it. You want someone to help you stop falling, and you feel that there is no one there. But Jesus is there, and He will never let you go. He will be the one to help you. Don't wait until the last minute because it might be too late. Call for Him and He will come to you without even thinking about it. Jesus loves you so much that He gave His own life for you and me.

— Irvin Dominguez, Class of 2016

Peace
To Know

'He will wipe every tear from their eyes. There will be no more death' or mourning or crying or pain, for the old order of things has passed away. (Revelation 21:4, NIV)

Losing a loved one is very hard and painful. You experience so many emotions when a loved one passes away. You may feel numb, angry, or sad. People take it very differently, and it will definitely take time for you to be okay.

I recently lost my grandmother and let me tell you, it has been hard for me. It's not an easy thing losing someone you love and someone that you were so close and attached to. I know it will take a long time for me to recover, because I still can't even believe that she is actually gone. In my head, I was convincing myself that she wasn't dead, that she is still alive, and that I will see her in a couple months for Thanksgiving. I won't see her anymore, though, and I have finally realized that she is gone from this wicked place we live in and call home. I won't have to see her suffer anymore, and I know that she is at peace. God knows what He did and His will was done.

Through this difficult time we have experienced, God has comforted my family and me. I now know that God has always been there for us, even though at first, I thought He wasn't. I truly hope and desire to see my grandma in heaven because she was the godliest woman I have ever known in my entire life. I know she has her spot in heaven, and this world is coming to an end. All we have to do is be ready and wait for the day to come to finally be at peace.

— Karen Dominguez, Class of 2018

Let Go and Let God
To Know

Have I not commanded you? Be strong and courageous. Do not be frightened, and do not be dismayed, for the LORD your God is with you wherever you go. (Joshua 1:9, ESV)

Last year was my first year here at GCA, and it was what you could call a journey. When I was looking for a high school to enroll at, GCA wasn't even in the question. My parents wanted me to go to a Christian school but none really stood out to me. We had a church family member whose son went to GCA. I asked him how he liked it there? He said that it was the best experience that he had ever had. So I came here for Academy Days and he was right; I loved it here so much that I didn't even want to go back to middle school.

When it was time for me to move into the dorm I was ready for high school. Everybody that I know said that high school would be the best years of my life. I assumed that it would be a breeze. That first month was the most terrifying month I had ever experienced. Constantly throughout the month I felt home sick. The schoolwork was becoming too much to handle. I felt that God had led me to a place that was only going to bring me down. I was in a dark place and I felt that I wasn't going to be able to get out.

Some of my friends saw that I was not my perky self. They were talking to me and I started to cry because I felt that it was too much to bear. One of them started praying for me and it felt like a burden was lifted off of my shoulders. After a few weeks everything started falling into place. I knew that God didn't send me here just to be depressed and a loner, but He sent me here to strengthen my relationship with Him and realize that all I have to do is ask and He will guide me through any trials I may have.

— Zoe Dorsett, Class of 2018

Never Alone
To Know

Have I not commanded you? Be strong and courageous. Do not be afraid; do not be discouraged, for the LORD your God will be with you wherever you go. (Joshua 1:9, NIV)

I loved birthdays. Every time January 30 rolled around, my excitement level, on a scale of one to ten, went from a five to an eleven. This is because my mom always threw the most amazing birthday parties. The list of "must-haves" for these celebrations never failed to include a plethora of balloons in every color, giant bowls filled with what seemed like endless amounts of every child's sugary dreams, and incredibly amusing games. After 364 days of waiting, the time had finally come to celebrate my nine years of life. I could hardly wait. I expected the weekend of my party to be as wonderful as usual, but something happened that turned my world upside down. Thursday night, I walked through the doors into a completely different household. I found my pastor, my grief-stricken grandmother, my red-eyed father, and the news that my mom had passed away. My life changed forever.

After the death of my mom, I struggled with the thoughts of knowing she would never see me graduate, wouldn't be at my wedding, wouldn't be there to mentor me and be on my side just because I was her daughter. On top of these thoughts, I had the constant fear that the people I loved would leave me somehow. But over time, I learned that there is Someone who will never leave me. He won't die, or fade, or desert me. He attends every important event in my life, always listens to me, and is the ultimate counselor. He is my never failing Father.

Joshua 1:9 is a reminder that God is always with me, and even though it still hurts not having the best woman I knew in my life, I do know that I have Someone who will never leave. And that is what makes me strong.

— Aaryn Drapiza, Class of 2015

Pointless Worrying
To Love

Cast your cares on the LORD and he will sustain you; he will never let the righteous be shaken. (Psalm 55:22, NIV)

"How would I like it? Can I survive without continual parental guidance?" These are two of the many questions I had my freshman year at GCA. I hadn't had a good eighth grade year. I truly struggled that year and wondered if more would follow. The first semester I was here was difficult. I only knew a few people and was a loner. All my time was spent in my room. I wondered if I liked GCA, but second semester got a lot better. I finally got to know people and made friends. I had worried for no reason at all.

I tend to think about an entire situation and worry about it. According to the text there is no point in worrying. God has got your back. He loves and cares for you. My freshman year may have started off badly but it didn't stay that way. God's care for me will help me.

We all need to stop worrying about the future and what could happen. When we just focus on the bad, our struggles, and life in general, it makes it seem as if we don't believe God's word. He tells us in many verses that He will care for us and will never leave us. Just learn to trust your life to Him, and He will see you through.

— Ivan Egbunike, Class of 2016

My Journey on How to Know God
To Know

May the God of hope fill you with all joy and peace as you trust in him, so that you may overflow with hope by the power of the Holy Spirit. (Romans 15:13, NIV)

We have all heard stories of God's amazing power, but do we truly believe them? I grew up an Adventist, but not until recently have I truly believed that God could do the impossible. Through one major struggle within my family I learned how amazing God is.

One day in middle school my family and I were cleaning. With all the "fun" that we were having, we noticed my sister had sat down. My mom went over to her to see what was happening, and then she realized that she looked as if she was sleeping. My mom kept on trying to wake her up but she just kept on "sleeping." My mom then told my dad to call 911 because something was wrong. When she got to the hospital she was put in a hospital bed. Long story short, she had suffered a silent seizure. She had lost all control on the left side of her body. My family was devastated because she had never shown signs of this before. The process was long. She was in the hospital for almost a year, but, through prayer and devotion, she was healed.

Now this story seems very nice and all, but what is the point? People blame God for all the wrong in the world, but maybe He lets the bad happen to help others learn. From my sister's struggle, I learned that God has power to heal. Before that, I just went through life's motions without feeling as if God was strong. I read all the stories and thought they were cool but I did not know Him personally. Ever since then, I have been getting closer and closer to God. With God's power we need to believe that He can do it all.

— Ivan Egbunike, Class of 2016

Voice Lessons
To Serve

Make a joyful shout to the LORD all you lands! Serve the LORD with gladness; Come before His presence with singing.
(Psalm 100:1, 2, NKJV)

I always dreamed of joining a singing group or even singing in an opera like Pavorotti. So I registered for vocal lessons with GCA music instructor, Carmen Swigert. The lessons were going well. She played the music and I listened to the instructions. And it still went well as she played my simple tenor part. But then something strange happened. She played everyone's part at the same time and I sang everyone's part. I went up and down the scale jumping from one part to another and doing harmony and then the melody. After enduring a few of these sessions, she persuaded me to give up on my vocal career.

The verse above soothes my memories, because it doesn't say make a joyful sound or sing with a beautiful voice. It says make a joyful shout to the Lord. My voice lessons have long been forgotten, but God's praise still actively resounds in my heart and soul. The tune, pitch, or key may not be perfect, but God's praise is always on my lips. In Psalm 67:5 it says "Let the people praise You, O God. Let all the people praise You."

So let our lips and lives express
The holy Gospel we profess;
So let our words and virtues shine,
To prove the doctrine all divine (Isaac Watts, Public Domain)

As we experience many different situations each day, let's praise God in the good times and bad and the in-between times also. Remember that true worship comes from the heart. When we put our whole heart, mind, and soul in praising God's blessed name, great things can happen.

— Joe Ellsworth, Class of 1985

Half Baked
To Know

Ephraim is a cake unturned... But they do not return to the LORD their God. (Hosea 7:8, 10, NIV)

The prophet Hosea used the tribe of Ephraim as an example of something that is half-baked. The people of Israel in the northern kingdom had used God to their advantage, but followed after other gods to worship. Growing up baking and cooking, I thought I was pretty good at making cakes. I even went through the Wilton Course of Cake Decorating and probably made thirty cakes before the request came to me from Todd Hunt (my class of '85 friend from GCA).

He wanted a special cake made for his wedding. He and his girlfriend had worked at Cohutta Springs Youth Camp the whole summer and then decided to get married at the convention center. I checked their cake request and started my work on their three-tier wedding cake with pale yellow frosting. The service was beginning, and I was well on my way to finishing on time for the reception.

The cake was shaping up well and all ready to serve when suddenly the top tier with the bride and groom figurines collapsed. The top tier landed on the floor safe and sound, but the middle tier didn't fare as well. So I quickly shut and locked the door to the dining room and gathered up the pieces. The design was readjusted to look like a stack of large and medium-sized pancakes about thirty inches tall. After the reception, I went up to him and apologized for the style readjustment.

He told me, "It's okay, you're not a professional yet."

A few months later, I studied cake design from Roy Dingle at the Village Market and corrected my faults.

Today's verse is calling out those who are overconfident and pointing out the differences between the real and the fake. Sometimes it is hard to know the difference. My friend worked at the Incheon International Airport (ICN) in the Customs Office. His job was to try to catch smugglers from Southeast Asian countries who are bringing in fake products to sell or distribute in South Korea. He would entertain us with stories about the boldness of these frequent flyers. Many of them would fly out with an empty bag and come back in with a full bag and claim their purchases were under the legal amount. The zipper expansion "body" bags were popular at that time. So going out it was deflated, and coming back was overinflated with cheap imitations.

When people are half-baked as the Scripture says, God loses patience with them. It is the same fate for those in the lukewarm stage of Christian growth.

How about us? The completely baked bread is delicious to smell and also to eat. These people have the fragrance of Jesus in their presence. The half-baked individuals have the stink of death or the smell of garbage. God sees us as we really are and works on those defects by rubbing off the rough edges. Finally, the purity of the heart shines through.

May we always desire the pureness of God's character. May we be real and not fake Christians.

— Joe Ellsworth, Class of 1985

Judging Others
To Love

But the LORD said to Samuel, "Do not look at his appearance or at his physical stature, because I have refused him. For the LORD does not see as man sees; for man looks at the outward appearance, but the LORD looks at the heart. (1 Samuel 16:7, NKJV)

During my junior year at GCA, I had the privilege of going on the New England trip with my classmates. The purpose of this trip was to acquaint us with the location and stories behind the studies found in our literature and history books. It was a hands-on learning experience.

Traveling up and down the roads in our infamous blue school bus helped us all get well acquainted with each other. After sunset the seating would become segregated, with the boys on one side and the girls on the other. If one was lucky enough to find a spot under the seats, one could lie down and sleep. The bus was staffed with four sponsors who sat toward the front of the bus to make sure the traveling went smoothly. The large pieces of luggage were piled in the back of the bus taking over about eight of the seats in the back.

One night while staff member Mr. Ed Connell was driving, a form appeared on top of the luggage in the back of the bus. It looked as if a couple was making out in full view of everyone. The driver called out for the people to get down off the luggage because that type of action was not allowed on the bus. The guy tried to explain that he was alone and hugging himself. But not many believed him. The truth came to light, when he sat back down in his own bus seat. It looked like one thing was happening, but it was only a prank played on the staff at night.

Our eyes are often fooled by what we think we see. It is also very common to judge people and put them into boxes of our liking. Mother Teresa said this about our situation, "If you judge people, you have no time to love them." Wise words, in my opinion. Romans 14:13 (NIV) gives us some additional words of advice: "Therefore let us stop passing judgment on one another. Instead, make up your mind not to put any stumbling block or obstacle in your brother's way."

I would like to suggest that we find ways to bless, rather than judge each other. There is a blessing found in Numbers 6:24–26 (NIV) that we can personalize by inserting the name of a person in place of the word "you." By way of example, I will use the name of my classmate, Karla Peck Reel in the blessing.

"The Lord bless Karla and keep her;
The Lord make His face shine upon Karla and be gracious to her;
The Lord turn his face toward Karla and give her peace."

By praying this prayer for your family and friends, your thoughts go out to them and they are lifted up before God. Let's bless others instead of judging them.

— Joe Ellsworth, Class of 1985

Garbage Run
To Serve

Come to Me, all you who labor and are heavy laden, and I will give you rest. (Matthew 11:28, NKJV)

One of my work assignments as a student at GCA was working in maintenance for Arnold Basham. One of my responsibilities was doing the garbage run. This involved driving around campus emptying all of the tall garbage cans into the truck and picking up the food garbage from the cafeteria. It was a dirty and difficult job. My partner and I had to lift those heavy cans over our heads and dump the stuff in the back of the truck. Sometimes it would take three of us to do it properly. It was a dirty and difficult job, but it had its benefits! After an hour or so of hard labor, the drive to and from the dump was well worth the effort. It was like a reward for finishing the job.

God offers us some help—He says, give it to Me and I will carry your load. We reluctantly allow Him to carry two of the corners of our load. We carry it awhile together and then all of a sudden take it all back again. It would be like carrying the weight of those large garbage cans while standing in the bed of the truck. When we try to carry our own heavy loads we totally miss the point of having a Savior and having someone to carry the burden. He offers a solution for all of our problems and longs to have us trust him enough to let Him have them all.

As we encounter the problems in our daily lives I pray we will realize help is available. It is as close and quick as turning to God in prayer. May God help us learn to trust Him to carry all our burdens!

— Joe Ellsworth, Class of 1985

Angels
To Love

For He shall give His angels charge over you, to keep you in all your ways. (Psalm 91:11, NKJV)

The summer after graduating from GCA, I got a job at Cohutta Springs Youth Camp. My main duties were constructing buildings and cutting the grass with a weed eater. We had a team that built the Mountain Lore cabins that summer. My building partner was Jeff Clevenger, a fun-loving guy who made us all laugh a lot. But when it came to building log cabins, we were both in the same boat. We didn't have a clue about choosing the correct trees, skinning the trees, notching the trees, and putting the concrete chinking in the cracks.

All was going well with the construction, but then the weather turned nasty. We were cold one day, so we built a fire in the fire pit between the cabins. In the area of the fire, were two containers full of gas. One was for the lanterns and one was for the chainsaw. Jeff grabbed the nearest can and threw a cupful on the fire. We heard a quick pop and jumped out of the way as the explosion shot into the air. After picking ourselves up off the ground, we decided take a nap under the tin roof in the loft of the newly made log cabin. I'm sure our guardian angels were working double time on that day.

Another type of angel story is of those who come to us in disguise.

"Let brotherly love continue. Do not forget to entertain strangers, for by so doing some have unwittingly entertained angels" (Heb. 13:1–2, NKJV).

There were many volunteers on the building team at Cohutta Springs who came and helped out that summer. Most of them were involved with Pathfinders, who happened to have a few weeks or days off from their regular jobs. I remember clearly Walter Earle and Bob Bird would pop in and surprise us with a new building design and new pieces of furniture.

The cook that summer was also an angel in disguise. Not only did she cook the food, but also would deliver popsicles and drinking water to those on the string trimming teams.

Whether we have some safety issues that need an extra bodyguard or we need to be encouraged or cheered up, angels are at work all around us twenty-four hours a day. Thank God for His holy angels who help us!

— Joe Ellsworth, Class of 1985

A Special Spirit
To Love

Behold, how good and how pleasant it is for brethren to dwell together in unity! (Psalm 133:1, NKJV)

The yearbook for the year 1985 at GCA is entitled "A Special Spirit." There were thirteen special themes during the school year 1984–1985. The ones that really impressed me were the spirit of unity, sharing, supportiveness, friendship, and student involvement. All of these special themes combined, created an atmosphere of peace, love, and hope. And the song that summed it all up is, "We Are One in the Spirit."

I live in South Korea where there is a bond in their society called "Jung." It is the glue that keeps the society tight like a warm, happy family. Navigating down the streets of Seoul, Korea for the first time, I just closed my eyes and held on tight while the "Best Driver" taxi employee drove me to my destination. People drive every which way and reach their destination unscathed, but non-natives find the battle of the vehicles a bit of a hair-raising experience. However, once the door of the office is opened the atmosphere changes completely. Outside, we were fighting in this battle of the vehicles as strangers, but now we are best buddies at the office.

That is like our Christian experience. Each of us has our own battles to fight, but gather together as a team to build each other up. As in sports, whether we are watching, participating, coaching, counseling, or cheering we are all involved. All of us have our part to play in winning this event. Just like the "Jung" found among Koreans around the globe, we have a common bond with the players in our section. All of us can work together for the common goal of winning the game. Or we can even help the other side win by not giving our time, effort, money, and energy to God.

I pray we will have that special spirit of unity as we work as a team for God.

— Joe Ellsworth, Class of 1985

Forgiveness
To Love

Return, O Lord, rescue my soul; save me for the sake of your loving kindness. (Psalm 6:4, NASB)

There was a group of friends that always did everything together. They were the best of friends. If one of the friends got in trouble, the rest of the group would try as hard as they could to get him out. These friends were loyal to each other and would seem to have an unbreakable bond. One day one of the friends named Jerry started to persuade the group to steal from a gas station. The group said no, but Jerry still had the idea in mind. After school Jerry decided instead of hanging with his friends, he would go to his house and plot to steal from the nearest gas station. That same afternoon he went and robbed the gas station. Soon after he got away, the police caught up with him and captured him.

Psalm 6 is all about repenting from sin. It is also about how to stay away from Satan. We cannot be fooled by Satan's trickery. God wants us to stay on the right path. If we fail to stay on God's path, then He is waiting for us to come back to Him and ask for forgiveness. He wants us to ask Him to get us out of that hole and repent. The chapter is all about repentance. No matter who we've hurt or what we have done, God is waiting with open arms.

Jerry let Satan in his mind and allowed himself to be persuaded. In a way Jerry is like us. The group of friends is like God and His angels. Satan will do his best to try and separate us from God. In that time we must have the strongest of faith. If we fall into Satan's trap, we need to ask close friends or God to help us out in the situation. When we confess to God what we have done wrong, then He will forgive us with His loving kindness.

— Rafael Encarnacion, Class of 2019

Dear Future Me: The Game Plan
To Know

"For I know the plans I have for you," declares the LORD, "plans to prosper you and not to harm you, plans to give you hope and a future." (Jeremiah 29:11, NIV)

Look back a year from today. Chances are you cringed or wished to go back to those sweet, simple times. We think we know the basis of our future, but we really don't.

Last year I had to fake my way through a lot of things like, music, academics, and people. It was just a big game of pretending that I was fine, showing everyone that I could do it on my own, even though I wasn't fine. This year it's been different. I am the one helping others who are like I was last year. I would never have guessed that I would progress as much as I have in only a year. The thing that's changed the most is my walk with God. Before I was like a dog on a leash, running up ahead and tugging which way I wanted to go. This year it feels like I'm walking beside Him, letting Him lead. Let Him lead your life too. He has an amazing future planed for us! He won't make us go through those doors. We have to choose them ourselves.

"When you are going through something hard and wonder where God is, remember the teacher is always quiet during a test." –*The Toilet Paper*

He has something planned; we just have to have faith in Him. Think about next year, and the year after that. Perhaps you have a plan, but God has an even better one.

— Megan Epperson, Class of 2018

God Had a Plan
To Serve

Then I heard the voice of the LORD saying, "Whom shall I send? And who will go for us?" And I said, "Here am I send me! (Isaiah 6:8, NIV)

I had been packing and double checking all my things making sure I had everything to embark on our regular mission trip to Central/South America. This year our trip was to Panama. This was my first mission trip, and my first time out of the country, and I was super excited. I had always wanted to go to Panama, since I had Netflix splurged all of *Prison Break* with a whole season set in Panama (a pretty good show I must add). And I was honestly a little scared and excited about going to Panama. But God had wanted me to come to Panama. He provided the funds I needed, and we were blessed with smooth travelling. He had a plan for me.

In the book of Isaiah, God also had a plan for the prophet Isaiah. The stereotypical prophet would be shouting at the establishment from the street corner, but you could find Isaiah in the royal palace as a sacred adviser to the king himself.

I had originally gone to Panama with the wrong intentions, just thinking I'll be able to see the same stuff that the *Prison Break* cast did, and so on, but that was a quick turnaround because I was beginning to see the bigger picture at hand and the real reason for being there.

We see God take an unworthy human and turn him into a man who became very important to the fate of Judah. In verses 6 and 7 of Isaiah 6, a seraph (one of Gods messenger angels) takes a hot coal and presses it to Isaiah's lips and says, "See that this has touched your lips; your guilt is taken away and your sin is atoned for."

God had a plan for me, I was that "Isaiah," and I was the unworthy human being used as a tool willing to be used for Christ's mission. You don't have to go to a foreign land, or even Panama, to be a blessing to somebody. It can be as simple as holding the door for someone or giving a smile to someone looking down. Pick them up. He has a plan. Just let Him use you today.

— Truman Findley, Class of 2016

How Do I Help My Friends?
To Love

Jesus prayed, "I pray for them. I do not pray for the world, but for those whom You have given Me. For they are Yours. I do not pray that You should take them out of the world, but that You should keep them from the evil one." (John 17: 9, 15, NKJV)

Have you ever felt like you are not helping your friends enough? I know that personally, I sometimes feel very selfish and useless. I sometimes pray, "God! I'm not helping my friends! They are hurting! What am I doing wrong?" I'm scared to go out of my comfort zone to talk to someone who is crying. Am I letting God down?

This question was really plaguing me one night and I was really feeling bad. Suddenly, a scenario I had read in my Bible during religion class popped into my head.

Jesus was about to be crucified and He was terrified. He knew that in a few short hours, He would be taken into custody, be beaten, and then killed. But one of the most pressing things on His mind was us. What would happen when we no longer had Him with us in the flesh? How would we stand the trials that we would face? Even before the realizations of His helplessness to do anything hit Him, He was praying. And we are whom He prayed for.

So maybe, if you are feeling helpless to comfort a hurting friend, and all you want to do is fix their problems, but you can't, just pray for them. That's one of the best ways you can love them. No matter how big their problems and their hurt God knows what to do.

> Just love them like Jesus, carry them to Him
> His yoke is easy, His burden is light
> You don't need the answers to all of life's questions
> Just know that He loves them and stay by their side
> Love them like Jesus. ("Love Them Like Jesus," Casting Crowns)

— Rebekah Fink, Class of 2016

Looking Deeper
To Love

But the LORD said to Samuel, "Do not look on his appearance or on the height of his stature, because I have rejected him. For the LORD sees not as man sees: man looks on the outward appearance, but the LORD looks on the heart." (1 Samuel 16:7, ESV)

I didn't like her from the moment I saw her. Her curly red hair reached to her lower back and her light hazel eyes complimented her skin tone. Her nose fit the rest of her face perfectly, centered between her rosy cheeks. Like, who did she think she was? I thought she was pretty, and, because I had labeled her pretty, I also labeled her stuck up. I would never be friends with her.

If you haven't guessed it already, I judge. When I first lay eyes on someone, I automatically start disliking something about them. It doesn't matter who they are or where I meet them, but something about them will tick me off.

But wait a minute. Maybe it's something in me.

When Samuel the prophet was led by God to choose a new king, he got a little bit hung up on appearance. Even though Samuel was looking at David's brothers and thinking what good kings they would make, my judging what I dislike in people isn't much different.

As humans, all we focus on is what we see. However, God has given us a challenge to look deeper! His gentle scolding to Samuel still applies to us today. "Don't focus on what they look like," He says. "Use My eyes and My love to look deeper! I believe in you."

— Rebekah Fink, Class of 2016

God Has a Plan
To Know

The LORD is my strength and my song; He has become my salvation. There are shouts of joy and victory in the tents of the righteous: "The LORD's right hand performs valiantly! The LORD's right hand is raised. The LORD's right hand performs valiantly!"
(Psalm 118:14-16, HCSB)

It was November 29, 2014, the day after my eighteenth birthday. I was surrounded by friends and family on the way to an afternoon of food and fun. The joy was interrupted by a phone call. The voice on the other end was telling me something that almost sounded too surreal to accept. A plane crash had taken place. A crash involving my grandparents, my uncle and his girlfriend. The reason it seemed so outlandish is that I didn't even think that it could happen. I had flown with them countless times to Canada and back for summer fishing trips.

They had taken off and as they did so, the engine stalled. As the plane descended it was headed for a frozen river, for they were taking off from Berrien Springs, Michigan. Miraculously, they were able to get enough lift to make it over the river and land in a residential neighborhood, barely missing trees as well. After the crash my grandfather, in his 60's, pulled my unconscious uncle who had broken his jaw, my uncle's girlfriend who had broken her ankle, and my grandmother who shattered her pelvis out of the mangled wreckage. All with fractured vertebrae. This entire situation makes the verse above all too real for me.

There were many more negative outcomes that could have been a result of the crash. But they survived and are alive and well to this day. Nothing short of a miracle could have been responsible for that. God has a plan for us all and He loves us all the same. I have no doubt in my mind that God saved them. And whenever we are in trouble we can call on God for comfort and love.

— Jake Fisher, Class of 2015

God in My Life
To Know

Be still, and know that I am God. I will be exalted among the nations, I will be exalted in the earth! (Psalm 46.10, ESV)

My relationship with God started out very tough. Even though I went to church every weekend and went to an Adventist school all of my life, I still felt like He wasn't there for me during some of those years. Growing up, I never really had many friends in my own grade. Most of my friends were in the upper classes or in the lower classes. When my friends would talk about what they had done over the weekend and how everyone was there, someone I didn't really talk to would come up to me and say, "Were you at the party?" I then felt like I wanted to say yes even though I wasn't at the party.

God started to talk to me a lot more in my later years. I started to take baptismal lessons in the school year of 2010. In the summer of 2010 I went to Cohutta Springs Youth Camp thinking that it was a regular trip to camp like every year. But then I felt as if God started to speak to me, so on the Sabbath before I went home, I asked God to come in my heart and stay in my heart.

My freshman year started at the academy near my home, and I thought I still had all of my friends, but they still treated me like they did as we were growing up. At vespers one night I was alone. My parents walked over to me and asked if I was okay, and I said yes, but I really wanted to go home so I didn't have to be there. Leaving my friends and coming to a new school was tough for me. I told a handful of people that I was leaving and the rest didn't know until I was gone.

God pointed me to GCA. When I came for a tour, everyone was so nice they came up to me and started to talk to me, asking if I was going to go to school there or if I was just looking at the school. This school has kids from all over the United States and the world. Even though everyone's not perfect, they still show the respect and show that they are always there for me.

— Mike Fisher, Class of 2018

Service to Others
To Serve

As each has received a gift, use it to serve one another, as good stewards of God's varied grace. (1 Peter 4:10, ESV)

A couple years ago, on a Sabbath afternoon in the winter, I went with my church to go feed the homeless. We made sack lunches and handed them out to people. After a while we came across a mom with two little kids. They were sitting on a nearby bench. Approaching them, I could tell they were cold, and the clothes they had were ripped and worn. The mom had her clothes in the worst condition and her shoes were barely staying together.

After a while of talking with the family, one of the girls did something that really shocked us. She had just gotten a pair of new and expensive shoes, and she asked the woman what size her shoes were. Finding out that they were the same size, she gave her shoes to the homeless woman with no hesitation. For the next fifteen minutes they were hugging as the woman cried.

This is a story that has really helped me define what serving God and others means. The definition of service is to perform duties or services for another person. So many times in the Bible God talks about how we need to serve others and Him. In the Bible verse for this devotional, God says to use our gifts to serve one another. He gave us many gifts and talents that can be used to serve Him, whether it be singing, being a leader, or having that urge to share Jesus with other people. So many times we get caught up in ourselves and only care about what we want or what we need that we don't see the other people who have a much greater need than us. The girl in our group put herself out there and cared more about others than herself. God has called us to serve, and I think that we should do something about that.

— Sarah Fisher, Class of 2019

Gangster's Love
To Love

If I had the gift of prophecy, and if I understood all of God's secret plans and possessed all knowledge, and if I had such faith that I could move mountains, but didn't love others, I would be nothing. (1 Corinthians 13:2, NLT)

There was a rich man was traveling along a road minding his own business. Taking a stroll around the city, he accidentally walked into an alleyway. Suddenly POW! A black figure in the blink of an eye smacked him on the head. In pain he tried to cry out, but a big thick hand covered his mouth tightly. In only a few moments of strangling, turning, and struggling to break free, he was smacked again, even harder this time. With a cracking sound, the rich man's left hip broke. Since he couldn't do anything, the mysterious man threw him around beating him. This man took all his clothes and valuables and left the rich man to die of his wounds.

Next morning when dawn broke, a wealthy pastor that worked at the big church a few blocks down passed by. Seeing the gory figure, he walked at faster pace. With a disgusted voice he said, "These sinful people, they are all evil. At least I know the Bible and they don't."

Minutes later a Christian walked by. He looked at the bloody man thinking of what to do, but sadly walked by, thinking to himself, *The pastor at my church wouldn't be happy if I helped a sinner.*

Evening was coming. A gangster drove up to the beaten man who was losing blood slowly and found compassion for him. Slowly and gently, he put him in the back seat of the car. Using strips of cloth from a jacket he never wore that was in the back of his car, he made a tourniquet and stopped the bleeding, learning from his past experiences in gang fights. Finally getting to a nearby hospital, he called the rich man's wife to tell her what happened and told her where he was. The gangster stayed by the rich man in the hospital room until the doctors were ready to help him. Ever since that day the rich man never forgot about that gangster.

Sometimes we are like the Christian and pastor in this story. We are focused on ourselves, not others. Let's be more like the gangster in this example and always sow God's love.

— Geoffrey Fowler, Class of 2018

To Know the Incomprehensible
To Know

When you are brought before synagogues, rulers and authorities, do not worry about how you will defend yourselves or what you will say, for the Holy Spirit will teach you at that time what you should say. (Luke 12:11–12, NIV)

A struggle that has been pricking at my brain more often than not is knowledge. Many times I fear being asked many questions about my faith because I'm afraid of saying the wrong thing, or saying something that makes it all the more confusing. As a Christian, this walk with Christ is quite confusing to explain, and what we put our faith in is not always easily comprehended.

Over the summer, I wrestled with the fact that my memory is very weak. My brain holds on to the things it wants to hold on to. I would ask myself to think of some verses of Scripture and one or two might jump at me. However, when it comes to witnessing, which I believe is God's plan for me, I cannot just be spitting one or two verses trying to give evidence for God Himself and His word.

One day in religion class a real, relatable, controversial question came up that erupted a flow of many other mind-boggling questions. The teacher gave us the best answers he could. However, I was frustrated because I felt distant from God and did not feel like I knew enough. I wondered, *what would I tell someone with those questions? Would I just walk away? Would I just give one or two verses and tell them that we will struggle with this together?* I couldn't take it. It left me uneasy and confused.

I never questioned God's existence, but I did question why we aren't given complete knowledge and why His vastness cannot be shared with us so that we can spread it to the entire world. That night, my dean stopped all the girls that were present at the previous religion class. Many of us still had questions and were unsatisfied with the answers from earlier that day. The dean looked us all in the eye and told us that God has the answers. Those words sprinted back and forth in my mind. She went on to say that we don't always, and never will have all of the answers to completely grasp the unmatched power of God and why these things happen to us. We as humans don't have the mind to grasp the power of God. He is too much greater. That is why we are sharing about the One who can save us from our sins, and one day we can ask all the questions we want to the One who made us. For now we wait, we ponder, we study, we love.

To know God is to remember that we can't do this all on our own. God has a plan for us all. As long as we keep our eyes on the cross, we don't have to worry about the questions that may come our way. Luke 12:11 (NIV) says, "When you are brought before synagogues, rulers and authorities, do not worry about how you will defend yourselves or what you will say, for the Holy Spirit will teach you at that time what you will say." God has not left us here alone to defend Him and prove His existence. God is a just and loving God, He knows all and will give us exactly the words to say when the time comes. All God wants is for as many of His children to come home with Him as possible. He will not leave you when you need Him the most.

I challenge you to dig into the Creator's book and get to know Him like never before.

Prayer: Lord, help me with those in disbelief, so that I may be a vessel for you.

— Cassie Freeman, Class of 2017

Christmas Box Surprise
To Serve

Give, and it will be given to you. A good measure, pressed down, shaken together and running over, will be poured into your lap. For with the measure you use, it will be measured to you.
(Luke 6:38, NIV)

It's Christmas season, and at my church, we always collect boxes of non-perishable food and such in wrapped boxes and send it off to people who need them. But a few years ago, it hadn't been a happy season financially for us, since the company that my dad worked for had recently gone out of business, which left us with no incoming money, and Christmas is the worst season to get caught in without a job. So the pickings were a bit slim in our cupboards that year, but thankfully my grandparents had recently sent us a large Costco-sized box of assorted cans of veggie-meat. We were thankful because nothing is more depressing than a mostly empty cupboard to a seventh-grade guy's eyes.

One day my mom came with one of the decorated boxes for church food baskets and said it was time to sort out which cans of veggie meat we were going to donate. My little sister, not knowing the full circumstance our family was in, happily started helping by pulling out what it seemed to me our only lifeline and started putting them in the food basket. I, of course, started to object to this, asking how we ourselves are going to survive if we're giving away our almost non-existent food. My mom said that God wants everyone to share, even if we don't have much, and that we were only tithing our food. So for every ten cans we pulled out, we would put one of those in. After I carefully helped select the veggie-meat I least like to go into the box and put in a couple bags of pasta and such, the "torture" and the food basket were complete.

A few weeks after we brought the box to the church, my mom herded my sister and I into our van to run some errands on Sunday morning. Mom had a bit of a sparkle in her eye, which I'm not sure brought me hope or more worry. We drove to this small building off the side of the road that I didn't recognize at all. Then suddenly, after the doors opened, some people just started piling wrapped boxes of food into our van, so much that I had to lift my legs to fit everything in. This was mind-blowing. We were receiving more food that what we gave. When God gives us a small amount of blessing and we share it or give it back to Him, He will be good to overflow us with more blessing.

— Kody Futcher, Class of 2018

Faking It
To Know

And He said to them, "You are those who justify yourselves in the sight of men, but God knows your hearts; for that which is highly esteemed among men is detestable in the sight of God."
(Luke 16:15, NASB)

Kids nowadays will do anything to get out of going to school. Playing sick is by far the most cliché and frequently used technique in history. When I was in the ninth grade, I tried this method out for myself. It was a Tuesday night, and a big rough draft over *To Kill a Mockingbird* was due the next morning. Being the lazy freshman that I was, I had barely started on the paper, so I thought that playing sick was the best way to get out of turning it in the next morning.

My friend, Jasmine Ponce, was on sick list that day due to pink eye, so I decided that it would be the best thing to fake. That night I practiced irritating my eye by stupidly putting toothpaste on it. The next morning Dean Janet saw me and somehow believed my story. I was put on sick list, and the school nurse would check me when she was available. In an hour or so, the nurse saw me and knew that I was faking it. Although she didn't accuse me of lying to her and the dean, she took me off sick list and I was to go to the next period class.

Christians sometimes fake it like I did that day. Just how others thought that I was actually sick, other people can look at Christians and think that they are perfect, but only God knows how we really are. We must be careful where our heart is, so we aren't doing good acts just to appear as good Christians. Others can look at us and believe that our actions are pure, but just like the nurse knew I was faking it, God knows when we are too.

— Lily Gammada, Class of 2015

My Devotional Life
To Love

He will wipe away every tear from their eyes, and death shall be no more, neither shall there be mourning, nor crying, nor pain anymore, for the former things have passed away.
(Revelation 21:4, ESV)

This is going to be my testimony on how I got to know Christ. I will be telling you how my life was before Christ, how I met Him, and how my life was after Christ. It goes all the way back to 2010 when I went on a summer vacation to the Dominican Republic. I went to visit my family and to go visit a lot of places. I was staying at my cousin's house at the time and it was so much fun. I grew so close to my aunt and uncle during that time because I hadn't seen them in years. I was there for about a solid month, and at the time, I was loving life, even though I hadn't met Jesus yet. I have been going to church all my life but you know, I hadn't really met God spiritually and everything. So my life before I met Christ was all right.

Around 2012 I got news that my uncle from the Dominican Republic committed suicide. It was a very rough time in our family. He was an alcoholic. He wouldn't drink much, but still alcohol is really bad for you. So he committed suicide when he was drunk. I was very sad. I even got angry at God because he passed away. My life just wasn't good at the time and I was very depressed. My mom and I started reading the Bible in the morning. I never really wanted to, but she would force me to. I wouldn't even listen during those worships because I was mad at God. One day I just decided to listen, and it changed my life forever.

After I started having a daily devotional with God, my life started to become better. You are going to need God in your life. He makes you happy and He loves you. He gave up His only Son to die for all of us just to give us a chance of eternal life. I know that my uncle's death made me and a lot of other people realize that God is still in our lives waiting for us to follow Him. I would like to encourage all of you just to have a little devotional each morning. It will make you come closer to our one and only Savior, Jesus Christ, and have a better relationship with your friends and family at home and school. I have realized the difference, so if you want a closer relationship with God, I would highly recommend reading His wonderful Word called the Bible. I would start in the New Testament, but if you really want to change your life for the better read both testaments and some Ellen G. White books, like *Steps to Christ*. So this is my testimony that I have written. I hope have been blessed by it and I hope you think of having a serious relationship with Jesus Christ, our one and only Savior.

— Edgar Garcia, Class of 2018

He Knows What He Is Doing
To Know

Trust in the Lord with all your heart and lean not on your own understanding; in all your ways submit to him, and he will make your paths straight. (Proverbs 3:5-6, NIV)

It was the summer after my eighth grade year. I just finished a chapter in my life, graduating from middle school and moving up to high school. I graduated from a small Adventist middle school in Poughkeepsie, New York. I honestly didn't like it much there; I was excited to be leaving that school. I still wasn't sure yet what high school I was going to, but as long as I wasn't homeschooled I was fine. And I was pretty sure my parents wouldn't do that to me.

Mid-August my parents decided we were going to Georgia to visit some close family friends. We had visited them before, and I kind of liked it there. I was excited for the trip because I was bored at home and wasn't doing much. We got to Calhoun, Georgia and were excited to see our friends. We were having a good time there.

One morning I woke up and went downstairs, but I couldn't find my parents. I asked my friends, and they said that they went to see the academy. I asked why, and they told me that I'm going to go to school there. I did not want to move to Georgia. It's nice place and the people were friendly down here, but I did not want to move here. My parents came back holding papers in their hands. I asked them why they had visited the academy, and they told us that they decided that we're going to move here. My brother and I were very mad! Georgia was nice, but I didn't want to move down here. I liked New York a lot.

I hated the school at first. I didn't know anyone, I had no friends, and I was already a week behind. I was mad at God. I asked why Georgia. I didn't even want to talk to Him. But slowly I started making friends, and I started liking GCA. Now that I look back, I have made some of my best friends here, and I have gotten closer to God. GCA has changed my life and I thank God that we moved here. I have learned to always trust in the Lord, He knows what He is doing.

— Emil Garcia, Class of 2015

Knowing God and Driving
To Know

And this is eternal life, that they know you the only true God, and Jesus Christ whom you have sent. (John 17:3, ESV)

My first driving lesson was terrifying. My foot was too heavy on the pedal, while my hands were too light on the wheel. The car flew forwards, and then lurched to a stop. My driving frightened everyone within seeing distance. All involved were either angry, scared, or both, myself included. My instructor, however, was unusually patient. She silently guided me back on the road when I started drifting off, and told me exactly what I should be doing, even when I thought everything was under control. At first, I hated how she was always correcting my choices. I couldn't even understand why she was telling me what to do, when no one was dying because of my driving. As I continued my lessons with her, however, I began to anticipate what she expected from my driving. As I got better, corrections became fewer and fewer. Looking back, I understood why she kept correcting me. I didn't even need her anymore. I didn't think I did, anyway.

God acts almost exactly the same way. We might think we can do things on our own, when in reality, we are so lost without Him. No matter how many mistakes we continually make, He continues to guide us back to safety. However, unlike my instructor, He never grows tired of us. We may not understand what He's doing at the time, but in hindsight, we'll understand, and actually appreciate it. And as we get to know Him, we'll know what He wants, and we should know that His will is better. After all, He knows a lot more about His creation than we do. As we come to know Him more, we get to know what He expects from us, sometimes even before we ask Him. This doesn't mean we stop talking to Him. It means we talk to Him more, because we must continue to get to know Him.

— Meagan Gardner, Class of 2017

Lessons from an Angry Bird
To Know

"For I know the plans I have for you," declares the Lord, "plans to prosper you and not to harm you, plans to give you hope and a future." (Jeremiah 29:11, NIV)

Whack! I winced and an involuntary groan escaped my mouth as I watched the bird slam into the glass.

Why was this stunning male cardinal attacking our patio doors? His reflection in the glass obviously angered him. Perhaps his self-destructive attacks stemmed from territorialism and a need to keep perceived predators away. Or maybe he wanted to protect his female companions from the attentions of other male birds. Thinking in human terms, possibly he struggled with anger issues or experienced some sort of aviary emotional melt down.

Although curious, neither his motives nor his emotional health were my main concerns. Mostly, I wanted to keep the bird from killing himself and to protect the glass on our patio doors. Pulling beach towels from the closet, I hung them over the doors to minimize the mirror effect of the glass. This worked temporarily, until the bird discovered the lower portion of the door where the towels did not reach. I considered other solutions to halt the bird from his crazed rampage, but nothing practical came to mind.

Whack! Whack! The angry attacks continued. Realizing the failure of my towel-hanging efforts, I gave up.

My husband and I left town for several days and upon our return, seeing the dried body fluids on the glass, obviously the bird had continued his self-destructive encounters with the doors. Sadder still, the bird appeared gone for good. His relentless, angry attacks on our patio doors no doubt took their final toll.

As I cleaned the bird mess off the glass doors I pondered the human condition and reflected on how we so often behave similarly to the angry bird. Like this bird, people get caught in patterns of self-destruction. What makes us repeat behaviors that are killing us, but make no sense? God's heart must break as He watches us attack ourselves and hurt others through any number of insidious or blatant self-defeating behaviors.

The sad truth is we are broken people, living in a broken world. God may not always experience success in getting us to turn from our destructive ways, but that does not mean He ever stops trying!

If my small human heart desperately wanted to protect an angry cardinal from hurting himself, I can only imagine what our perfectly loving heavenly Father must experience as He watches us self-destruct. Jeremiah 29:11 (NIV) tells us of a God who envisions a bright future for us even when we can't see it for ourselves. "For I know the plans I have for you," declares the Lord, "Plans to prosper you and not to harm you, plans to give you hope and a future." He holds out the prospect of hope, even when we are in the midst of pain. He will even step in, if need be, redirecting our steps to a brighter future.

My heart overflows with gratitude for a compassionate God who sees and knows and cares enough about us to craft a beautiful life plan and provide direction when we stray from that plan and hurt ourselves and others in the process. I love God's willingness to risk His reputation by taking corrective measures, even when I don't like them, a God who constantly puts Himself out to save me from myself.

— Nancy Gerard, Staff

Bon Appetit!
To Love

Is anyone thirsty? Come and drink ... Why spend your money on food that does not give you strength? Why pay for food that does you no good? Listen to me, and you will eat what is good. You will enjoy the finest food. Come to me with your ears wide open. Listen, and you will find life. (Isaiah 55:1–3, NLT)

Summer 1976: Europe wilted in the grip of a record-breaking heat wave. In an effort to keep from suffocating in our un-air-conditioned Paris hotel room, my roommate and I opened the French doors that led onto the balcony. Across the street we could see a family in an upstairs apartment, enjoying their evening meal. As sleep eluded us, we continued to watch the family. An hour passed, then another hour and finally around midnight they cleared the table, turned off the lights and apparently went to bed.

The French really know how to enjoy a satisfying meal. Gatherings around food are almost sacred; the fare is wonderful, but perhaps more important is what happens during the time spent at the table. Mealtime is a means for people to connect and Europeans take it very seriously!

As a mom of grown children, I treasure those special times when our kids return home with their spouses. I love creating their favorite foods and serving wonderful meals that remind them of home and family. More important than the food, however, are the conversations that take place around the table—the laughter, the stories, the stimulating discussions over dinner and long past when the dishes are cleared.

But let's say my son or daughter stop at a mini-mart on their way home and fill up on chips, candy, and soda while I am in the kitchen making final preparations for a wonderful home cooked meal. They come through the door, give me a hug, say, "Wow! The food smells wonderful!" But when it comes time to sit down to dinner they refuse. "No thanks. We stopped at the gas station for some snacks on the way into town so we're not hungry." Ridiculous! A home-cooked meal awaits, but they chose to fill up on junk food. Thankfully, that has never happened in our home.

But are we guilty of stopping at the mini-mart, so to speak, filling up on junk food, and refusing the eternally satisfying fare God offers? God extends an invitation to us in Isaiah 55 to come and feast at His table. He invites us, "Is anyone thirsty? Come and drink ... Why spend your money on food that does not give you strength? Why pay for food that does you no good? Listen to me, and you will eat what is good. You will enjoy the finest food. Come to me with your ears wide open. Listen, and you will find life ..." (Isa. 55:1–3, NLT)

The "finest food" God wants to share with us is His mercy and forgiveness, freely offered if we will only join Him at the table (Isa. 55:7). Jesus continued the metaphor of food and drink when He described Himself as "living water" and the "bread of life."

Don't settle for junk food! Accept God's invitation to come to the table and enjoy the soul-satisfying fare He offers in Jesus. Mercy, forgiveness and friendship await and He promises you won't be disappointed!

— Nancy Gerard, Staff

In Perfect Harmony
To Serve

Live in harmony with each other. Don't be too proud to enjoy the company of ordinary people. And don't think you know it all!
(Romans 12:16, NLT)

We are called as Christ followers to live in harmony with each other. But is this an unrealistic expectation?

In 1971 Coca Cola came out with an ad that went down in history as one of the best of all times. The advertisement featured young people representing the nations of the world, standing on a hillside in Italy, singing while holding bottles of Coke. Soon the bouncy tune and feel-good lyrics had people around the world singing along. Two of the more familiar lines from the jingle are:

I'd like to teach the world to sing in perfect harmony
I'd like to buy the world a Coke and keep it company.

What is it about singing in "perfect harmony" that we find so pleasing? Notes that compliment each other work together to bring us beauty in sound, whether by instrument or the human voice, and something responds within us to this harmony. No matter the size of the group, rich harmonies thrill us!

Perhaps one reason we respond the way we do to harmony in music is that harmony speaks to our deep need for human connection and cooperation. Voices or instruments blending, with no particular voice being heard over another, represent this. Harmonies complement rather than compete. No individual voice strives for domination; all voices blend to form a balanced sound.

Maybe the analogy of musical harmony is helpful in understanding how harmony works in relationships. If one part of the harmonic structure (say, the tenor section) overpowers the other parts the sound is not pleasing. If the altos or basses decide to really belt out their part in an effort to make sure they are heard, the results are disastrous.

When sub-groups of people within a community of faith decide that their cause or their opinions or beliefs are more important than anyone else's, they may dominate to make sure their voice is heard. But the overall sound will suffer and the "audience" will be repulsed rather than enthralled by what they hear.

The apostle Paul's call to live in harmony is followed by a couple of how-to's. First, get over your pride, and don't think you are better than others. Your part in the choir is no better than any other. Then he makes sure we really understand by adding, "And don't think you know it all!" Harmony cannot happen within a community if the choir is full of prideful know-it-alls.

Maybe the words of the Coke jingle could be re-written for communities of faith:

I'd like to teach the church to sing in perfect harmony
If love and grace adorn our space, the world will come to see.

— Nancy Gerard, Staff

Don't Go It Alone
To Know

I have given them the glory that you gave me, that they may be one as we are one—I in them and you in me—so that they may be brought to complete unity. Then the world will know that you sent me and have loved them even as you have loved me.
(John 17:22–23, NIV)

Fourteen travelers ranging in age from 17–62 signed on for a tour of Israel and Istanbul, Turkey. All were seasoned world travelers. Any of them, mostly leaders, business owners and strong, independent types, were capable of doing this trip solo.

The adventure started in Tel Aviv, Israel. Some were complete strangers before meeting that first day and our diverse ages made us potentially incompatible—not to mention our Israeli guide and the Palestinian driver. Our final number equaled sixteen.

With group travel you are at the mercy of the tour planners. They determine the hotels, restaurants, and the sites you'll see. However, on the up side, you don't have to worry about a thing. Jerusalem today, the Dead Sea tomorrow—it doesn't matter. All you need to do is meet the group at the bus on time.

Eating together, spending all day seeing the sites, listening to lectures by the tour guide, and meeting for worship in the evenings is an intense dose of people. Yet shared experiences tend to bond people. When those experiences include crossing the Sea of Galilee on a boat, visiting sites where Jesus preached and healed people, and being on top of Mount Carmel where the prophet Elijah met up with the prophets of Baal, you are drawn even closer by your shared faith.

Traveling in close quarters is sure to result in little irritations and inconveniences. Yet such travel helps develop patience and endurance. We become better people when we share or defer to the needs of others.

Perhaps group travel serves as a metaphor for the church. Travelers of all ages sign on for a group travel experience when joining a community of faith. Many could manage on their own, needing no one's support through life. But Christians are warned against the dangers of going it alone. We need each other. Shared faith bridges the cultural, economic, gender and age divisions.

So why travel through life as a group—a community of faith—a church? Surely our shared experiences serve to bind us together. Friendships are formed, and group experiences build us into the kind of community Jesus had in mind when establishing His kingdom on this earth.

In His final hours Jesus prayed for His disciples, those with Him and those of us who follow. His intercession included community. May we be willing to risk inconvenience and some loss of personal independence in order to know the deep connections and joys of group travel through life, thus experiencing a taste of the joys of heaven to come.

— Nancy Gerard, Staff

Moose Crossing
To Serve

I can do all things through Christ which strengtheneth me.
(Philippians 4:13, KJV)

If you ever ran over a squirrel with your car or barely missed a deer you know the awful, helpless feeling of wishing for the ability to communicate with animals about their reckless behavior. Warning signs alert us to areas with high animal activity, but any animal, from armadillos to zebras, can create problems for drivers.

Too bad animals can't read signs. I once saw a cartoon depicting animals about to cross a busy highway, but seeing a car crossing warning sign, they changed their minds. If only …

Animals cross busy roads because roads are built over their travel routes. Humans don't consult animals when we build roads. Sometimes if an area of highway becomes especially dangerous to both traffic and animals, special animal passages are built over the road so animals can cross safely from one side to the other. Experts once constructed a tunnel under a busy Southern California freeway because after the road was built they discovered the highway bisected a well-traveled route of mountain lions and they needed a way to safely cross the freeway.

As frustrated as we may be at animals and their lack of sensibility when it comes to crossing roads, we humans aren't much different. Once we get into the habit of doing something a certain way we often continue the behavior even if it isn't working, and may be downright harmful.

Are we like animals that simply follow their instincts? Is it that we don't know any better? If that were the case anyone practicing a harmful behavior like smoking, eating poorly, or not exercising would remedy their behavior once they were informed of the negative consequences.

Let's face it: behavior modification is very difficult. Anyone trying to lose weight or quit smoking will tell you how hard it is. But to not change, to continue doing reckless or dangerous behaviors that impact our quality of life and relationships is hurtful to everyone.

Unlike animals that rely on instinct, humans have higher cognitive abilities. We can reason, linking behaviors with consequences much better than most animals. The good news is that God has equipped us with what we need to quit crossing dangerous highways like deer or moose.

Perhaps the place to begin is with a reality check. Fill in the blank with your personal human equivalent: "I don't dart in front of cars like squirrels, but I _____." Once you've stated reality, educate yourself on what positive behaviors you need to substitute. Find someone to provide support and accountability. Pray for wisdom. Pray for perseverance. Pray for motivation and will power.

God's Word tells us, "I can do all things through Christ which strengtheneth me." (Phil.4:13, KJV) He doesn't say it will be easy, but He does promise success when we partner with Him.

— Nancy Gerard, Staff

Dancing or Marching?
To Know

Take delight in the LORD. (Psalm 37:4, NIV)

Don't ask me to dance! No, sir. Except for a brief period of life in the early 1980's when aerobic dancing (for exercise) was all the rage, my people did not dance.

Fast forward and we are aboard a boat on the Sea of Galilee with a GCA tour group. The Israeli crew clears the chairs away from the middle of the boat, puts on some traditional Jewish folk music and in their minimal English, motion for us to join them on the dance floor. No one budges. Finally, one of the crew members smilingly takes one of the women by the hand and pulls her up. He motions for the rest of us to join them. One or two join the circle perhaps out of sympathy for their friend. *Oh, this is going to be good*, I think. He shows them how to move their feet to the music, holding hands, going round and round.

Soon enough, the whole group is laughing, smiling and dancing in a circle to the Jewish folk tunes. What a crazy, clumsy sight we are, but what fun we are having! The sheer joy and sense of camaraderie among the group is irrepressible!

In comparison to marching, dancing offers freedom of movement and individualistic expression, while marching is more disciplined. Marching involves everyone doing the same thing in time—left foot, right foot, left foot, right foot. We don't typically think of marching as fun. Dancing, on the other hand, seems to set our spirits free. Just watch toddlers when you play upbeat music. They can't help but dance! Their little bodies bob and sway to the music, their little hands clapping as joy oozes out of them.

Is your Christian experience more like dancing or marching? If your walk with God is more duty than delight, perhaps it is time to reassess your relationship.

David admonishes us to, "Delight yourself in The Lord …" (Ps. 37:4, NIV)). Nehemiah 8:10 reminds us that "The joy of The Lord is your strength." So where did we get the idea that our relationship with God should be joyless, all work and no play? There will certainly be days when we put one foot in front of the other and life feels more like a march than a dance. But on the whole, God wants us to experience the joy of a full and abundant life (John 10:10).

There is nothing that pleases God more than for us to find our greatest delight in Him! When we radiate the joy of the Lord, we honor Him by showing the world how good He is and how complete life is in Him. When we dance rather than march through life, people on the sidelines will join us on the dance floor, clumsy though we may be. And hand in hand, we will find that we are enjoying the sense of true joy and camaraderie that comes from sharing the dance of life together.

— Nancy Gerard, Staff

Learning to Love
To Love

Beloved, let us love one another, for love is from God, and whoever loves has been born of God and knows God. Anyone who does not love does not know God, because God is love. (1 John 4:7–8, ESV)

The first day of middle school I remember looking across the room at a petite, quiet girl sitting awkwardly in a green chair with obvious thoughts racing through her mind. Never knowing that she was immediately acknowledged by all the boys and envied by all the girls, she grew up talented and intelligent, but never recognized it in herself. As years went on she became one of my dearest friends.

As we got older, things got harder, mistakes were made and fights developed; some leading me to think it would be the end of our friendship, but it never was. Praying to God, He helped me realize even though we disagreed it wasn't worth losing a friend over. Though I was almost always the first one to apologize, I never regret reaching out and trying to fix our problems.

Always comparing herself to everyone else, saying she was different, she struggled to see how much everyone loved her despite her imperfections. She was said to be "perfect" by everyone she came in contact with, but her differences got the best of her and the many worldly forms of sin consumed her. She went through phases of life trying to find herself through multiple types of things and people. Looking to God to lead her, but never understanding why He was letting things in her life fall apart. I always tried to encourage her and tell her to hang on because I know God has a plan for her and her many talents. Though some looked down upon her because of the past mistakes she had made, I looked at her no differently. She was still the same caring, petite, little girl, who I had met in middle school. She had been led astray by the wickedness of this world, but continued to ask God to lead in her life daily.

Pushing on through it all, she has been an inspiration in my life. Through the trials of this earth I have been shown Gods love through some of the worst circumstances and have learned to love Him more and more every day. The Greek word love for is agapao, which means to totally give ourselves over to something. To love God is to make Him number the one priority in our lives, striving every day to be involved and changed by Him. I find it amazing how God can work through the worst things in people's lives to bring us closer to Him.

— Candace Gettys, Class of 2017

Not Your Parents' Religion
To Know

Wherefore, my beloved, as ye have always obeyed, not as in my presence only, but now much more in my absence, work out your own salvation with fear and trembling.
(Philippians 2:12–13, KJV)

I grew up in a very conservative SDA home. We did not have a TV, we were homeschooled, and had a list of things we were not allowed to do. When I went to GCA for high school, suddenly I had more freedom than I had ever had. (I know this is hard for my classmates to understand, because when I graduated in 1988 the power in the dorms turned off at 10 p.m., and we had no cell phones or computers.)

I always equated my spirituality with that of my parents. I thought that since they were very religious and strict that I was "covered" by them, too. I always prayed, but I knew I didn't want to be so strict like them so I kept Jesus at a distance. It didn't occur to me until much later that each of us has to discover Jesus for ourselves, and once we feel His love and get to know Him for ourselves, it will be our own relationship!

My relationship with Jesus does not look the same as my parents still to this day! My father does not really like laughing during worships, his prayers are more structured, and our music is very different. However, all this works for them and I am not saying it is wrong, just that for your relationship to be real and personal, it has to be unique to you.

I challenge each of us to make Jesus real in our lives today!

— Liz Theus Glass, Class of 1988

Embrace Who You Are
To Serve

You shaped me before I was born; you put my bones together while I was still in my mother's womb. I praise you, for this body is incredibly and wonderfully made.
(Psalm. 139:13–14 Clear Word)

I was so insecure as a teenager. I found myself trying to find my self-worth in friends, boys, or being a little rebellious. I compared my insides with other people's outsides. I didn't think that maybe they were all struggling with some of the same things that I was.

The Bible tells us that Jesus made us—you and me. He knows everything that we like and dislike about our faces, bodies, and personalities. He wants us to give these "dislikes" over to Him. He wants us to be self-confident, not prideful or "full or ourselves," but to be content. Talk to Him about areas of your life that you want to be more confident in. Try to find five things about yourself that you like and you can thank Jesus for.

After I graduated from GCA and Southern, I went to graduate school for social work. While getting my master's degree, I learned that positive affirmations or "self-talk" could really change negative patterns of thinking into positive ones. If someone puts you down or you are tempted to put yourself down, do what a popular singer says and "Shake It Off," then pray and thank Jesus for making you incredible and wonderful!

— Liz Theus Glass, Class of 1988

Solid Ground
To Know

In a desert land he found him, in a barren and howling waste. He shielded him and cared for him; he guarded him as the apple of his eye, like an eagle that stirs up its nest and hovers over its young, that spreads its wings to catch them and carries them aloft. (Deuteronomy 32:10–11, NIV)

Have you ever jumped off of something and the moment your feet left the safety of solid ground you realized that the drop was a lot farther than it looked when you first climbed up? When I was around six years old I had an experience like this. My family and I went to Wisconsin to visit my grandparents on their farm. They had just finished bailing hay so there were huge cylinders of it scattered throughout the field. Well, of course I wanted to climb up on them, so my dad picked me up and plopped me on top. I thought it was the greatest thing to be taller than everyone else, but after a while the excitement wore off, and I was ready to come back down. My dad saw that it was a pretty big jump for my stubby six-year-old self, so he offered to help me, but I refused. I wanted to prove that I could do it all by myself. As I stood at the edge it looked a little steeper than when I first climbed up, but I was still going to jump, although now I was a little nervous. I tested my weight on the edge to take my leap and the hay started to cave in along the side, which threw me off balance and I was forced to jump. It felt like an eternity as I was falling and all I could think of was *Daddy, help me!* And before I hit the ground, he swooped in and saved the day. He had never left me the whole time and had stayed within arm's reach just in case I needed him.

Just like my dad stayed there right beside me, even when at the moment I told him that I did not need him, God is always right there with us. Even when we try to push Him away, He will never leave. He stays in arms' reach just waiting for us to call out to Him. And the very second we humble ourselves to cry out to God He swoops in like an eagle to catch us.

Sometimes in life we don't want any help, we'd rather try to prove that we can do things on our own. It can be hard to humble yourself to ask for help, but we need to remember that we are God's children. He finds us in our deepest struggles and He protects us, because to Him we are worth so much more then we can imagine. And even if we push Him away, He stays right beside us just waiting to catch us. All we have to do is accept His help.

— Megan Goffin, Class of 2016

Call and He Will Answer
To Know

Then you will call on me and come and pray to me, and I will listen to you. You will seek me and find me when you seek me with all your heart. (Jeremiah 29:12–13, NIV)

While walking through New York City on our junior New England trip, my group got lost. We were following the rest of the group with the teacher in the lead, but then all of a sudden we had no clue where we were, and we couldn't see any familiar faces on the street. We just kept walking hoping that we would eventually catch up with the rest of the group. Because we had no idea where we were going, we got even more lost. Finally, someone decided to call the teacher and tell him our problem. Before we knew it, we were reunited with the rest of our class and could continue with our trip.

This story reminds me of how some of us go through life. We get separated from God and we are completely lost. We have no clue which way to go, but we just stumble along hoping that we will make it through. If we actually got to know God and were able to call out to Him, we would know that as soon as He hears our cry for help, He is right there by our side leading us back on the right path.

Today I encourage you to get to know God. Know that He is always there for you to help you along your journey. Just know that whenever you get lost or are in trouble, all you have to do is call on Him and He will be right there beside you.

— Megan Goffin, Class of 2016

Back to School
To Know

Call to me and I will answer you, and will tell you great and hidden things that you have not known. (Jeremiah 33:3, ESV)

I had always dreamed of going to school. The sixth-grader version of me was anti-social and awkward, but also desperate for a friend. Since I had been homeschooled my whole life up until sixth grade, I was lonely almost every day, having no one to talk to during my "school hours" except my mom. It got so bad that I was crying and begging on my knees for my parents to let me go to an actual school with kids my age.

However, it hadn't always been that way. My siblings were homeschooled too, and I was used to doing my schoolwork with them. Unfortunately, because of our great age difference, all of them left me all at once to further continue their education in a university somewhere out of the state. Not only that, but around the same time, my family decided to move our church membership to another, leaving behind the only place where I actually did have friends. All at once, it felt like everything was taken from me, and I think that was the first time I had actually experienced anxiety at such a high level.

The idea of school had always been in my mind before then, but I had never wanted it as much as I did now. When I asked my mother about it the first time, she told me that if I were to enroll in one, it would have to be a Seventh-day Adventist private school. She wanted me to learn in a religious environment, but the costs for those schools were too high for us. The only way I would be able to go was if she also got a job to help my dad. And as the number of prayers a day grew, so did my relationship with God. I knew and understood that if God wanted me to go to school, He would cause something to happen so that my enrollment in school was possible.

Sure enough, one day our former church pastor, a good friend of ours, called up my mom to ask her if she would like to take a job at the Seventh-day Adventist Conference. Not only was it an answer to prayer, but God also made sure to give my mother a job she where she could easily serve Him through her work. And just one month later, when all the kids come back to school after Christmas break, they would see the face of a young, eleven year-old girl walking down the hallway to the sixth grade classroom that they hadn't seen before.

We as human beings often doubt the power of prayer. We often don't understand that God already has a plan set out for us, and believe that He doesn't care enough about us to listen. But in reality, all we have to do is ask Him. Like it says in Jeremiah, God always knows the best path to lead us down, and if we take the time to call to Him, He will answer our prayers.

— Aleyra Gonzalez, Class of 2019

God Does His Works for Good
To Know

Can anything separate us from Christ's love? Can trouble or problems or persecution separate us from his love? If we have no food or clothes or face danger or even death, will that separate us from his love? (Romans 8:35, ERV)

Sometimes I ask myself why God allows bad things to happen to good people. The apostle Paul assures us that no one can separate us from the love of God. It's said that God is for us and never against us, and if God is with us, then who is against us. Satan tries to separate us from God, but the declaration of the apostle Paul is certain, to say that nothing will separate us from the love of God, because He is for us.

Look at the story of Job. God, the King of the universe and the protector of life, gave Satan permission to mess with His servant Job. God could've silenced Satan, but he didn't do it. This is what is hard to comprehend and hard to accept. We would like it if God would intervene in our story and put an end to the pain, sufferings, accidents, earthquakes, tsunamis, etc. People ask themselves where God is in the book of Job. God first blesses and protects Job, but in the middle of his suffering Job feels abandoned by God. There seemed to be no logic in the situation for Job. But throughout the book of Job we see God's presence, and in the end, God's love won.

When I lost my dad, I had a similar suffering experience just like Job. He was a good man, who loved God, worked for God, a minister of God, a servant of God. He worked hard and did the best he could for God. Then one day I was told that he was diagnosed with cancer. But his faith never failed. And I asked myself, Why him, why do good people have to go through so much suffering, why did God allow this all to happen? But as

I said before we need to learn to live with questions without answers and trust that God's love will never leave us alone.

In conclusion, the problems of life—sufferings and persecution—don't have the power to create faith in us, but these situations reveal our faith. The difficulties of life help us discover our faith. And they can help us to grow and fertilize our faith. God does His works for good. God has special plans for us in the future.

— Carlos Gonzalez, Class of 2018

Light in the Dark
To Know

Thy word is a lamp unto my feet, and a light unto my path.
(Psalm 119:105, KJV)

Darkness. At one point or another we all fear it. We do not always know what is in the darkness, or what is lurking in the dark places.

The summer of 2014 I had the opportunity to work at summer camp. During my summer at Kulaqua, I was asked to be the counselor of our fifty-seven-year-old blind camper, Leslie. I was excited and terrified all at the same time. That week was very difficult, trying, and demanding, but it was completely and totally worth it. Being Leslie's counselor, I got to do absolutely everything with her. I was her sole caretaker for one week, and it was an incredible experience. I did not feel prepared or equipped to take on such a task, but God knew what He was doing. I helped feed her, bathe her, transport her, and so much more. I always took her by her hand to lead her to where we needed to go.

Being in this situation, it made me realize many different things. It made me recognize that Leslie was not the one without sight, I was. It also helped me to see how God is taking us through life. He is the one who provides every miniscule thing for us. Like Leslie, we are all blind, but instead we have a spiritual blindness. We do not have any insight to what is going on all around us in the spiritual realm. God is guiding us, otherwise we would be blindly running around. A lot of times we think we can get through things ourselves, and we prefer to run around in the darkness. When we run around in the dark, we end up running into things. (I accidentally ran Leslie into a wall once or twice.) Thankfully, God is always ready to help us. He is always ready to take us by the hand and lead us to our destination. He illuminates our paths, so we can make it. He is not going to let us down. In the daily darkness of our spiritual lives God is going to see us through. God is my leader and my guide. I cannot do anything without Him. According to the Message Bible, Psalm 31 says, "Be my safe leader, be my true mountain guide." God can and will be your leader and guide. You just have to let Him.

— Kayla Goodman, Class of 2017

The Floating Glasses
To Know

But as one of them was cutting a tree, his ax head fell into the river. "Oh, sir!" he cried. "It was a borrowed ax!" "Where did it fall?" the man of God asked. When he showed him the place, Elisha cut a stick and threw it into the water at that spot. Then the ax head floated to the surface. "Grab it," Elisha said. And the man reached out and grabbed it. (2 Kings 6:5–7, NLT)

Summers are very hot and humid in South Carolina, and it was time for their annual mother-daughter get-a-way to Kiawah Island Beach a little over eighty miles from home. Jamie, age twelve, and Melissa, almost fifteen, excitedly assisted Mom pack a lunch and beach paraphernalia to head out for a day in the sun. Kiawah Island Beach was their favorite, non-commercialized, almost private beach—and the weather forecast was perfect!

It was early morning and everyone was packed and ready to go! As they traveled down the highway in their 27-foot Tioga motor home, they had a wonderful time laughing and chatting about what they would do and what shells they may find at the beach. Nearing the coastline, they saw lots of Spanish moss hanging from tall cypress trees. They spotted saw palmettos, South Carolina's state tree, here and there, as they made their way down the narrow, beach road. Arriving in time for an early lunch, they unpacked their belongings to set up a spot on the beach, only to notice that the "yellow caution flag" was flying. Jamie just knew it meant there were *sharks* in the water. She had just been studying about sharks in their home school that very week! No way was she going in *that* water, even though the lifeguard said it only meant that an occasional jellyfish had been spotted. So as an alternative they all decided to go shell hunting in the nearby tidal pools acquiring quite a collection of shells and over a dozen sand dollars.

Afterwards, Melissa pleaded for Mom to go in the water with her, and so they did, leaving Jamie behind to look after their beach gear and watch them have fun! In time, they were eventually able to coax Jamie to join them in the water.

She warned them, "I'm only going in knee-deep, there are *sharks* out there!"

So she waded out into the water and almost immediately, *something* bumped her leg. She screamed and scrambled to get out of the water as fast she could, all the while shouting, "I told you there's something in the water and it's trying to get *me*! I'm just going to sit on the blanket and watch our shells and stuff and *you* can go in the water if you want!"

Mom and Melissa assured her that nothing was trying to get her, and so they went back to the water's edge, when mom, shockingly and unexpectedly, got barbed in the side of her foot by some sea creature near the *same* exact spot where Jamie had just felt something hit her leg!

Mom's puncture wound was bleeding quite a bit by then, so she went to get first aid at the lifeguard station. The lifeguard didn't seem to think much of the situation until a man stepped in the same area, came stumbling out of the water and fell flat on his beach blanket trembling all over. That area of the beach was definitely inhabited by something—and Jamie had already advised us that this was *not* the day to get in the water!

After Mom recovered from that incident, Melissa thought it would be such a waste not to go in the water since they had come so far to enjoy the beach! Mom agreed, so they decided to play it safe and not go near that particular area, and they would ride their inner-tubes so their feet wouldn't touch the ocean floor where some illusive sea creature may be lurking.

Since Mom needed to wear her glasses to see, she only went in the ocean as far as where the first line of waves was breaking to catch a ride in on her inner tube. What she hadn't counted on was being "flipped" by a wave! And that's exactly what happened. Then, as you've already guessed, her glasses fell into the waste-deep water! She knew she'd never find them, especially since she couldn't see well without them. She really didn't want to feel the ocean floor with her hands or feet to find her glasses because of her recent experience getting her foot barbed. So she began walking the fifty feet to shore, tugging her inner tube behind her.

As she reached knee-deep water, she whispered this simple prayer, "Lord you know I can't see to drive home without my glasses, so I depend on You to solve our dilemma."

Just then, something hit her leg—at first she was fearful to reach down to feel what it was. No, something had just latched around her calf! As she reached down, she pulled the object away from her leg—you won't believe this—it was her *glasses*! No way! She had already walked about twenty-five feet from where she had lost them! Glasses don't float! She knew immediately that only God could have orchestrated that! God placed the glasses where she could *feel* them because He knew that even if they had washed ashore, she wouldn't have been able to *see* them.

She shouted to Melissa, "I found my glasses! It's unbelievable!"

Melissa was astounded, but corrected her mom as she said, "No, God found your glasses!"

When they both reached shore, they excitedly ran to tell Jamie of the miracle! Thanking God for their own personal miracle, they decided it was time to call it a day and get home to tell Dad about their exciting day at the beach and the "floating glasses!"

— Sonia Thompson Gott, Class of 1972

A Child's Faith
To Know

If you believe, you will receive whatever you ask for in prayer.
(Matthew 21:22, NIV)

Several years ago my family and I lived in Illinois. Our winters were always full of freezing cold and several feet of snow. To the adults in my life, this time of year was several months of terrible driving conditions that made them late for everything. But for my little brother and I, it was the most magical season of them all.

Every morning, during winters, when my brother was younger, we would put on all of our protective gear and play for hours outside. Snowball fights and forts, snowmen and snow angels filled our hours until we were too tired to play anymore. Every winter we could look forward to frolicking in a winter wonderland.

Every year, that is, except the year my brother would be turning five. For whatever reason, instead of bone-chilling cold and fluffy snow, we experienced the mildest winter since anyone could remember. My parents were overjoyed that they could get to work safely, but my little brother and I were devastated. What will we do all winter? My parents assured us that it would snow eventually, but day after day my brother rushed to window, and still there was no snow. Thanksgiving passed, then so did Christmas, and still the sky refused to yield its snow to us.

For a while, I kept hoping that the snow would come. But after we experienced a dreary "green" Christmas, I had decided to forget about it. I was just going to have to deal with the snowless state, and I told Noah that he would too.

But when I told my little brother this, instead of whining, he just looked at me and said, "Ty, it's going to snow on my birthday. I already asked Jesus, He said so."

Of course I reminded him that it hadn't snowed all year. But he just kept assuring me that on January 12, there would be snow.

My little brother's birthday rolled around, and everyone in my family rushed to the window and what did we see? A beautiful sea of sparkling white snow.

When we are little, it's easy for us to have faith that Jesus will give us the desires of our hearts. But when we get older, we become more cynical and distrusting. Jesus told us to become like little children, and trust in Him like my little brother did.

— Tyleigh Griswold, Class of 2017

Trusting God During Devastation
To Serve

Trust in the Lord with all thine heart; and lean not unto thine own understanding. In all thy ways acknowledge him, and he shall direct thy paths. (Proverbs 3: 5–6, KJV)

Throughout Jamil's four years of attendance at Georgia-Cumberland Academy (GCA), God always protected and cared for our family. Jamil was the first child in our immediate and extended family to attend GCA. During the summer following Jamil's eighth-grade graduation I fasted and prayed, asking God to lead me in which academy to send Jamil. This was not an easy decision because we lived four miles away from a day academy where the majority of his elementary friends were planning to attend, and where he wanted to attend as well.

I talked to Jamil and told him that I was not totally convinced that God was directing me to send him to the local academy. A few months prior to Jamil's eighth-grade graduation we had the opportunity of touring GCA during Academy Days. A seed was planted in my soul that germinated over the course of time following our visit. The spiritual atmosphere is what sold me on GCA, and I wanted Jamil in a spiritual environment during his high school years. GCA is where my son's personal relationship, love, and total trust in God were cultivated.

In Jamil's senior year, he was put to the test after injuring his shoulder during gymnastics. The muscles in Jamil's right shoulder were torn requiring major surgery. Following the MRI, we were told that his rehabilitation period would be one to two years. This was devastating since it was Jamil's dream to try out for the Gym-Master's Gymnastic Team at Southern Adventist University. That evening Jamil cried out to God for comfort and strength because it seemed that his dreams would not become a reality. He asked God to give him an understanding of His plan for his life and acceptance of His plan.

The following week the Advanced Anatomy and Physiology class visited Southern Adventist University's cadaver lab for the day. Prior to returning to GCA Jamil felt God leading him to share with the Gym-Master's coach his injury, plans for surgery in the summer, and his mother's decision to enroll him at Adventist University of Health Sciences (ADU) where his mother would be working during his rehabilitation process. He assured Coach Rick Schwarz he would try out for Gym-Masters during his sophomore year of college following his recovery from surgery.

Immediately, God's plan in Jamil's life path was clearly revealed. Coach Schwarz informed Jamil that he would be offering him a Gym-Master's scholarship, and he could rehab with the other students that had surgeries planned for the summer months, and would automatically be a Gym-Master. Coach Schwarz had been watching Jamil's gymnastics performances throughout the year, and Jamil's God-given gift of tumbling and pressing had already been revealed to Coach Schwarz. Jamil trusted God in the midst of devastation, and he was able to witness God turn what the devil meant for bad into a miraculous blessing. Jamil is currently attending SAU studying Clinical Psychology, and he is a second year Gym-Master gymnast.

— Lynelle Callender (Jamil's Mother)
— Rodney Jamil Hairston, II, Class of 2014

Costa Rican Mission Trip
To Serve

And in that day shall ye say, Praise the Lord, call upon his name, declare his doings among the people, make mention that his name is exalted. (Isaiah 12:4 KJV)

When I was much younger, I embarked on a mission trip to Costa Rica. I had a lot of fun helping people paint schools and help out the less fortunate. Before we started painting, we always sang worship songs and gave short devotionals to the missionaries and school members alike. I will never forget the looks of gratitude that we got for helping people and how much they appreciated the things we did for them.

I feel like God calls us out to be missionaries to people who need help and can't help themselves. The Golden Rule: "Do unto others as you wish them to do unto you," definitely applies here. Would you not want others to help you out in a time of need? I strongly suggest to those that have not gone on a mission trip to take part in one, because it will expand your relationship with Christ and fill you with joy for helping others. It will also give you a sense of understanding that you might not have had before by seeing what the people that live there go through on a day to day basis.

God will reward you for your good deeds, and you will gain a sense of pride and joy as you watch yourself and others impact the people that need it. Going on a mission trip positively affected my relationship with Christ and showed me how to effectively impact others that need it most. You will feel good about helping others, you will gain a sense of understanding like no other, and most important of all, you will spread the word of the Lord and give people hope by helping them do things that they can't do themselves while strengthening or giving them faith in God.

— Cameron Hamilton, Class of 2016

Failure and Disappointment
To Love

Jesus Christ is the same yesterday and today and forever.
(Hebrews 13: 8, NKJV)

There are some phrases in life you never want to hear. "Your father and I are getting a divorce," happens to be at the top of my list. After spending a week with our grandparents, my mom came to pick us up from their house. Before we left, she sat my nine-year-old brother and me down on the couch to break the news.

Neither of us had been expecting to hear those words come out of her mouth. My brother ran into the other room and slammed the door, while I on the other hand, was inwardly fuming. Being nine and eleven we didn't handle this information well. We proceeded to make the awkward drive home, and we weren't really sure what to expect. What we never expected to happen was for our dad to have already moved in with his girlfriend. Needless to say, things were weird. It was really hard for me, for a long time, to not be horribly angry with my dad. Coming to terms with the fact that my daddy wasn't the superhero I had always thought he was, really took a toll on our relationship. It has taken years for our relationship to be okay.

Luckily, as much as my earthly father can fail and disappoint me, I have a heavenly Father who will never do that. No matter where I am in my life, I can know that God will not let me down. He tells us in Isaiah, "For my thoughts are not your thoughts, neither are your ways my ways."

— Christian Hamilton, Class of 2015

Angel from Heaven
To Know

He will cover you with his pinions, and under his wings you will find refuge; his faithfulness is a shield and buckler.
(Psalm 91:4, ESV)

There was a time when I was placed right in front of menacing danger. It was an unusual day, a Sabbath, when I was ten-year-old girl. Why did I remember it as an unusual day? Because there was something different in my clothing. I rarely wore dresses for church attire because of my proclivity to mess my wardrobe up with dirt, mud, or food, etc. But on that day, my mom gave me a cute dress to wear. So I went church in a cobalt–blue-colored one-piece dress, skipping all the way to the church with mirth.

It seemed great until I met a huge, ferocious-looking dog. By then, I was by myself since my brother left home earlier to play at the playground with other guys. I prayed to God, desperately hoping that the dog would not notice me. However, the dog saw me and started barking. I was frightened, and didn't know what to do but to pray.

Fortuitously, a middle-aged woman passing by saw the dog barking furiously at me, and she came over to get me out of my predicament. She seemed like an angel sent from heaven for me at that time. I thanked the woman, but I also thanked God. Further, I was convinced that God is listening to our prayers and He is ready to provide us refuge.

In the Bible, it says that God will protect us with His wings and He will be a shield and a buckler for us. Therefore, we should not be afraid, but feel secure regardless of the situation since we are in God's protection.

Sometimes we tend to forget that God is always there to help us. But it is crucial to keep in mind that no matter when, by any means, God will save us from the plight whether it is by deviating the point of the arrow Himself, or by sending people to help us. Prayer is the way we on earth connect with God in heaven. Hence, we should pray when we are dealing with difficult situation, to let Him know that we are mired in unpleasant circumstances. He will be our shelter.

— Jiwon Han, Class of 2016

We Can Find Hope in Jesus Christ
To Know

I warn everyone who hears the words of the prophecy of this scroll: If anyone adds anything to them, God will add to that person the plagues described in this scroll. And if anyone takes words away from this scroll of prophecy, God will take away from that person any share in the tree of life and in the Holy City, which are described in this scroll. He who testifies to these things says, "Yes, I am coming soon." Amen. Come, Lord Jesus. The grace of the Lord Jesus be with God's people. Amen. (Revelation 22:18–21, NIV)

Allison cringed at her reflection in the mirror as she gently dabbed concealer over the bruises circling her eye. The makeup only hid so much. When she turned and saw her son watching from the hallway, Allison knew it was time to break free from her abusive partner and the father of her son.

"I blocked a lot of things out to survive the eight years I had to deal with him," Allison says of her abusive partner. "I had to write down what he wanted for dinner, because if I asked him a second time, I'd get punched in the face."

This is a story about Allison from *Women Against Abuse*. People often times can be confronted with domestic violence that is especially targeted for women. One in four women experience domestic violence in their life.

When we face difficulties like this, we are inclined to look for something to rely on. In her case, God was there for her to rely on. She prayed every day hoping for this nightmare to cease. Finally, she could divorce with her horrible husband and was able to take her lovely son with her.

Believing in God and trusting Jesus is really important. Don't forget that Jesus is coming soon to save us. Keep praying. He is always with us!

— Jiwon Han, Class of 2016

Uncomfortable Much?
To Know

And now Israel, what does the LORD your God require of you, but to fear the LORD your God, to walk in all his ways, to love him, to serve the LORD your God with all your heart and with all your soul. (Deuteronomy 10:12, ESV)

A few years ago, I had the wonderful opportunity to do an outreach program with the women's ministry at my church. Titled "God in Shoes," it was an event where we gave shoes, makeup, nail polish, and hair products to women. It was just little stuff to make them feel beautiful. At first, I didn't have much of an idea of where we were going, but I looked forward to blessing others.

We finally got there and the place felt secluded from the world—as if it was its own neighborhood. The place was for women who had been abused by their husbands. It really was a sanctuary for them so they could be protected from men hunting for them. I felt so scared and uncomfortable as soon as I heard that.

We started to prepare the place where the women would enjoy themselves. We made stations where the women could get new shoes, massages, manicures, pedicures, food, haircuts, and even a day care for the kids. Lucky for me, I was chosen to take care of the kids. This helped the mothers to relax without children constantly hanging on them.

I felt that the working environment was kind of unclean, so I didn't move around or grab stuff. It was a workout because the kids were so rowdy and jumpy. At first, I didn't know what to do with them. The kids were just as uncomfortable with me. Off the top of my head, I tried so hard to keep them entertained with games. Some were still bored and got on their phones.

When the event was finally done, some women went outside to smoke. I imagined they were smokers because of all they had gone through. I didn't want to sit down and talk with them because getting second-hand smoke scares me. Watching them smile made my day and the work I did worth it. It made me think about how Jesus would have handled the situation. Many times, I feel uncomfortable with helping others, whether it is an old stranger off the side of the road, or at a ministry event. Yet, I want to be like Jesus—and He was different. Jesus got out of His comfort zone to love those who needed Him. I didn't realize that what I had done made me feel so good because I had done it with all my heart. Yes, I was uncomfortable, but God was with me.

— Angeline Harper, Class of 2017

Uplifting Others
To Serve

Who comforts us in all our troubles, so that we can comfort those in any trouble with the comfort we ourselves receive from God.
(2 Corinthians 1:4, NIV)

As I am writing this I am having the worst day ever. I woke up late for class, I missed PSAT and I have sooo much homework. I wish I could just start my day over. I am sitting in physical science and I am thinking about all of my classes today, and I remembered that I have drama today. I was thinking why drama makes me happy. I love drama class because it is a place where I can be myself and not worry about all the other things I have to do. It's a place where I can calm down and a place where I can explode. It's a place where I feel happy. It is also a place where I don't think about myself, but others. In drama we are practicing skits for parents' weekend. I am thinking about all the people that are going to be there and how God will use me to reach them and teach them lessons. I find joy in helping others. It reminds me that although my day is going bad and there is nothing I can do about that, I can do something about other people's lives if their day is going bad. I can be the light and joy to bring their spirits up. If you are having a horrible day, and you just can't stand to be in school or even around people, just think about others and how someone is probably having a worse day than you. Thank God that you can help others and comfort others. Remember the verse for today and think about how you can make their day better.

— Annabelle Harper, Class of 2018

Loss to Hope
To Know

Brothers and sisters, we do not want you to be uninformed about those who sleep in death, so that you do not grieve like the rest of mankind, who have no hope. ... Therefore, encourage one another with these words. (1 Thessalonians 4:13–18, NIV)

From the time I was a year old until I was about twelve years old, I had one babysitter. She helped raise me, teaching me right from wrong and learning to do for myself. She was one of the most important people in my life and most influential. She was like a second mother to my sister and me. She kept us every day while my parents were working, and after school, once we were old enough to go. Sometimes we even spent the weekend with her just because we loved her. I would go to her house more than a friend's house just because of how much I enjoyed being with her. She was a huge part of my childhood and I would never want to take back a second of it.

A death in the family can always be hard, but it is equally as hard if it is someone that is like family. She passed away about six months ago, and I can't go a day without thinking about her. She's a big part of why I am the way I am. Dealing with death is always hard, but it makes it easier knowing that I will see her again someday. Even though I have the hope that I will see her again, that doesn't mean that I don't still grieve her loss. I still think about the little things she used to do for me, and I remember the perfume she wore and the type of purses she used to carry. I will connect those things to losing her, but also to the hope I have in seeing her smiling face once again.

— Sara Harper, Class of 2015

Heavenly Home
To Know

And if I go and prepare a place for you, I will come again, and receive you unto myself; that where I am, there ye may be also. (John 14:3, KJV)

Growing up I never felt as if I belonged. At every school I went to I had no friends. I would do anything for friend, only to be ridiculed even more when I would get in trouble for my efforts. Even when I did make friends, they weren't good ones. They'd always put me down or not invite me to things, secretly talking about me behind my back. And my teachers were no different. Neither were my parents, it seemed. Sometimes my dad would be there for me, but he was very violent towards me. So it was like being friends with the same person who would stab you in the back. I don't know how God got me to, but through all of this I never stopped smiling. I never stopped being my joyful happy self even though inside I felt worthless and very lonely.

I always asked God why he placed me here on earth to live such a miserable and unhappy life. Then I began reading books about Jesus' second coming. And it hit me, God allows our lives here on earth to uncomfortable or hard because He wants us to look forward to the heavenly home that is being prepared. If life here was perfect and comfortable, we wouldn't want to leave and that is exactly the opposite of God's plan for my life and your life too. So if you might be having a bad day or are feeling depressed just remember that this earth is not our home. God is making a better one for us up in heaven.

— Jessica Harris, Class of 2015

The Whole World in His Hands
To Know

You will laugh at destruction and famine, and need not fear the wild animals. (Job 5:22, NIV)

There I was, sitting on my front porch around ten o'clock at night, the only light coming from the bright moon hanging in the sky. Since we lived in a cabin out in the woods, I always enjoyed taking some time to myself, sitting out in nature, enjoying the serenity. However, *this* night wasn't as peaceful as I had hoped. As I was sitting there, staring off into the woods, I began to notice a pair of bright yellow dots off in the distance. I tilted my head, trying to get a better glimpse, but the dots seemed to be coming closer. By the time I realized that the dots were actually a pair of eyes, it was too late.

A large grizzly bear, about the size of a car, stalked up to me. I sat frozen, as it began to come closer. It stopped a few feet away from where I was sitting and watched me, while I watched it right back. I could feel my heart beating a mile a minute and I could barely breathe. A couple seconds later, I hear the front door open, and thought to myself, *Oh, thank goodness! I'm saved!*

It was my dad, who called, "I'm letting the cat out, okay?"

I waited for him to notice the bear, but he never made a sound. I began to mumble unintelligent words, trying to form an accurate sentence and let him know my problem. But, after a couple seconds, I heard the door shut and I realized he had gone back inside.

Frightened beyond belief, I began to pray. And I prayed like I had never prayed before.

Dear Lord, please don't let me get eaten by a bear. I promise to always listen to my parents and do my homework and eat my Brussels sprouts. But please don't let me get eaten. Amen.

The minute I ended my prayer, the bear turned on its heel and headed back into the woods where it came from.

In Job, there are many passages about fear and how, as long as we know that God is who He says He is, we have no reason to be afraid. Every day, we may go through struggles or obstacles that scare us unlike anything else we've ever encountered. And it's so easy to stress and freak out, possibly even scream or cry. Often times, we forget that God has the whole world in His hands. He sees every sparrow that falls and knows every hair on our heads. He knows when we're hurting or when we're in trouble. All we need to do is pray for protection and He immediately sends our guardian angels to our side.

In that very instance, I was so worried about what the bear might do, that I didn't automatically think to pray. But once I remembered that if God can calm a storm and give the power to a man to walk on water, He could protect me from anything. Now, whenever I recognize trouble, I pray and instantly feel a calm wave of security settle over me.

— Malissa Harris, Class of 2016

The Icing on Top of the Cake
To Know

So then, if someone comes along and presents you with a Jesus different from the one we told you about, or if you receive a spirit different from the one gifted through our Lord Jesus, or even if you hear a gospel different from the one you heard through us; then you're ready to go with it. (2 Corinthians 11: 4, The Voice)

When I was about six or seven years old, I was fooled into believing one of the most deceitful lies ever told. I walked into our kitchen and was immediately attracted to a large mixing bowl that sat in the middle of the counter. I instantly recognized it as the bowl that my mother used to make the icing that she would apply on her homemade cakes. So, naturally, I became very excited and ran over to the bowl, grabbing a big spoon on my way. I looked around suspiciously, hoping nobody was watching me, and I dipped the spoon into the bowl, getting a huge spoonful.

The minute I put the spoon into my mouth, I noticed that something didn't taste right. It was the most awful thing I had ever tasted in my life. I forced myself to swallow it, before guzzling down a glass of juice in order to get rid of the taste. I ran to find my mother and demanded to know what was in the bowl. She laughed when she told me she has been making lotion from a recipe she saw online.

Many times, Satan makes things look appealing and delicious, only to lure us into the web that he's spinning. It can be very hard to decide if something that looks good is actually good for us. In the garden, Lucifer was able to convince Eve that the fruit was good for her. It looked good, it smelled good, and so it probably tasted good as well. But, in the end, she started the chain reaction that caused humanity to fall into a dark hole. So, next time we see something that we want to devour, we need to take a step back and pray, asking if what we're about to encounter is really God's will for us.

— Malissa Harris, Class of 2016

To Know God
To Know

"For I know the plans I have for you," declares the LORD, "plans to prosper you and not to harm you, plans to give you hope and a future." (Jeremiah 29:11, NIV)

Here is my story, whether or not I relate to you is for you to decide, but what I do know is that the situation I am in does relate to a lot of people here at GCA first hand. Since the time I was born, I felt as though I literally lived in the church. Since I could first remember, I was being told what was true, and what was not. Who I can hang out with, or whom I cannot. It seemed like I was being told that from Friday night to Sabbath you need to be different and do different things in order to make God happy. This became a nuisance to me the older I got.

In elementary school these rules and guidelines of things I could not do on Sabbath weren't an issue, but then in middle school is where it became worse. I couldn't play flag football on Saturdays because it was the "Sabbath." I couldn't try out for basketball because they had Saturday practices and games and parties weren't an option either as they were on Friday night. I didn't know where to turn because everything that seemed pleasurable to me was being obstructed all because being an Adventist wasn't letting me.

As I have gotten older I can now study and comprehend the Bible when it explains to me why I must protect the Sabbath. While some moments in life seem to reek because of what you cannot do, then you realize that as you go through life, it is not a sprint, but a marathon. Jeremiah 29:11 shows us that God works on His own time. If you persevere in your studies of the Bible and work with those that are there for you, then I believe that God will speak to you. Then you will know Him and understand why you must not be doing those worldly things. So let me leave you with this, whenever you are not positive if you should do this or that, just pray and study the Scriptures, and when God is ready to answer He will. Just know that He works on Holy God Time and not Eastern Standard Time.

— Vincent Hayes, Class of 2017

Know God by Trusting
To Know

When I am afraid, I put my trust in you. (Psalm 56:3 NIV)

On January 17, 2013, the most incredible yet scariest thing happened to my family. My sister had been pregnant for six months with my little nephew, and things had been going well. They were both healthy until a sudden twist happened when my sister's blood pressure shot up and wouldn't come down. She went to the doctor to see what was wrong, and the doctors came to the conclusion that she had preeclampsia. This meant that her life and the baby's life were in danger. They ran tests on her and found an aneurism in her brain. They said if it burst she would most likely die. That brought the whole family to a sudden shock, and we all were trying to figure out what to do.

On the day when my nephew was born, my sister's life was hanging on by a thread, and they had to do an immediate Caesarean section. My nephew was born at one pound and twelve ounces. The length of his diaper was the length of a Q-tip, and he could pretty much fit in your hand when you held him. His chances of living were very slim and it was a very hard time for my family. My sister recovered slowly but surely, and after three months of my nephew being in the ICU, he finally got to come home.

It was a complete miracle from God that they both survived and that they are thriving. During this time my faith in God was not very strong. It was wavering a little bit, because I kept asking, *why would You let this happen?* In Psalm 56:3 I found hope in the short, concise verse that says, "When I am afraid, I put my trust in you." It helped me through the struggles, and it continues to give me guidance every day of my life. I know that God let this happen to strengthen my trust in Him, and it showed me a snippet of His character. Remember that when you're scared, worried, or stressed to put your trust in God, and He will listen and give you an answer when the time is right.

— Emily Hehn, Class of 2017

The Modern Day Samaritans
To Serve

He said, "The one who showed him mercy." And Jesus said to him, "You go, and do likewise." (Luke 10:37 ESV)

My parents and I go downtown to a homeless shelter to feed the people there, and sometimes we bring them clothes because they can't afford much. Some people are really nice and kind to us. Others are some of the rudest people I have ever come across, even though we just gave them a warm meal for free that they can't afford. Even though they are rude and disrespectful, we don't take away their food or stop serving them. Instead we come back to help them again and again every single month. Just like the good Samaritan in the Bible, we are asked to help people who can't do anything in return. As a matter of fact, my parents have spent money and time doing this, yet we don't stop. The good Samaritan spent money and time from his trip to help the man who got robbed, unlike the others who just passed him.

People all over the world have dedicated their lives to helping others. Helping is what God created us to do, as it says in Genesis 1:28 (NIV), "God blessed them and said to them, "Be fruitful and increase in number; fill the earth and subdue it. Rule over the fish in the sea and the birds in the sky and over every living creature that moves on the ground." Creatures means animals and humans alike. The only job that God has given us is to multiply and take care of the animals and help each other out. Are we really doing that, or are we like the priest in the good Samaritan that Jesus spoke about, skipping over people and not helping them. What if you were starving and cold but didn't have anything to eat or to cover you up at night? Wouldn't you want someone to help you and give you a blanket or something warm to eat? Just like the good Samaritan we should help others and become modern day Samaritans even if they reject us and curse at us we should still show them mercy.

— Joshua Hendrix, Class of 2018

Lost with 47,000 People
To Know

You will seek me and find me, when you seek me with all your heart. (Jeremiah 29:13, ESV)

This verse makes me think of Oshkosh, Wisconsin. Some will know what I am talking about, but for those who don't know what Oshkosh is, it's a big Pathfinder Camporee with Pathfinder Clubs from all over the world. You trade pins that are super rare and get pins from all over. You get to make friends from different parts of the world, and you also get to eat their food. Let me just say Italy's pizza is the best in all the world. I remember getting lost so many times. The first time was very scary, so the first thing that always popped to my brain was this verse.

I was only twelve, I think, or I just turned twelve when all of this happened. The first time I got lost was when our group was going back to camp from worship. I think I was on my phone or something, and when I glanced up I was lost. I kept walking in the direction that I thought was right, but when I got to the place where I thought the camp should be, it wasn't there. Then for some reason (I really don't know why I did this) I took out my phone and called my mom who was home in Georgia while I was in Wisconsin. When I started talking to her she got so scared that she called everybody in our group. Soon everybody knew that I called my mom just to tell her I was lost in Wisconsin. About thirty minutes later they found me. But the most hilarious part was that I was literally only about fifty feet away from the camp.

Then the very next day I was walking with a good friend named Dylan. We were going to worship where they would do a skit when here came a girl he liked. We kept talking and walking, slowing down so much that we lost the group. When I finally looked around, the group was gone. I told Dylan, and we told the girl goodbye and started to look for the group. Soon we heard this loud shout that startled us, but we realized it was our leader and he took us back to the group. And we lived happily ever after for that day.

Another day we were going to the same place again with friends. I knew this time for sure that I wasn't going to get lost. Yet again, we got lost, but this time there were several of us, so we found our group in no time.

In this story I was lost, but I got help from my friends. So will the King of kings help us when we need Him? When we call on Him in prayer, He will answer. Don't just come to God when you are lost. You should also come to Him even if you are not lost. Talk to Him like a friend. Tell Him how your day was, or ask for what you might want. But just as you don't always get what you want for Christmas, God doesn't always give you what you want. But He will always give you what He knows is best for you.

— Carlos Hernandez, Class of 2018

The Power of Love
To Love

But love your enemies, do good to them, and lend to them without expecting to get anything back. Then your reward will be great, and you will be children of the Most High, because he is kind to the ungrateful and wicked. (Luke 6:35, NIV)

Growing up as a Christian I was always expected to love everyone I encountered. Unfortunately, I found that harder to do than it seemed or looked. As a child I had a major anger problem. I would cry and throw tantrums for little things, but the main cause of my anger would be competitive sports. Being on a losing team in any sport would make me so mad, and I would always blame the loss of the game on everyone else except myself. When I was in the fourth grade, my class decided to play a game of kickball at recess one day. Of course, the competitive side of me came out, and I wanted to pick the best team possible to play on. I picked every strong kicker in our class. I thought we had won the game well before we even started the game. After two innings of this game we were losing by five points, and the fumes of my anger began to rise up inside of me. Pretty soon we were losing by ten points. I couldn't hold it in anymore, and I started to scream and yell and grab the ball and kick it at the members of my team or kick it out of the playing field.

I never fully grew out of my anger for losing until the end of eighth grade, after losing a basketball game. The game was very tight the whole way through. Sometimes we were up on the scoreboard and other times they were up. It wasn't until the last thirty seconds that we were down by two points. I was open on the three-point line and I got the ball and I shot it, but I missed the shot. I felt so bad after this, but I kept it in. After the game I didn't stay to shake people's hands, instead I went behind the stage and began to cry. My father came to me and asked me why I didn't shake the people's hands.

I said, "I hate every single person on my team and the others."

After this he said this verse: "But love your enemies, do well to them, and lend to them without expecting to get anything back. Then your reward will be great, and you will be sons of the Most High, because he is kind to the ungrateful and wicked." After this, every time I got angry I thought about that verse. It helped me to love, and to not care so much, and to focus on encouraging people instead of putting them down.

How can you start loving others today? Is there someone that you hate and need to apologize and mend broken relationships with?

— Jonathan Hernandez, Class of 2016

Actions, Not Words
To Serve

For even the Son of Man did not come to be served, but to serve, and to give his life as a ransom for many. (Mark 10:45, NIV)

Each student at GCA is offered a chance to go on at least three school-organized missionary trips a year. As a pastor's son, I am used to evangelism and hearing stories of how people served others. Missionary work has always been a part of me so much that I can't resist. My very first missionary trip was to Guatemala to help build a church during my freshman year of high school. At the time I was a student at Atlanta Adventist Academy. I heard that GCA had a missionary trip every year, so I wanted to see what it was like to serve others in a different country away from my parents' influence.

In Guatemala, we built two churches in one and a half weeks. Although it was tough work and tiring labor, what motivated me to work harder were the looks and smiles on the faces of the locals that we were helping. Our hotel didn't have hot water and had cockroaches under the beds and the living situation wasn't ideal. All of that went aside as I was there because of this verse in Mark 10:45 that Pastor Greg quoted: "For even the Son of Man did not come to be served, but to serve, and to give his life as a ransom for many." After hearing that verse I reevaluated the real reason I wanted to go overseas in the first place. Learning how to serve others and putting them first helped give me a new appreciation for my life. It taught me a new appreciation of how blessed I am and how helping others will bring them closer to our God. In Matthew 5:16 (ESV) it says, "In the same way, let your light shine before others, so that they may see your good works and give glory to your Father who is in heaven." By going on mission trips many people have been brought closer to God, and that has brought glory to God. Pray and ask God to lead you into a direction that will bring glory to His name today.

— Jonathan Hernandez, Class of 2016

Valleys
To Know

Even though I walk through the darkest valley, I will fear no evil, for you are with me; your rod and your staff, they comfort me.
(Psalm 23:4, NIV)

Who is God to you? To me, He is my heavenly Father. He knows my every want and need, and it is His most passionate desire to put His plans to motion in the lives of His children. This verse really gives me a picture of who God is. He is always present, and He guides our paths when we ask Him to.

We all make mistakes—I know I do. I have constantly found myself walking through "the darkest valley." I tend to look at the things I'm doing and say to myself that it's really not that bad, and that at least I'm not doing what those other people are doing.

God doesn't want us to compare ourselves with others. Instead, He wants us to look up to Him and follow His example and not the example of others. He wants us to be with Him. When we attach ourselves to God and let Him guide us, we will end up in a better place. Even when we do fall, when we ignore God, and when we ignore His gentle guidance, He is still there with us. All we have to do is call out to Him. In Matthew 28:20 (NIV) it says, "And surely I am with you always, to the very end of the age."

No matter the circumstance and no matter how dark a valley you believe you've lost yourself in, God is always present. He cares for His children and nothing makes Him happier than when we call for His hand to pick us up and to carry us out of the low places that we lose ourselves in.

— Alise Hirsch, Class of 2016

The Wrong Plan
To Know

Trust in the LORD with all your heart and lean not on your own understanding; in all your ways submit to him, and he will make your paths straight. (Proverbs 3:5–6, NIV)

When I was younger, I played the piano. I never liked playing, and I never wanted to practice or put effort into it. My parents were the ones making me go to the lessons, and they told me that I was not allowed to quit until I came to GCA.

It all began with my brother. He started taking lessons at the age of five. When I was born only a year later, they decided to continue the tradition in the family. I started lessons at the age of three and was forced to continue until I reached sixteen. My parents would not let me quit no matter how much I tried. It was as though they were trying to punish me. There were many fights and arguments over the matter. Eventually, I figured out that it wasn't because they hated me. They forced me to continue it because they love me. They knew how piano would help me in many different ways. They knew what was best for me even though I thought different.

Isn't it that way with God? We think we know what is best for us. We have our life planned out because we know what we want, but that's not always what God wants for us. His plan is greater, even though we may not like it, we need to trust Him because He knows what He's doing. He doesn't want to punish us. He does it because He loves us.

— Rylan Hissong, Class of 2016

The Baker
To Love

I will praise You, for I am fearfully and wonderfully made; marvelous are Your works, and that my soul knows very well. (Psalm 139:14, NKJV)

While working in a kitchen one morning, a certain baker was tasked with the special job of making bread. He gathered all the ingredients, and all the tools he would need to complete the job. He began to mix the flours, sugars, and liquids together, and got a wonderful brown blob of dough. It wouldn't look like much to others, but to him it was the best color brown he had ever seen. The baker took the dough out of the bowl and began cutting it into portions. If the dough was not cut right, the bread would either be too big or too small. It was a delicate situation that needed expert concentration. When he was finished, there were little round hills of dough all over the counter, ready and waiting to fulfill their purpose. He gathered the rising dough one at a time, and beat and pounded them to a flat circle. Then the bread maker sculpted the dough until it was according to how he liked it. The loaves were then put into an oven to bake.

When the bread had come out of the oven, none of the loaves' appearances was the same. Not that the bread was made wrong, but all were different in some way. Some loaves had wrinkles, while others were smooth. Some were lean, while others were bulky. Each one also had a purpose—whether it was to feed a crowd, or to feed someone in need, each one was needed to fulfill what the baker wanted them to do.

We, as God's chosen, are a lot like the bread. He made us with love and precision, and wouldn't change a thing about us. He made us in His image, after all. How can we say something is wrong with us? We are all special to Him, and He wants us to trust Him that He knows what's best for us. So the next time you feel down about yourself, remember the baker and his precious bread.

— Hannah Hoey, Class of 2017

Why God?
To Know

"For I know the plans I have for you," declares the Lord, "plans to prosper you and not to harm you, plans to give you hope and a future." (Jeremiah 29:11, NIV)

I'm looking down at this giant of a man and starting to yell, trying to get response. No sound or anything, his pulse is very faint. It begins to rain; the temperature drops. We start CPR immediately with all the motivation we could muster, afraid to stop because we don't want to lose the chance of him coming back. He never regained consciousness.

In my mind, I was praying the whole time. Where are you God? Why are you allowing my pastor, an innocent, strong, godly leader, to just collapse and die? The very one who introduced me to Jesus and baptized me, now dies in front of my face.

Previously we had been on a mission trip to Panama with a group of teens preaching an evangelistic series, sponsored by my home church. We had taken a little trip to hike out in the native mountainous jungle. But during this sad incident, I wasn't sure how to respond. It was all so sudden and happened so fast.

Our coordinator stayed with the body, waiting for the EMS, as we walked down the mountain, to take a taxi van back to the city where our hotel was. Our church back home wanted us to come home as soon as possible, but we decided that we would stay to finish what we started. Eventually, when we did come home, it was awkward and very weird. Coming to your home church and seeing everyone, but no pastor. It was a real struggle just going to my church.

I started to doubt God, but I couldn't because He provided so many miracles in getting us there and getting us back. So I knew He was there with us, but why did He let that happen? A year later I enrolled at GCA, and that changed my whole view on God. I began to see how God was working in my life. I began to see answers to the deep questions I had, but I was too shy to ask. Yet God knew, and He was answering. What has happened, what is happening, and what's my future, He knows it all.

The painful things that happen to us are not punishments for our errors, nor are they in any way part of some grand design on God's part. Tragedy is not God's will. We do not need to feel hurt or betrayed by God when tragedy strikes. Instead, we can turn to Him for help in overcoming it, precisely because we can tell ourselves that God is as outraged by it as we are.

We are not guaranteed life on this earth. Jesus died for our sins and paid the penalty we should have had, but granted us eternal life with Him. There is war going on for our souls! God does have a plan for our lives . We may never see the full picture, but He does. Bad things happen to good people only because we are in this sinful world. It's not His plan for innocent people to die, but I believe He can use those instances to touch people and make them stronger for Him.

— Caleb Holland, Class of 2017

What It Means to Serve
To Serve

But if serving the Lord seems undesirable to you, then choose for yourselves this day whom you will serve, whether the gods your ancestors served beyond the Euphrates, or the gods of the Amorites, in whose land you are living. But as for me and my household, we will serve the Lord. (Joshua 24:15, NIV)

For students, colleagues, or classmates, they know what it means to serve. To serve means to give up selfish ways in order to fulfill other people's needs. Jesus was sent by God to preach and serve others. He helped people, healed the sick, and preached to the people. Last year, I went to Panama for a mission trip. Over in Cerro Campania, GCA students helped build a church, helped with VBS, and painted another church.

In one week I helped with building of the church. Work was hard, but we built the majority of the church. After coming back to America, I realized that this is what the disciples did long ago. In Mark 16:15 (NIV) it says, "He said unto them, Go into all the world and preach the gospel to all creation." God wants us to serve others and to preach the gospel as well.

Also, God has sent missionaries to other countries to do His work so others can be saved and go to Heaven with Him. When Jesus came to this earth, He showed us how to serve others. Because of what He did, Jesus wants us to serve the way He did for us. Jesus wants us to tell other people about Him. He never wants us to be lost, so He sent Jesus to be our missionary.

— Joshua Holland, Class of 2018

God Has a Plan
To Serve

I alone know the plans I have for you, plans to bring you prosperity and not disaster, plans to bring about the future you hope for. (Jeremiah 29:11, GNT)

Every day seemingly normal families struggle through daily life due to divorce or separation. When I was only two years old, my parents made the decision to separate. My mom got custody of my sister and me, and we headed down to the small town of Calhoun, Georgia, to live with my grandparents. As I grew up, I began to understand what was really happening, traveling to our old house in Kentucky to spend every other weekend with my dad. Within a year, it was time for my sister to start elementary school. The Seventh-day Adventist school in the area was Coble Elementary, only 20 minutes from our new home.

In Jeremiah 29 verse 11 God promises us that He knows the plans He has for you, plans to prosper you and not to harm you, plans to give you hope and a future. When we go through struggles in life, we must learn to trust God even more. No matter what happens, whether good or bad, God's plan for us will work out in the end. Even though my situation looked horrible, in time, it got better.

In the summer of 2001, my parents got remarried, and the whole family moved to Knoxville, Tennessee. If they had not split, it isn't likely that I would be graduating from Georgia-Cumberland Academy in 2016. Because of my and my sister's time in Calhoun at Coble, I got to learn of, and begin to associate myself with GCA. Through GCA I have had the opportunity and privilege to go on three mission trips so far, including my first trip out of the country to Panama. Trust your life in God's hands and you will come out victorious in the end.

— Jason Hollenbeck, Class of 2016

Without Boundaries
To Love

But love your enemies, do good to them, and lend to them without expecting to get anything back. Then your reward will be great, and you will be children of the Most High, because he is kind to the ungrateful and wicked. (Luke 6:35, NIV)

Many people have the same generalization when thinking of love. It's a feeling toward someone that is usually mutual. Think about an enemy or a group that does not appreciate you that much. God asks us to love them, but how do we love someone who clearly despises us, or someone we may despise?

To look back at records in the Bible, in the story of the good Samaritan, a Samaritan loves his enemy, by helping him when it would be in his best interest to keep on walking. So by helping someone even if they may not want your help, or if they are one of your most rivaled enemies you are showing love for your enemy. Doing this is often hard, and many of us choose not to, because we do not want to sacrifice our pride to do what the Bible instructs us to do. In an attempt to make this easier, you can try to think of your enemies in a different perspective. By understanding them, you can often justify many of their actions. Which will hopefully soften your pride. Or by looking at them without bias, as only someone in need regardless of what you think of them will change your mood towards them.

Loving your enemies isn't just about fulfilling one of the Bible's many requests. It's about learning compassion, and doing what is right, no matter how much it contradicts your agenda. Being loving to our enemies might even change their hearts and opinions towards you, diffusing the tension. It may not always happen, but through love you might just change an enemy to a friend.

— Elijah Hooker, Class of 2018

Friendship in Light
To Love

Anyone who claims to be in the light but hates a brother or sister is still in the darkness. (1 John 2:9, NIV)

Have you ever met someone that you didn't click with or didn't like? Well one day I met this girl at camp and we instinctively hated each other, for what reason no one knows. When I came around her, I felt like she was talking about me, and when she came around me I wouldn't be any better. Then one day we were walking by ourselves, and I tripped and fell. She asked if I was okay and helped me up.

She said, "You know, you're not that bad, Charnae, your demeanor is just hard to come by."

I was shocked we were talking and asked her what she meant. She explained and we sat together and talked about it. As we sat talking, we got into our lives and how we ended up at camp. At the end of that day we prayed and hugged out our differences.

In 1 John 2:9 it says how we must be true to ourselves in order to be a light, to not only ourselves, but to others as well. While at camp we are supposed to be good and show God in our hearts, but how can we claim to be light, if we are being mean to each other. If we think we are light, while also being mean with hatred, then we are really living in darkness.

Do you love yourself? Do you love others around you? If you do, think about what you want your life to represent, then love the people around you, for you will live a life of love in the light.

— Charnae Horton, Class of 2016

Knowing God in the Midst of Hardship
To Know

I keep asking that the God of our Lord Jesus Christ, the glorious Father, may give you the Spirit of wisdom and revelation, so that you may know him better. (Ephesians 1:17, NIV)

"Help, help," are the echoes I heard myself scream as I laid there on the concrete, after I stepped into space and fell thirty feet down an elevator shaft. Finally, someone found me down on the bottom floor of the house, blood everywhere. As family and friends stood around to keep me awake, we sang songs of praise and love to God. I was rushed to the hospital in a helicopter because I was bleeding from my head, and the house was on a gravel road. After a day and a half in the hospital, I found out that I had a hairline fracture in my nose and skull.

Once I got out of the hospital, it was hard because I couldn't do the regular things I was used to. I wasn't allowed to go to school, ride my bike, and even had problems eating right. I learned I had to get to know God and depend on Him. Some nights I would cry myself to sleep and wonder why me. If God loved me, why would He allow me to go through the things I was going through? Not to mention I was about to be baptized in two weeks. I was on a search to know who God really was.

One night as I was crying and reflecting on what had happened to me in that past week, I prayed that God would help me understand, and so He did. I closed my eyes as I went over what happened to me the day I fell. With my eyes closed, I felt myself falling. I saw white, I saw angels, guardian angels, lifting me to the floor as I stood there and then collapsed on the concrete. In that moment I realized I could've died. I knew His love for me when He placed the right people around me during that time to pray and sing in His honor and presence.

I don't know where God is leading me, but I know that I am here for a reason and a purpose. Everyone can use their situation and turn it in to a way to know God better. God loves you and wants you give Him a chance, even if it is going through a hard situation first. Getting to know God can and will be hard sometimes, but when people are on the search for something it's never easy. God wants to have a relationship with you, but in order for that to happen you have to give Him a chance and get to know Him.

— Charnae Horton, Class of 2016

Messed Up
To Love

"Love is patient and kind. Love is not jealous, it does not brag, and it is not proud. Love is not rude, it is not selfish, and it cannot be made angry easily. Love does not remember wrongs done against it. Love is never happy when others do wrong, but it is always happy with the truth. Love never gives up on people. It never stops trusting, never loses hope, and never quits."
(1 Corinthians 13:4–7, ERV)

The dictionary's definition of love is to have a feeling of strong or constant affection for a person. Paul told the Corinthians that love never quits, and to me that's the part of the verse that sticks.

One time at work, a coworker and I were messing around with the soundboard in the fellowship hall at church. We were taking a break when somehow it got turned on, and the whole church started to shake. When I say it was shaking, it was. A humming noise was coming from somewhere, and for a while we had no idea what it was. But luckily, Mr. Kelch was there and ran in and fixed it, then he called us over to tell us what we did wrong. He may have yelled at us, but he was doing it so later on we wouldn't get in worse trouble. He did that because he had to, not because he was mad at us or loved us any less. Another example would be every time we sin. We mess up and God will discipline us, but He still loves us the same. See, love never quits.

Next time you mess up, remember someone will always love you. Be it God, your wife/husband, your parent, or your friends, because love never quits.

— Brandon Hudson, Class of 2018

The Abundant Life
To Know

I have come that they may have life, and that they may have it more abundantly. (John 10:10, NKJV)

This is a verse that we quote often. We crave an abundant life. But just what does this mean? More money, more houses, more cars, more stuff? This verse comes in the middle of a passage with 3 main characters:

1) The Sheep (ok, this is more than one character).

The sheep are need of help, guidance, and support. The sheep can't provide their own food, they get lost, and they wander away from the one who wants to take care of them. They often put themselves in a place of danger (knowingly or unknowingly). They need help.

2) The Thief

The thief has no good intentions for the sheep. He tries to sneak in (10:1). His only purpose is to steal, or even worse, to kill and destroy (10:10). The sheep should run away from the thief, but sheep are not always so bright. Sometimes they follow after this one who only wants to harm them.

3) The Good Shepherd

This is the main character of the whole passage. The Good Shepherd desires to help the sheep (who often run away). The Shepherd wants to protect from the dangers of the thief. The Shepherd protects the sheep. He even says He is the "Door" (10:7), keeping back the dangers of the thief.

There is only one character in this story who wants what is best for us. Not the thief (he wants to harm). Not the sheep (they don't know what is best). Only the Good Shepherd. He is the one that tells about the abundant life.

He even talks about knowing His sheep and the sheep knowing Him (10:14). As we (the sheep) hear the voice of Jesus (the Good Shepherd), He will lead us to places that lead to a life more abundant.

Remember the words of the familiar Twenty-third Psalm:

The LORD is my shepherd; I shall not want.
He makes me to lie down in green pastures;
He leads me beside the still waters. He restores my soul;
He leads me in the paths of righteousness for His name's sake.

Yea, though I walk through the valley of the shadow of death, I will fear no evil;
For You are with me; Your rod and Your staff, they comfort me.
You prepare a table before me in the presence of my enemies;
You anoint my head with oil; my cup runs over.
Surely goodness and mercy shall follow me all the days of my life;
And I will dwell in the house of the LORD forever.
(NKJV)

— Pastor Greg Hudson, Church Pastor

High Up
To Serve

I lift up my eyes to the mountains— where does my help come from? My help comes from the LORD, the Maker of heaven and earth. (Psalm 121:1-2)

What is the highest place you have been? I have been up Cheaha Mt. (2413 ft.—highest point in Alabama). I have been up Mt. LeConte (6593 ft) and Clingmans Dome, Tennessee (6643 ft.— the highest point in Tennessee). I have been up Mt. Mitchell (6683 ft.—highest point in N.Carolina). But the highest I have been (outside of an airplane) is Mt. Evans, Colorado, making my way to 14, 240 ft. of elevation (it is an easy trip … the highest paved road in the US). But each time I went up a mountain, I had to come back down.

Sometimes life is like that. Life is full of ups and downs, highs and lows. Sometimes all goes well, sometimes it seems like all goes wrong. We talk about "mountain-top experiences" and how we come down after a spiritual or emotional "high."

The Bible often talks about the "high places," places of worship, but also places of spiritual warfare, as often people turned their eyes away from God while at the high places. But the Bible is about being victorious. Abraham went to the mountain with his son as the sacrifice, but came down with the Lamb of God as his Savior. Moses went in the fiery mountain of Sinai and saw the glory of God revealed through His law. Elijah prayed on the mountain, and the fire fell and the people worshipped the true God.

Jesus also climbed the mountain. From the mountaintop, He preached the blessings of the Beatitudes, He spent nights in prayer on the mountain, He was encouraged by Moses and Elijah, but then came off the mountain to share His power to heal. He climbed a mountain carrying a cross to give the ultimate gift of Salvation.

But as Jesus went up mountains, He also lived in the valley, to share life, grace, and eternity.

Where is your life right now? Are you climbing? Are you in the valley of despair? Are you stuck in the rut of routine? Wherever you are, know that Jesus is there.

— Greg Hudson, Church Pastor

Outreach
To Serve

For the grace of God that brings salvation has appeared to all men,
(Titus 2:11, NKJV)

Outreach ... Reach Out ... What do these words mean to you?

A picture of going beyond the walls of what is normal? Stretching yourself for the sake of someone else? It is easy to spend all our time with people we know, to spend all of our energy on programs for our friends and family. Could we be missing out on something very important?

> The church is God's appointed agency for the salvation of men. It was **organized for service**, and its mission is to **carry the gospel to the world.** From the beginning it has been God's plan that through His church shall be reflected to the world His fullness and His sufficiency. The **members of the church**, those whom He has called out of darkness into His marvelous light, **are to show forth His glory.** (White, *Acts of the Apostles*, p.9)

There are lots of clichés that we use to talk about showing Jesus to others:

Get outside your comfort zone.
Fishing for men.
Live the sermon.

Be a sermon in shoes (remember that old song?).

Preach the gospel, if necessary use words (Attributed to St. Francis of Assisi, although he was from a preaching order).

The Bible (as usual) is incredibly balanced. It speaks clearly about our actions to help others

Whatever you did for the least of these ... (Matthew 25:40, NIV).

Visit orphans and widows in their trouble ... (James 1:27, NKJV).

But the Bible also speaks clearly about using our words to lead others to the foot of the cross

Go ... and make disciples ... teaching them ..." (Matthew 28:19, NKJV)

How shall they believe in Him of whom they have not heard? And how shall they hear without a preacher? (Romans 10:14, NKJV)

Preach the Word! Be ready in season and out of season ... (2 Timothy 4:2, NKJV)

So live out your faith by serving others and looking for opportunities to speak words of truth that will introduce others to your Savior.

— Greg Hudson, Church Pastor

The Power of Prayer
To Love

Be anxious for nothing, but in everything by prayer and supplication, with thanksgiving, let your requests be made known to God; and the peace of God, which surpasses all understanding will guard your hearts and minds through Christ Jesus.
(Philippians 4:6–7, NKJV)

Throughout Scripture, the power of prayer is seen. In the early church, the believers gathered to pray in good times and bad (Acts 1:14, 2:42). And amazing things took place. The Holy Spirit was poured out (Acts 2:4), thousands were baptized (Acts 2:41), they were given boldness to share the gospel (Acts 4:31), and people were even healed (Acts 5:16)!

The stories of prayer and power continue as your read through the book of Acts. We continue to need prayer today.

> Prayer is the opening of the heart to God as to a friend. Not that it is necessary in order to make known to God what we are, but in order to enable us to receive Him. Prayer does not bring God down to us, but brings us up to Him (White, *Steps to Christ*, p. 93)

> A revival of true godliness among us is the greatest and most urgent of all our needs. To seek this should be our first work. ... Our heavenly Father is more willing to give His Holy Spirit to them that ask Him, than are earthly parents to give good gifts to their children. But it is our work, by confession, humiliation, repentance, and earnest prayer, to fulfill the conditions upon which God has promised to grant us His blessings. **A revival need be expected only in answer to prayer.** (White, *Selected Messages*, vol. 1, p. 121)

Note the four elements in this last passage: Confession, humiliation, repentance, and earnest prayer. We may have the best program, a beautiful church, smiling members, and a climate-controlled sanctuary. But without prayer, we are missing out on what is most important, we are not letting the full potential of God's grace to change our hearts and our lives.

— Greg Hudson, Church Pastor

Spring
To Love

But who am I, and who are my people, that we should be able to offer so willingly as this? For all things come from You, and of Your own we have given You. (1 Chronicles 29:14, NKJV)

After a few weeks of cold, and a few days of snow, March is here, and that means spring is soon to follow. Even while the snow lay on the ground, the daffodil plants at my house were reaching to the warmth of the sun. The starkness of winter will begin to give way to redbuds and dogwoods, to budding trees and blossoming flowers. This is our yearly reminder that God is the great giver of life.

As humans, we have only one source of life. God is our Creator, our Savior, and He sustains our life day by day. We have not done anything to deserve this all-encompassing love. But how can we respond to what we have received?

David reminds us that everything comes from God, even our abilities and skills. When we serve God, when we return a tithe or offering, when we honor His Sabbath, we are simply acknowledging that God is not only our Savior, but He is also the Lord of our life.

We are called to give our whole life:

> I beseech you therefore, brethren, by the mercies of God, that you present your bodies a living sacrifice, holy, acceptable to God, which is your reasonable service. And do not be conformed to this world, but be transformed by the renewing of your mind, that you may prove what is that good and acceptable and perfect will of God. (Romans 12:1–2, NKJV)

What does it mean to be a living sacrifice? It is more than climbing on an altar, but daily acknowledging that everything we have belongs to God—our time, talents, treasure, influence, service, and skills. What has God given to you?

— Greg Hudson, Church Pastor

The Sower
To Love

But the seed on good soil stands for those with a noble and good heart, who hear the word, retain it, and by persevering produce a crop. (Luke 8:15, NIV)

Early spring brings flowers and warm temperatures. I was working in the garden, trying to get a head start so the veggies can beat the drought and heat of July. I tilled, hoed, pulled weeds, and planted rows of cucumber, zucchini, beans, and lots of other veggies my kids don't like. As I was working, I was reminded of the parable of the sower (I am sure in a few weeks, I will be reminded of the parable of the weeds).

Luke 8 tells the story. The sower sows the seed (the Word of God). Some falls in the path, the rocks, or the thorns. The seed on the Path represents those who allow Satan to snatch the word from their heart. The rocky soil is those who hear the Word, but have no root, so when it gets hot (when challenges come), the plants wither and die. The thorny ground represents people that allow God's Word to be choked out by "life's worries, riches, and pleasures."

My garden has hard ground, it has rocks, it has weeds and thorns. It takes work to get them out, to prepare the soil, to till, to weed, to compost, to plant. What about my life?

What about your lives? Are you allowing anything to choke out, to dry up, to snatch away the Word of God in your life? Are you preparing the soil each day by spending time in God's word?

I hope to soon have a good harvest, to eat fresh tomatoes and cucumbers. But even more important is to allow the Word of God to daily grow in my heart, to make a difference in the life I live.

May you have a bountiful harvest!

— Greg Hudson, Church Pastor

Awaiting the Advent
To Know

Therefore the Lord Himself will give you a sign: Behold, the virgin shall conceive and bear a Son, and shall call His name Immanuel.
(Isaiah 7:14, NKJV)

Many people greatly anticipate the closing months of the year. Children look forward to the hope of presents. Students dream of Thanksgiving break followed shortly by the extra-long Christmas break. Employees enjoy some extra days off work. Grandparents and parents plan for families to be reunited after times of separation. Business owners hope for a boost in sales.

In ancient Palestine the world was waiting for something special. For centuries they anticipated a coming king:

> For unto us a Child is born,
> Unto us a Son is given;
> And the government will be upon His shoulder.

And His name will be called
Wonderful, Counselor, Mighty God,
Everlasting Father, Prince of Peace. (Isaiah 9:6, NKJV)
I see Him, but not now;
I behold Him, but not near;
A Star shall come out of Jacob;
A Scepter shall rise out of Israel. ... (Numbers 24:17, NKJV)

But you, Bethlehem Ephrathah, though you are little among the thousands of Judah, yet out of you shall come forth to Me the One to be Ruler in Israel, whose goings forth are from of old, from everlasting. (Micah 5:2, NKJV)

All this waiting and anticipation. But they missed Jesus when He was born on this earth. The king remained in the palace. The priests remained in the temple. The people continued their daily routine, even though the King of the universe was in their midst.

Our time is busy these days. Parties, baking, banquets, concerts, plays, parades, and pageants vie for spots on your calendar. Lots of fun activities! Will you make time for what is most important, both in the last month of the year, and in the new year to come. Set your priority on what is most important. Set your focus on Jesus!

— Greg Hudson, Church Pastor

Truth from a Mummy
To Know

They received the word with all readiness, and searched the Scriptures daily to find out whether these things were so.
(Acts 17:11, NKJV)

A recently studied mummy mask[2], made of scraps of linen and paper (like papier mâché), appears to contain a scrap of the Gospel of Mark. This scrap appears to be dated around AD 90, making it the oldest scrap of this gospel that has yet to be found (only about thirty years after it was written). On one hand, this is a fascinating find to lend even more credibility to the historical significance of the gospel story, but on the other hand, the Word of God was forgotten, simply used as a scrap of paper for an art project.

Perhaps you remember the story of the Waldenses**[3], a group of Christians living in the mountains of Italy during the Dark Ages. The Waldenses were persecuted because of their faith in the Bible, but it remained precious to them. They translated it (into their language), copied it (by hand), shared it (by smuggling it in the hem of their clothes), and lived it (some of them even kept the seventh-day Sabbath). They are known for their dedication to the Word of God.

Where do you find yourself? You probably have a Bible (or several). You probably have one in your house, maybe even on your phone. But how do you relate to it? Is it just a book, a piece of scrap paper? Is it something you carry to church? Do you read it every so often (when your favorite show is over)? Or have you allowed the Bible to be precious to you, to be something that guides your life, that brings you peace, that points you to Jesus?

Maybe you started a new Bible reading plan for the new year. Are you keeping at it? If not, start again. Do you have a Bible study plan? I encourage you to keep it up, to share with someone else the blessings you are learning.

---

2 http://www.livescience.com/49489-oldest-known-gospel-mummy-mask.html (accessed November 13, 2015)

3 Read more about the Waldenses in chapter 4 of *The Great Controversy*

More to be desired are they than gold, Yea, than much fine gold; Sweeter also than honey and the honeycomb. Moreover by them Your servant is warned, And in keeping them there is great reward. (Psalm 19:10–11, NKJV)

The Bereans in Acts 17 are well known for their devotion to God's Word. They studied it and learned it. What about you?

— Greg Hudson, Church Pastor

Wise Words
To Serve

Let no one despise you for your youth, but set the believers an example in speech, in conduct, in love, in faith, in purity.
(1 Timothy 4:12, ESV)

When we think back to our years in elementary school, everyone has one main thing that comes to mind. Whether it is old friends, recess, lunch, etc. For me, it isn't any of those things. It's the teachers. And I always think of one first. Most kids love their first teachers. They're the ones that start them on their journey through their schooling experience. I didn't have that same experience. Pre-K and Kindergarten were my worst years in elementary school.

I cannot remember if I was excited to start school. To be honest, I probably didn't even understand what was going on. I remember getting there, my Thomas the Train roller backpack and all, ready to go inside. I saw some friends there, and it was good. Then I met the teacher. While they were nice to all of us, they made me step out of my comfort zone. I'm a picky eater, and while over the years I've learned to like a lot more, I didn't back then.

Something occurred at school that ended up having us eating olives. We had the choice of trying a black or green olive. Being the kid I was, I wanted neither. So, when the time came to choose, I said none. So, being as hard headed as I am, they decided to shove both of them in my mouth. The kids thought it was cool that I said no and took none. So then I got other kids doing it.

Another time, we had hot lunch, and carrots were the side item. I told the kids "let's not eat the carrots," and again I said "no." So they take the carrots one by one, and force them in my mouth. After a while, I had quite a few kids doing this. I became a leader, in the wrong direction.

One day, the teacher pulled me aside and said something along the lines of, "If you are leading everyone to do the bad things, who's going to do the good things? You should practice being good, so the others can follow you."

While that seems really simple, that's the reason it stuck with me that long ago. A good verse that I can relate with this story is 1 Timothy 4:12 (ESV), that says "Let no one despise you for your youth, but set the believers an example in speech, in conduct, in love, in faith, in purity." Here at GCA, we try to live by the motto "To Know, To Love, To Serve". Sometimes I don't always practice that, like in my story. We all need to look at that, and take it to heart. If we go to GCA, we should live by their motto, shouldn't we?

— Gage Hufstetler, Class of 2018

Doing a Service
To Serve

You, my brothers and sisters, were called to be free. But do not use your freedom to indulge the flesh; rather, serve one another humbly in love. (Galatians 5:13, NIV)

One day I was doing laundry to prepare for my next week of school. When I opened the dryer I was surprised to find that my brother had clothes inside of it. Instead of tossing them to the side, I decide to fold them and put them in his drawer. My brother was later gracious and thanked me for this small deed that I did. It's the small things in life that can really change the path of people's days. Try to be that small positive change in someone's day to push them on.

In serving others you are really serving yourself. When you serve others you are building a bridge connecting that person to an image of what God truly is. As Christians, we are called to build bridges between God and mankind. As a Christian you can either be a bridge or a barrier. Barriers are people who make an obstacle in the paths of the walks of others. It should be your goal to be a Christian connection to Jesus.

The easiest way to create this spiritual connection to others is to do small deeds for the people you know. You don't have to buy them a new

Rolex or a new car. What really encourages and changes people is when people do small meaningful deeds for each other. Helping someone study for a test, taking out someone's trash, doing the dishes at home, all the little unseen things are brilliant things to do to make others' day just a little bit brighter, and it will also probably make yours the same way.

Jesus is the greatest example of this. Jesus came down to be the lowest of the low to serve others so that one day those people might go out and do the same to others in need. Jesus gave us freedom. The freedom to do good for the world. We should use this to benefit not just ourselves but everyone God created.

— Noah Humphrey, Class of 2016

One People, One God
To Know

There is neither Jew nor Greek, there is neither bond nor free, there is neither male nor female: for ye are all one in Christ Jesus.
(Galatians 3:28, KJV)

I was born and raised in the South. Tennessee is one very cultural southern state. In 1861 the Civil War began in the United States. Tennessee fought with the Confederates. As most people see it, the Confederates wanted slaves while the Union didn't. So, being a child of the South, I've grown up with racial controversy.

My dad's side of the family comes from a line of slave owners, so they have dealt with discrimination. Although I'd been around different races, I'd never thought much about it. Seeing racism firsthand caught me off guard because the Adventist community had shielded me from it.

My eighth grade, year my class was trying to pick a Bible verse motto. We went with the idea of unity and uniqueness. We were looking up Bible verses, and found Galatians 3:28. Pleased with it, our teacher asked us to talk to each other about what it meant. I thought about racism, and prejudices. It opened my eyes. I thought about growing up in the South, and seeing racial tension. Though it isn't horrible, it's there. I am very lucky to have grown up in a time where most everyone is treated fairly. That's what Galatians 3:28 is talking about. It doesn't matter if you are a man or a woman, black or white, poor or rich, we are all one in Jesus. We are no better than the last, but make up a body of people in Christ. Sometimes, I know I've thought it myself,

Some Adventists think we are better than other religions, but we aren't. God created us all equal. Because of this, we need to accept everyone. It's not an easy task, and it won't ever be, but that's OK. As long as we are treating everyone as equal and not pointing at minor things like race or an accent, we are taking God's word to heart. We are all one in Christ Jesus. We are one.

Prayer: Dear God, help me to see others as one with me, in You. Give me the strength to treat everyone equal, no matter their differences. Amen.

— Aimee Hunt, Class of 2018

You Are Loved
To Love

But who are you, a human being, to talk back to God? "Shall what is formed say to the one who formed it, 'Why did you make me like this?' Does not the potter have the right to make out of the same lump of clay some pottery for special purposes and some for common use?" (Romans 9:20–21, NIV)

You are meant to be loved. Not just by the people around you, but by yourself as well. You are a masterpiece created by the most brilliant artist. Often times, you won't see the beautiful things about you because you are so focused on searching for the flaws. Don't spend your time in front of the mirror pointing out all of your blemishes. Instead, look for the perfections that God has blessed you with. You are worth more than your downgraded opinion of yourself.

Believing that you are a piece of art is such an important thing. Loving yourself is so important to be able to continue showing the love of God to others around you. I understand that when you look in the mirror, you automatically pick out the flaws. You aren't the only one! We all have a tendency to somewhat downgrade ourselves because it's what society has taught us to do. The world today teaches that we are never good enough. Never. It wouldn't matter if you became the president because someone would still criticize you. If we value our self-worth through the world's eyes, we will never be good enough, and if we depend on people to give us the validation we crave, we will always be disappointed.

Search for God and you will find your self-worth in Him. He genuinely loves you and thinks the world of you. Even when society's opinion tells you that you are worthless and not important to anyone, know that society is wrong. You are a beautiful individual, and don't let others get in the way of God's view of you. Who are you to judge God's art? He thought about each individual characteristic and personalized it just for you. You are truly priceless, and you are loved. Remember that as you go throughout your day.

— Shelby Huse, Class of 2018

It Is Easy to Serve
To Serve

As each has received a gift, use it to serve one another, as good stewards of God's varied grace. (1 Peter 4:10, ESV)

Every year, GCA provides us several opportunities to serve others, whether through community service or mission trips. But being an international student here has taught me that there is another simpler (but not less important) way to serve your neighbor: by being a helpful roommate.

I remember that my first months at GCA were tough for me. I came to this school speaking very little English and with the responsibility of catching on all my classes, because I arrived in the United States a few weeks after school had started. I was feeling discouraged and sad at that time. I thought that no one would help me, and that I would not be able to make any friends here. This is where I was wrong, and my roommate is the best proof of it.

My roommate was the one who told me in the first weeks where I was supposed to go or what I was supposed to do next; who patiently answered all my English questions; who explained the assignments to me; and who repeated the announcements of the dormitory or chapel again for me. She was also the one who became my first friend and who introduced me to the people who would later on become my friends too. And she was not the only one who helped me. There are many more people that I could list here that have also supported and encouraged me through these years at GCA: classmates, teachers, students, deans, RA's, nurses … All of them have showed care and love for me in one way or another, even by just giving me a smile.

You do not have to go very far away from your house to serve others. There are many people around you who need help. Maybe they are an international student like me, or someone who is going through difficult times. The Bible says in 1 Peter 4:10 (ESV): "As each has received a gift, use it to serve one another, as good stewards of God's varied grace." God gave to each one of us different gifts, and He expects us to use them for the benefit of others. Even if you are not sure what your gift is, you can do the same thing as my roommate did, be ready and willing to serve.

— Narumi Imayuki, Class of 2018

Simple Instructions
To Know

Children, obey your parents in the Lord, for this is right. "Honor your father and mother"—which is the first commandment with a promise—so that it may go well with you and that you may enjoy long life on the earth. (Ephesians 6:1–3, NIV)

"Don't run in the warehouse." Those were words going through my head as I ran down one of the isles. I turned around a shelf and started sprinting down another isle, running as fast my 8-year-old legs could carry me. The next thing I knew I was flat on my back, blood pouring out of my head. I had run into the corner of a desk, leaving a half-inch gash in the corner of my forehead.

I would not have the scar today if I had listened to what my dad had told me. We often brush off what our parents say. Later in life we begin to realize how much they actually know. Crazy, right? Our parents give us simple instructions and all we have to do is listen and follow them. Not exactly what every teenager wants to hear. We may complain, but in the end we know they're right.

That's how it is with God. God gave the Israelites simple instructions to follow. They experienced the consequences form their actions, leaving a scar. When God gives us direction or instructions we must listen and act upon them. Next time your parents tell you something, realize that they may actually know what they are talking about.

— Skylar Jacobs, Class of 2016

The Narrow Path
To Serve

You can enter God's Kingdom only through the narrow gate. The highway to hell is broad, and its gate is wide for the many who choose that way. But the gateway to life is very narrow and the road is difficult, and only a few ever find it.
(Matthew 7:13–14, NLT)

I'm sure many of you have seen the movie, *Facing the Giants*. The movie is about a Christian high school football team that is struggling to find victory. They thought their whole goal was to win, but what their coach realized was that God is victory, and that through God, you will always win. He brought their faith back into action and found victory in football, academics, and faith.

This coach had several challenges in life. His car wouldn't run well, the stove would break, he felt that he couldn't provide for his wife, but one of the biggest challenges he faced was that he couldn't give his wife a child.

The football team had struggled in past seasons to get a winning season. Many of the player's dads wanted a new coach for the team, because they thought that he wasn't capable of winning. After the coach realized that they weren't following the narrow path, he put his effort into showing his team the rights and wrongs of life. They would pray and give God the praise whether they won or lost the game, but they started winning.

The team finally had a winning season, and made it to the state championship. The game was fought hard, but they were down by two points with two seconds left on the clock. They were on about the 35-yard line, and the coach knew they couldn't throw the ball and try to win, so he brought out the kicking team. It was a 51-yard field goal. The down side was that they were down to their backup kicker who only weighed about 150 pounds, plus he had to kick into the wind. Suddenly the direction of the wind changed and started blowing towards the goal posts. The kicker kicked it, and it went through, so they won the biggest game in the state.

What I really like about this movie is that it points out that if we follow the narrow path, we find victory through God. They pointed out that kicking a field goal is just like following the narrow path. To score the three points you have to kick it through the posts, but if you don't, you don't score. It's just like the narrow path, if you follow the path, then you find victory through God, and you get the three points, and the win.

— David Jenkins, Class of 2019

Perfect Peace
To Know

O taste and see that the LORD is good; how blessed is the man who takes refuge in Him! (Psalm 34:8, NASB)

Everyone has different relationships with God. How can we have strong a relationship with God like most Christians strive for? Many of my friends have told me that they have never really felt a real connection with God, especially those who grew up as Christians. That's sad because there's no meaning for them in worship. It is very difficult to believe in something invisible and easy for us to question God.

I just want you to know this one thing: God loves you. We are His masterpieces and He chose us. God only asks for one thing. He wants us to choose Him in every situation. Whatever situation we are in, we should trust God. As teenagers, we often get caught up with our schoolwork, stress, and relationships. We care about other things so much that we sometimes forget to spend time with God.

When I first came to GCA, I thought I was all settled, but I was wrong. I was depressed and sad for no reason. I kept telling myself I couldn't handle my problems. Finally, I got to the point where I realized couldn't handle the situation by myself, so I told Mrs. Short about it. She told me many things that made me feel loved, and valuable. The only problem was Satan, trying to drag me down. Also, she told me to pray and spend time with God, because she already knew that it was the only solution. I've heard that so many times in my life, I should pray and really ask God for help through trials. I never listened or at least I never tried. This time, it was different. I prayed and read some Scripture, and cliché it might sound, I improved so much. I had a perfect peace that I'd never felt before.

When I think back, I am so thankful that I was in that situation. I realized how important God is. Now I want you to get to know my God, and you don't need a dramatic situation to make it happen. Just taste and see the Lord is good, always trust in the Lord with all your heart!

— Annie Jeong, Class of 2016

Relationship Between Me and God
To Know

And the Lord God said, Behold, the man is become as one of us, to know good and evil: and now, lest he put forth his hand, and take also of the tree of life, and eat, and live for ever:
(Genesis 3:22, KJV)

There are people in the world who don't know about God. Occasionally, someone will start to believe in God if there is something to affect the person strongly.

For me, when I was young and was in Korea, I felt myself as hypocrite. Because when I first become a SDA student, the reason why I became SDA was to go to the middle school where my mother wanted me to go. I was baptized, but I barely prayed to God, and only when I was in trouble or just to tell Him to show a miracle to me to get what I wanted to have. Whenever I went to any food court to have some food, I ate everything. I ate beef, duck meat, or even pork, which Christians should not eat. I also went to a computer building where a lot of computers are, and people play games or search for something on the computer and pay for it during the Sabbath day during the time I had to go to the church. Even though I didn't act like it, I called myself a Christian. However, I changed after I came to America. I went to the school called Georgia-Cumberland Academy. This school is an SDA school, and it also called God Chosen Academy. In this school, people are required to go to the church during Friday and Sabbath. There was a religion class, and lots of activities that relate religion. In my first year in GCA, I was kind of bored and had no interest about religion, because I did nothing about religion in Korea. But after many days that I have been in GCA, I don't know when, but I started to have interest in Christianity. I heard about what the pastor says in the church, and I tried to pray at least once in a day. When I was in GCA, I saw lots of friends who talked about God or the Bible in the dorm. Every time I heard it, I honestly wanted to be like a person who has lots of knowledge about Christ, and I learned lot of things about Christians from my friends.

In conclusion, I learned and knew lots of things about Christians in GCA, and GCA connected me to Christ. If I did not come to GCA, there would be no other thing that connects me to my religion.

— Bobby Jeong, Class of 2018

Faith It, Till You Make It
To Serve

Jesus replied, "You do not realize now what I am doing, but later you will understand" (John 13:7, NIV)

This summer, I made a fairly difficult decision. My two options were to stay home for the summer and do nothing, or go to California and join the Youth Rush canvassing program. I chose the latter. While I was in California I had many different door-to-door experiences, but there is one that really stuck out to me.

It was a very hot day and I was making my way up a hill. I saw a young woman in a black Mercedes pull up to a house, so I ran to it. When I peered in, I noticed a Bible in the seat next to the woman. I proceeded to show her one of our message books but she stopped me abruptly. She explained to me that she was aware that I was a literature evangelist and that she already had all of the books that I was selling, and that she had just arrived at a house that was holding an Adventist Bible study. At that moment I knew that I'd be able to empty my bag of books in that home because they were all Adventists and would surely support me. I was wrong.

Things didn't work out at that home, and I left without selling a single book there. The people were simply uninterested. I questioned God, asking for the rest of the day, "These people claim to be Yours, but why won't they even help out another one of Your sons?" The day was long after that and I was only able to sell a few books.

My leader noticed that our team's morale had died, so when it was time for pickup at the end of the night, she took us all to a bubble tea shop. While we were there, still in uniform, a man asked us if we were part of Youth Rush. I told him that we were, and he asked to see all of our books. That night he ended up buying every book that I showed him, which put me at the highest number of books that I had ever sold.

Had it not been for the bad experience at that one house, I would have never been able to sell that many books. The events that took place that day proved to me that God always has a plan in store for us, no matter if we feel like we've missed our opportunity or if nothing seems to be going right. Always keep your trust in God and just faith it, till you make it.

— Joel Joa, Class of 2016

Ultimate Love
To Love

The Lord our God is merciful and forgiving, even though we have rebelled against him. (Daniel 9:9, NIV)

As a child I would always get into trouble for fighting with my sister and doing other bad things that I wasn't supposed to. There was one time when I was about ten years old that I was playing a game on my dad's computer without permission. I knew that I wasn't supposed to because it was a Sabbath, and I wasn't supposed to be playing video games. Once I was done I tried to turn off the computer, but I, unknowingly, shut it off incorrectly. When I shut it off, I had accidentally managed to wipe the memory from the computer, which resulted in us losing all of our digital copies of our family pictures. Later that evening my dad came to me and asked me what I had done. I knew that I was probably going to get in very big trouble for being on the computer, but I told him what I had done. He was disappointed that I had done it, but he forgave me for it.

A lot of times I've misbehaved and done bad things, but my parents have always forgiven me. The reason that they have forgiven me is because they love me. If my parents can forgive me and love me, then imagine how much more God forgives all of our sins and loves us. God's love for us is unending and He will always love and forgive us.

— Joel Joa, Class of 2016

God's Still Working on Me
To Know

But he knoweth the way that I take: when he hath tried me I shall come forth as gold. (Job 23:10, KJV)

Let's face it—the average teenager doesn't really know who they are. Some of us don't really know ourselves until we hit rock bottom, whatever rock bottom may be for us personally. For some it may be when they are five years old, for others, when they are forty-five years old. Sometimes what a person's been through changes the way they view life or even how they view themselves. But let's be real—even when we hit rock bottom, we have a lot of growing to do. It's a process.

As a little girl growing up in DeKalb County, I didn't understand a lot of what happened around me. All I knew was I went to school for a few hours, then came back home and did it all over again the next day. I remember I would listen to my friends' stories about their family sitting together at dinner and laughing. I used to always feel envious because my parents argued all the time and never slept in the same bed. When it was movie night, I had to choose which parent I was going to watch a movie with. Things between my parents got worse, but I never noticed, because they were always mean to each other. One day their relationship ran its course, and my parents divorced. My imperfect world shattered even further. I soon realized I was a reflection of everything around me, and now I had to figure who I really was all by myself. I was around twelve now, with no role model. I bounced around from clique to clique trying to find where I fit in. I was trying to find myself in a generation where we are known by our status. We are taught to love things and use people instead of the other way around. This is the world I was trying to live in and figure out who I was.

In the midst of this, God was trying to reach me and show me how to love again. I couldn't hear Him because I was too prideful. I remember asking God why everyone around me had a perfect life, and He helped me to realize that it is through the hard times that we grow in Him and can become a better person. I'm still trying to figure out who I am, but I think this quote that my grandma shared with me sums it up—"coal—dark, cold, hard, and dusty. Coal has no beauty of its own. When it is consumed, it is beautiful and becomes what it's designed to be." God's still working on me.

— Alyssa Johnson, Class of 2017

The Happy Children of India
To Serve

But may the righteous be glad and rejoice before God; may they be happy and joyful. (Psalm 68:3, NIV)

The Lord your God is with you, the Mighty Warrior who saves. He will take great delight in you; in his love he will no longer rebuke you, but will rejoice over you with singing. (Zephaniah 3:17, NIV)

The small off-road tires of the group's Tata Magic (4-wheel passenger vehicle built in India) come to a halt as we stop at the gate of Irvine Adventist School. It's 6 a.m. I am resting my head on the old torn up seat in front of me. Deric sits next to me. He has his head resting on my shoulder. I think I can feel his drool soaking through my shirt and onto my sticky skin. I think this is the most humid weather I have ever been in. We have only been in India's Manas Forest for three days, my book bag already has mold on it, and all my clothes have a haunting stench. My bed is so moist it's like sleeping on a damp sponge.

We step out of the Tata Magic and onto the poorly paved road. Deric and I trudged through the gates of the small school anticipating what our tasks for the day would be. We walk down the small pebble path to the school's cafeteria. You can't even call it a cafeteria but it is the only thing that these kids have. We sit down on long wooden benches, so warped from the humidity that they are uncomfortable. They fed us the same thing every day—rice with dal.

I finish my food hastily, I'm anxious to go see the children of the school. All of the kids wear the same thing—a washed-out red tie with a washed-out blue shirt, and some black pants that don't look like they have been washed in weeks. I walk out into the field where all the kids are, they swarm around me and start jumping on me. I can feel their consistent joy.

All of these children are so happy, yet they have nothing. It doesn't make sense. I think that these children have found the secret to be happy. The kids have true happiness despite their situations and what material objects they have. They have happiness in God. They know that God is there for them unconditionally and that makes them happy. God gives them peace.

We have all that we need. We have a nice place to sleep, we have warm water, and we have a way to efficiently wash our clothes. We have all of these things and yet we are still unhappy, we still think that God has somehow forgotten about us. He hasn't! God says many times in the Bible that He cares about us, and that He is always by our side. Zephaniah 3:17 says that the Lord delights in us, and He wants to make us happy. It was a struggle for me to understand how these children had real happiness. The kids had nothing, and yet they had a strong relationship with God, which made them at peace with their current situations. God wants us to know Him, and He wants us to walk with Him in our everyday life. God wants us to be happy! Psalm 68:3 (NIV) says, "But may the righteous be glad and rejoice before God; may they be happy and joyful." Remember everything that God has blessed you with in your life. Be happy and know that God is always there, right by your side.

My challenge to you is to remind yourself that God is always there for you, no matter how alone you feel.

Prayer: Dear Father, please guide me through my daily life, and strengthen my relationship with You.

— Carter Johnson, Class of 2017

Righteous Hand
To Know

Fear not, for I am with you; be not dismayed, for I am your God; I will strengthen you, yes, I will help you, I will uphold you with my righteous right hand. (Isaiah 41:10, NKJV)

When was the first time you learned how to swim without a tube? Or when was the last time you drowned in water?

For years, after Sabbath, a boy named Ted and his family went on a picnic. In summer, they went to the river. There was no noise, and there were no people. It was perfect to enjoy the creation of God. The wind blew whispers through the tree branches. The birds sang in light pure tones. The river flow slowed down. The huge stones blocking the water way made the water dance side to side. Ted had been singing and smiling with the indescribable excitement he felt to swim in the river. After a short worship with family, he immediately asked for permission to go to the river first. By the time Ted was ready, he was wearing a pair of dark blue swimming trunks, dark goggles, and a bright yellow tube.

His parents said, "Sure go ahead, son."

Right after he received permission to swim, he sprinted like a wild boar with his head forward. And SPLASH! After few second he saw his parents, and without any word, he just smiled. After swimming for ten minutes the sun came out from behind a cloud, and he saw the bottom of the river. He saw something like a dark flat fish with a long tail, which was the reflection of himself in the tube with the string. But in his imagination it looked like a sting ray. Even though he did not have any idea where it came from, he knew it was dangerous. Ted hesitated to ask for help from his parents because he thought he was old enough to handle his problem. Since he was so scared, he twisted his leg close to the tube to move away from the shadow, which he thought was a dangerous fish. After swimming closer to the land, he looked down through his goggles to see if he could see where the sting ray was. It was swimming closer to him. So he panicked. He cried out loud, "Help!!! Father!!! Help!!!" Within a second, Father was right beside Ted (his phone and wallet was in his pocket). The boy wept and cried on his father's white T-shirt. Father hugged him close, patted his back and said, "I am here. I am here. Don't be afraid."

Later, Ted told his father about the creature in the river. So Father went in and checked what it really was. After a few minutes Father came out of the water with laughter.

The boy was sure of what he saw. "It is a ray. Ya? Is it?"

Father looked at him and said, "It was your shadow. The sun made a shadow with the tube."

This story is based on a childhood experience. From this story we can relate to our social lives. Satan is always making us scared and weak over nothing. We are so confident in our tube and swimming skill that we can handle our problem. We are often times scared to admit our sins and actions. We want to do everything by ourselves. However, we can do better with help from our heavenly Father.

— Min U Jun, Class of 2015

Milah's Death
To Serve

He will wipe away every tear from their eyes, and death shall be no more, neither shall there be mourning, nor crying, nor pain anymore, for the former things have passed away.
(Revelation 21:4, ESV)

Have you ever wondered if God was there? Well Milah did. Milah was a Seventh-day Adventist, and recently her grandmother died. Her grandmother was diagnosed with cancer and didn't have much time to live. Milah was praying to God for her grandmother to live, but God was saying that it was her time to go. When her grandmother died, she hated and cursed God and asked, "Why did You allow this to happen to my family?" She thought God had turned away from her.

She cried for days, months actually. On one particular day, Milah's mother witnessed her crying and told her that everything happens for a reason, and that she will see her grandmother again when Jesus comes. Then she showed her a beautiful verse in Revelation 21:4 (ESV) that says "He will wipe away every tear from their eyes, and death shall be no more, neither shall there be mourning, nor crying, nor pain anymore, for the former things have passed away."

When I first heard this story it made me think of how the devil throws little balls of distractions in your life, whether it's a death in the family or a bad grade you got on your latest test, etc. But this verse, Revelation 21:4, says that when Jesus comes there will be no more pain, no more sorrow, no murdering, nothing bad like that, when we come home with our Heavenly Father. To Milah, the way she understood the verse was that even though her grandmother died, she knows that she's going to see her again in heaven. Then she can rejoice and be with her forever.

— Ngady Kabia, Class of 2019

Know Your Enemy!
To Know

For our struggle is not against flesh and blood, but against the rulers, against the authorities, against the powers of this dark world and against the spiritual forces of evil in the heavenly realms. (Ephesians 6:12, NIV)

Is Satan powerful? Yes. Is God more powerful? Absolutely.

Writing in *Moody Monthly*, Carl Armerding recounted his experience of watching a wildcat in a zoo. "As I stood there," he said, "an attendant entered the cage through a door on the opposite side. He had nothing in his hands but a broom. Carefully closing the door, he proceeded to sweep the floor of the cage."

He observed that the worker had no weapon to ward off an attack by the beast. In fact, when he got to the corner of the cage where the wildcat was lying, he poked the animal with the broom. The wildcat hissed at him and then lay down in another corner of the enclosure.

Armerding remarked to the attendant, "You certainly are a brave man."

"No, I ain't brave," he replied as he continued to sweep.

"Well, then, that cat must be tame."

"No," came the reply, "he ain't tame."

"If you aren't brave and the wildcat isn't tame, then I can't understand why he doesn't attack you."

Armerding said the man chuckled, then replied with an air of confidence, "Mister, he's old—and he ain't got no teeth."

That's the devil. Ever since Jesus died on the cross, he "ain't got no teeth." He can growl and he can roar, but he's a defeated foe. As long as you stay in league with Jesus, there is nothing he can do to hurt you.

But ignore him. Pretend he isn't there. He'll be all over you. You have to be up to the spiritual battle. You must always be on your guard. One final verse.

Be alert and of sober mind. Your enemy the devil prowls around like a roaring lion looking for someone to devour. Resist him, standing firm in the faith, because you know that the family of believers throughout the world is undergoing the same kind of sufferings. And the God of all grace, who called you to his eternal glory in Christ, after you have suffered a

little while, will himself restore you and make you strong, firm and steadfast. To him be the power for ever and ever. Amen. (1 Peter 5:8–11, NIV)
— Don Keele Jr., Church Pastor

The Love Response
To Love

You see, at just the right time, when we were still powerless, Christ died for the ungodly. Very rarely will anyone die for a righteous man, though for a good man someone might possibly dare to die. But God demonstrates his own love for us in this: While we were still sinners, Christ died for us.
(Romans 5:6–8, NIV)

When it comes to the word sacrifice, we must look at attitudes. Our attitudes. Have they grown selfish and inward, or are they ever expanding to include our fellow man? Are we learning to share more, love more, and show God's love more, or are we too busy, too important or too calloused to be bothered by it all?

Eric Fellman speaks of meeting a Chinese couple in Hong Kong, while traveling to China. He said, "A friend took me down a narrow alley to a second-floor flat to meet a man recently released from prison in China. I knew I would be pressed to carry Bibles and literature on my trip. But I was hesitant and tried to mask my fear with rationalizations about legalities and other concerns.

"A Chinese man in his 60s opened the door. His smile was radiant, but his back was bent almost double. He led us to a sparsely furnished room. A Chinese woman of about the same age came in to serve tea. As she lingered, I couldn't help but notice how they touched and lovingly looked at each other. My staring apparently didn't go unnoticed, for soon they were both giggling.

"'What is it?' I asked my friend.

"'Oh nothing,' he said with a smile. 'They just wanted you to know it was OK—they're newlyweds.' I learned they had been engaged in 1949, when he was a student at Nanking Seminary.

"On the day of their wedding rehearsal, Chinese communists seized the seminary. They took the students to a hard-labor prison. For the next thirty years, the bride-to-be was allowed only one visit per year. Each time, following their brief minutes together, the man would be called to the warden's office.

"'You may go home with your bride,' he said, 'if you will renounce Christianity.' Year after year, this man replied with just one word: 'No.' I was stunned. How had he been able to stand the strain for so long, being denied his family, his marriage, and even his health? When I asked, he seemed astonished at my question.

"He replied, 'With all that Jesus has done for me, how could I betray Him?' The next day, I requested that my suitcase be crammed with Bibles and training literature for Chinese Christians. I determined not to lie about the materials, yet lost not one minute of sleep worrying about the consequences. And as God had planned, my suitcases were never inspected." (Fellman, Eric. *Moody Monthly*, January 1986, p. 33.)

Sacrifice comes from realizing that someone already sacrificed for you. It is a love response. And here's the kicker. If there is no love response, it means, quite frankly, there is no love. In other words, if you are not willing to sacrifice for the sake of Christ, you really don't love Him. Love means sacrificial action.

— Don Keele Jr., Church Pastor

I Am a Soldier
To Serve

Endure suffering along with me, as a good soldier of Christ Jesus. Soldiers don't get tied up in the affairs of civilian life, for then they cannot please the officer who enlisted them.
(2 Timothy 2:3–4, NLT)

Remind everyone about these things, and command them in God's presence to stop fighting over words. Such arguments are useless, and they can ruin those who hear them. Work hard so you can present yourself to God and receive his approval. Be a good worker, one who does not need to be ashamed and who correctly explains the word of truth. Avoid worthless, foolish talk that only leads to more godless behavior. This kind of talk spreads like cancer. (2 Timothy 2:14–17 NLT)

I was reading an old book the other day about the Huguenots, the Waldensians and others that tried to remain true to the commands of God during the Dark Ages, and the contrast between them and us is absolutely incredible.

Thousands died cruel deaths; burned at the stake, hurled over cliffs, hung up with meat hooks, starved in prison, and yet very few, if any, turned back from following God.

Yet today, it seems the slightest thing can turn many of us back from following Jesus. Our feelings get hurt, so we quit. Our leadership gets criticized, so we quit. A pastor doesn't come visit us at the right time, so we quit. We don't want to get involved, so we don't. We are afraid to make our neighbor uncomfortable, so we don't share. Church doesn't suit our tastes, so we stop attending. At the slightest hint of resistance, we turn back. Could it be that the worst enemy the church has is prosperity?

I mentioned this to a friend in another state, and he sent me this piece, which I think needs to be our rallying cry. Read it and see where you stand. It is titled, "I am a Soldier."

> I am a soldier.
> I am a soldier in the army of my God;
> The Lord Jesus Christ is my Commanding Officer.
> The Holy Bible is my code of conduct.
> Faith, prayer and the Word are my weapons of warfare.
> I have been taught by the Holy Spirit, trained by experience, tried by adversity and tested by fire.
>
> I am a volunteer in this army and I have enlisted for eternity
> I will either retire from this army at the Second Coming or die in this army; but I will not get out, sell out, be talked out or pushed out.
> I am faithful, reliable and dependable.
>
> If my God needs me, I am there.
> If He needs me in Sabbath School to teach children, work with youth, help with adults or just sit and learn, He can use me, because I am there.
>
> If He needs me in church Sabbath morning, Vespers, Wednesday, revival or
> special services' I am there.
> I am there to preach, teach, sing, play, pray, work or worship.
> God can use me because I am there.

I am a Soldier. I am not a baby.
I do not need to be pampered, petted, primed up, pumped up, picked up or
pepped up.

I am a Soldier. No one has to call me, remind me, write me, visit me, entice me or lure me.

I am a Soldier. I am not a wimp.
I am in place saluting my King, obeying His orders, praising His name and serving in His Kingdom.
No one has to send me flowers, gifts, food, cards, candy or give me handouts.
I do not need to be cuddled, cradled, cared for or catered to.
I am a Soldier, and I am committed.

I cannot have my feelings hurt badly enough to turn me around.
I cannot be discouraged enough to turn me aside.
I cannot lose enough to cause me to quit,
When Jesus called me into this army, I had nothing,
And if I end up with nothing I will still break even.

I am a Soldier, I am committed, I will win.
My God will supply all my needs.
I am more than a conqueror, I will always triumph.
I can do all things through Christ.

Devils cannot defeat me. People cannot disillusion me. Weather cannot
weary me. Sickness cannot stop me. Battles cannot beat me. Money cannot buy
me. Governments cannot silence me and Hell cannot handle me.
I am a soldier. I am committed. Even death cannot destroy me.

When my Commander calls me from this battlefield He will promote me and
then bring me back to rule this world with Him.
I am a Soldier in the army and I am marching, claiming victory.
I will not give up, I will not turn around. I am a Soldier marching Heaven bound. –Author Unknown

I am a Soldier. Will you stand with me?
If God is in it, you can do it.

— Don Keele Jr., Church Pastor

God's Big Plans
To Serve

And this same God who takes care of me will supply all your needs from his glorious riches, which have been given to us in Christ Jesus. (Philippians 4:19, NLT)

In 2009 I received a call from Carl Rodriguez, the youth director of the Chesapeake Conference, asking if I would be interested in serving as leader of a worship team for all Pathfinder and youth leadership training events that the conference planned each year. I was excited about the opportunity, but I was also hesitant. I had just gotten in to coordinating the praise time at our church, and it was just me on the piano with some singers. I had never played with a band before or led worship, especially not in front of a bunch of kids.

My passion for worship, music, and youth overrode my fear of the unknown, and I jumped into the new role with enthusiasm, bringing with me my audio technician husband. But all of that excitement was replaced with a severe case of nerves a few weeks later when we took the stage to lead worship for the youth division at camp meeting and were welcomed with blank stares. I did my best to engage the audience, but my words and our music seemed to fall on deaf ears. It was horrible, and I wanted to crawl under my piano!

Fast forward four years, and my family and I were preparing to move to Calhoun. It was April, and we had just finished our last weekend leading worship for a conference event. We had enjoyed highs and lows and many incredible worship moments over the years of our ministry with the conference. We were saying goodbye to Carl and thanking him for mentoring us and helping us grow in what was now a ministry we loved!

I'll never forget what he said before we left: "I know God has something bigger in store for you and your ministry. I can't wait to see what doors He opens for you in Georgia."

Little did I know back in 2009 when Carl called me that God was training me for His purposes and His role for me at GCA. Little did I know that He was supplying my needs even before I asked Him, because I wouldn't have been prepared to help with the praise and worship class at GCA without the training I received working with Carl and our worship band.

You never know what God has in store for your life, but I guarantee you that it will be an adventure you don't want to miss. I promise you that if you give your life to God He will supply your every need to accomplish the opportunities He places in your path.

— Kalie Kelch, Staff

To Know Him
To Know

But the fruit of the Spirit is love, joy, peace, patience, kindness, goodness, faithfulness, gentleness and self-control. Against such things there is no law. (Galatians 5:22-23, WEB)

As a kid, my parents had me memorize this verse because it is a very important verse. At the end of this verse it says, "Against such things there is no law." This means that if people don't have all of these character traits, we will not be Christ-like. Each one of these fruits is important in their own way.

When I was about six years old, my parents decided to renovate our basement. In order to renovate the basement, they had to get rid of everything in the basement and remove the walls. Since the basement was one big open space, I thought it would be fun to ride my bike around the basement. I got out of control, and I hit the ironing board with the iron on it. The iron was warmed up and ready to be used.

As I hit the ironing board, the iron should have fallen on me, but for some reason, it didn't. I am very convinced that my angel protected me that night and made sure the iron would not touch me. This is an example of not having self-control. One of the most important fruits is self-control. You need to have control in life, and know what is going on, and not be like me and run into hot irons in your life.

Love is important because God told us to love one another as ourselves. In order to love others, you must first love yourself.

Joy is very important because you need to be happy in life. It is scientifically proven that people who are happy do better in life and are healthier than people who are always negative.

Peace is the next fruit that is one of the most important ones on the list. You must have peace in life because without peace, people will constantly be fighting with one another.

Patience is one of the hardest fruits to have. If you feel that people are taking too long and you're about to blow up, you need to pray for patience that you will be like God.

Kindness is essential. If you see someone having a bad day, go over and talk to them, cheer them up and try to make them feel better, that is kind.

Goodness is almost like common sense. If you know that what you're doing isn't good, then don't do it and be a good person.

Faithfulness is key to having a relationship with God. You always need to be faithful to what you believe in and do your part also.

Gentleness is very important. Whenever I hear the word gentleness I think of being careful. I think God is telling us, "Be careful in the world around you, and don't fall into temptations."

Self-Control is what you have to go through every day. Control yourself on what you're about to do. Don't let yourself fall into temptations, control yourself.

I challenge you as you are reading this to pray that you will demonstrate every fruit today and to know God better today than you did yesterday.

— Zach Kirstein, Class of 2019

Influence Never Dies
To Love

He gives generously to those in need. His deeds will never be forgotten. He shall have influence and honor. (Psalm 112:9, TLB)

Fall semester of my junior year at Southern was a very dark time for me. Thinking there was no hope that my life would get any better, I started planning my suicide. I put a lot of thought into it and came up with a method, a location, and a time that would ensure I would not be found until it was too late. As I planned it all out, I thought, "This is going to be so easy!" Immediately I recalled something from Survey of English Literature the previous year.

The lecture was about the devilish debate scene from Paradise Lost where Satan and his hosts were discussing various ways of getting back at God. My professor, Dr. Haluska*, pointed out that as the scene progresses and suggestions are made, that they get progressively easier. The final, most despicable, evil idea is to get to God through hurting His human children, which is also the easiest thing for them to attempt.

After a short pause, Dr. Haluska said, "If you ever find yourself at a time of decision, considering the easiest path to take, be careful, for it often will also be the worst possible thing you could do, with the most potential for evil."

Remembering that lecture, I realized I could not carry out what I was planning, because I would be choosing the easiest path.

I was so upset I yelled at God and told Him, "I don't understand why You would want me to continue living such a horrible life, but I'll keep going, since You've just taken away my only other option." In making that decision, I inadvertently gave God more opportunities to continue to work in my life and put me on the path toward healing.

Prior to that day, I might never have said that taking a literature class could be so important. However, because of that lecture, because Dr. Haluska consistently invited God into the classroom, and because he used his ministry of teaching to impart wisdom, I am alive. I will be forever grateful to him for allowing God to use him that day and giving me the tools I needed to choose to live.

*Dr. Jan Haluska taught at GCA from 1974-1981. The rest of Jan Haluska's career was spent in the English department of Southern

Adventist University until he retired in 2014. Dr. Haluska passed away on September 25, 2015.

— Eve Parker Knight, Class of 1993

A Hold on Fear
To Know

Because God is always at work in you to make you willing and able to obey his own purpose. (Philippians 2:13, GNT)

I have always been afraid of water. My parents don't know why, but have told me when I was a baby, I would scream so loudly during bath time my dad would have to leave the house. Fortunately, I overcame the aversion to bathing, and I eventually figured out the focus of the fear was putting my face in water or going under water. This was never a big problem for me until my junior year at GCA when God impressed me to be baptized.

I wanted very much to follow His leading, but my fear got in the way. My courage flagged when I wondered if the chaplain—who was slightly shorter than me—could successfully dip me backwards into the water with me in the midst of a full-blown panic attack. I went to talk to him and started to think maybe I could do this. Then he told me the baptisms every year were done at Sloppy Floyd Park in a lake.

Horrified, I said, "No way I'm doing that."

The next year I again felt the impression that I needed to be baptized. I tried to ignore it, but it persisted and then got even stronger.

Finally, I prayed, "God, if You really want me to do this, then You need to send someone taller than me, and make sure it happens in the baptismal tank in the chapel. If you do that, then I will get baptized." I walked away from that prayer certain I had stymied God with my requirements.

A couple weeks later I walked into the first meeting for our Week of Prayer, and stumbled when I saw the speaker. Pastor Doug Martin was well over six feet tall. I wondered if I should worry about that, but then reassured myself that baptisms never happened anywhere other than at the lake.

Wednesday of that week, my friend and co-worker casually said, "Oh, by the way, I'm getting baptized at vespers on Friday night." My heart may have stopped beating for a few seconds, but I finally managed to squeak out a question about who was doing it and where. Sure enough, it was Pastor Martin in the chapel baptismal.

God had clearly come through with His part of the bargain, which meant it was my turn. With great fear and trembling, I went to the chaplain and added my name to the small list of students for the baptism.

Friday night arrived, and I gathered with four other students to receive our final instructions. One of the girls noticed the look on my face and asked, "Are you ok?"

"I'm afraid of water," I whispered.

"Oh," she nodded. The pastor came back in, and she said, "Be sure and be careful with my friend here, because she's afraid of water."

"Ok," he said, and walked up the stairs to the tank.

When I joined him there later, he asked me if it was true. I nodded, and he said, "Don't worry, it'll be ok." Surprisingly, it was. From that moment until after he brought me back up out of the water, I felt only peace. Fear was completely absent. It was the only time in my life I ever experienced not being afraid of water.

I learned that day that no matter what God asks of me, no matter how fearful I am of the task, I can boldly step forward in faith. Fear is no barrier for Him. God is love and "There is no fear in love; perfect love drives out all fear" (1 John 4:18a, GNB).

— Eve Parker Knight, Class of 1993

The Falls of Prayer
To Know

The Lord is near to all them that call on him, to all that call on him in truth. (Psalm 145:18, NIV)

One beautiful Sabbath day, my dad and I decided to head to the Ocoee White Water Center. As we arrived, we found a perfect swimming hole with a 7-foot waterfall.

Unbeknownst to me, this waterfall was not the only thing that resided there. As the waterfall crashed to the bottom of the swimming hole, the water created a whirlpool, which was waiting to strike. I swam towards the waterfall and the whirlpool saw its chance. It pulled with all its might and I grabbed on to the nearest rock and held on for dear life. The tug-of-war ended with the whirlpool in victory. It dragged me under the water.

I paddled hard in hopes to get my head above the water for that all-important breath. The whirlpool was determined to not let me go. I gave one last, final push towards the surface and broke free. As I popped up, I tried to swim out from the circular movement that I knew would take me back under if I didn't get out fast. Every muscle was working as I put each arm in front of me and pushed myself forward.

The whirlpool had the advantage and decided it wasn't done with me. It swung my body around and slammed me back under. My adrenaline was wearing thin, and I knew I couldn't do this again, so I turned to the One I knew who could, my God. I said three short words to Him, "God, help me!" A new, refreshing power surged through my body and suddenly, the whirlpool had absolutely nothing on me. I flew forward and pushed out of the whirlpool with ease.

God is always there. You may not feel like it, but He is always right next to you. Satan will try to drag you down and take you from God, and believe me, he is good at it. Don't let Satan do that to you, let God take control. God has an outstretched hand for you, call upon Him and take that hand and He will always pull you through. Let God take the wheel in your life, and He will guide you to all the right choices because His plan is the best plan, and only wants the best for you.

— Andrew Korp, Class of 2016

Radical Trust
To Love

But when he (Peter) saw the wind boisterous, he was afraid; and beginning to sink, he cried, saying, Lord, save me. And immediately Jesus stretched forth his hand, and caught him, and said unto him, O thou of little faith, wherefore didst thou doubt.
(Matthew 14:30–31, KJV)

How many times have we wanted to do something for God, or He has called us to come to Him? At first it seems great but when the storm assails us we are terrified. We take our eyes off Jesus and look at our circumstances. We forget that Jesus would never ask us to do anything that we can't handle with Him. When we cry out in terror His hand is always right there. The rebuke is gentle, "Where is your faith?" We are safe anywhere in Jesus' hands.

Peter and the other disciples were probably on a spiritual high after all the events of the previous few days. Between the crowds of people, the incredible miracles, and the feeding of the five thousand, they must have been feeling pretty great. Maybe they even expected Jesus to announce that He was going to be king. Then Jesus sent the disciples away and they were off for a night on the stormy sea. I'm sure they were disappointed. Many times I have felt that spiritual high and maybe even expected God to do something my way. When it doesn't happen, I must admit I have a lapse in my faith.

GCA provided many opportunities to be spiritually uplifted and I truly felt that my relationship with Jesus grew through my high school years. Bible and prayer conferences were highlights for me, and I generally came back on fire for Christ. Those spiritually uplifting moments were wonderful, but there was always the other side. The valley experiences have taught me to trust in Jesus, and keep faith no matter how I feel.

In the darkest part of the night Jesus walked across the sea to His disciples. Jesus was prepared because He had spent the whole evening with His Father in prayer. When Peter walked on the water, he lost sight of the Savior and only focused on himself and his fear.

Are we limiting what Jesus can do in our lives because of our lack of faith? Or even because of our fear? Our God is limitless; we are the ones that place limits on Him because of our unbelief. Though our relationship with Jesus may have it's up and down moments, do we have faith to keep our eyes on Him no matter what the circumstances are? I have found in my life that feelings come and go, but my Jesus is always there. God is looking for people to walk with Him today. It's a constant walk, with our eyes continually focused on Him. Are you willing to walk that walk today? He will be with you every step of the way. You can count on it.

I have felt the same way as Peter, God has asked me to step out in faith and to allow Him to be my only safety net. When I stopped relying on my own plans, and started trusting in the Lord, I found that I could feel His hands holding me. When I trust Jesus with everything, I have found that He is everything that I need.

— Julie Kretschmar, Almuni, Class of 2010

Light My Fire
To Know

For I know the thoughts that I think toward you, says the LORD, thoughts of peace and not of evil, to give you a future and a hope.
(Jeremiah 29:11, NKJV)

Have you ever looked back on your life and seen how God has been leading you all along? For me, it has been very gradual. In fact, I don't remember ever knowing exactly what I wanted to do with my life. I had vague ideas that changed frequently, and I was half way through my senior year at GCA before I decided on nursing. It was more of a rational decision as a reaction to my desire to do missions and to serve others. Now, I wouldn't choose any other profession.

During my senior year, I got to go to GYC (Generation of Youth for Christ) and heard a talk that lit a fire in my soul to do mission work. What I didn't realize was that the embers had been simmering all through my GCA experience. Four Appalachian mission trips to rural Kentucky made me realize how fulfilling a life of service can be, and how much I have to be grateful for.

Have you thought about the mission field that may be waiting for you in your own home? While mission work has been rather varied for me, and I haven't always served in the USA, the missions in my backyard are often the most fulfilling. I must admit, while I am writing this I am deep in the bush of Papua New Guinea, but the backyard missions prepared me for where I am today.

Turns out the God of the universe has incredible plans for our lives, if only we will allow ourselves to be led by Him. Have you thought about giving yourself fully to Him today? It's the best adventure that you could ever have. When you have given your life into his hands He holds you. One of the best things I have learned in the short twisty path of my life is that He is there, just waiting to reveal Himself.

I challenge you today to see God working in your backyard, in your life. Ask Him to reveal Himself and surrender to the incredible plan He has for your life. Are you feeling down and depressed about life? Seeing Jesus in your day-to-day life is one of the most encouraging things and serving others is the best pick-me-up you could ask for. He's there, just waiting for you! Won't you seek him today? "Trust in the LORD with all your heart, and lean not on your own understanding; In all your ways acknowledge Him, and He shall direct your paths." (Prov. 3:5-6, NKJV)

— Julie Kretschmar, Class of 2010

Working
To Serve

You, my brothers and sisters, were called to be free. But do not use your freedom to indulge the flesh; rather, serve one another humbly in love. For the entire law is fulfilled in keeping this one command: "Love your neighbor as yourself."
(Galatians 5: 13-14, NIV)

Working on a Sunday morning is rarely an anticipated experience, especially at a boarding academy. Leather gloves, straining against railroad ties, digging through a never-ending mesh of tree roots; the only thing that makes Sunday labor more bearable is working with friends. In the spring of my senior year at Georgia-Cumberland Academy, there were a few Sundays when I worked with my classmates to build an amphitheater. The big goal since freshman year (sadly I did not join the class until junior year) was a mission trip, and to save money our class put some "sweat equity" into building an amphitheater as a class gift. There was much perturbation about this gift, because providing more supervision areas is understandably an added hassle for the staff. However, after much debate we were allowed to clear an area between the girl's dorm and the ad building for some anticipated outdoor gatherings. Trees were felled, railroad ties laid, and tiers routed during long weary hours. In the end, we were able to raise/save enough money to fly to the Virgin Islands and spend more "sweat equity" on a bus shelter, bleachers, and playground for a sister academy on St. Thomas.

Service is an important aspect of any Christian's life, and especially for a young Christian's life. Young people feel important when they are able to contribute to a common goal in a meaningful way. Our contributions were probably more a nuisance than an actual help (when we put the playground together in St. Thomas we bolted the slide on upside down, and I'm sure trying to build an amphitheater with a bunch of seniors was like herding cats). But I was fortunate to be in a class that valued service and hard work, and we were also fortunate to have sponsors and parents that were willing to sweat and save with us.

So much of Christ's ministry on earth was centered on service to others. His ability to heal and comfort gave the people He encountered a reason to get to know God better. Programs that foster this desire for service are essential for young people everywhere and I am fortunate that service was emphasized for me while a student at GCA.

— Bliss McClellan Kuntz, Class of 2000

Last Day at the Beach
To Know

Have I not commanded you? Be strong and courageous. Do not be afraid; do not be discouraged, for the Lord your God will be with you wherever you go. (Joshua 1:9 NIV)

It was the last day of our vacation in Daytona Beach, Florida. I did not want to swim because I had already taken a shower the night before. However, my mom insisted that I swim because it was the last day and I would miss out. I was having fun in the ocean and swimming around people I did not know, but I wanted to go further out.

On this day the current was different. Rather than pulling to the side, it pulled me back out to make another bigger wave. The current was worse than when I just swim around in it and jump the waves. The tide was up closer than normal and all the waves were bigger. After my grandma and sisters left I wanted to go out farther and I got stuck in a rip tide. I remembered what my family always said, "Swim parallel to the shore," but the water kept smacking me in the face and going over my head.

Not knowing what else to do, I prayed to God to help me get out of the ocean. I remember floating up on a wave and being able to see the lifeguard waving his flag in the distance. I did not know if it was for me, but I hoped so. He was telling me to come in but I could not. I started to wave my hands and yell for help as I struggled to stay above the water. Eventually a lifeguard came to tell me to come in, but heard me calling for help. He got to me and tried to help me, but was not strong enough to get anywhere. Before I knew it, there were five lifeguards helping me get out.

God is like the lifeguards. He is always there when you need help. Remember even in your times of trouble that God is always right there beside you.

— Krystena Land, Class of 2017

Protection
To Know

He who dwells in the secret place of the Most High shall abide under the shadow of the Almighty. I will say of the Lord, "He is my refuge and my fortress; My God, in Him I will trust." Surely He shall deliver you from the snare of the fowler and from the perilous pestilence. (Psalm 91:1–3, NKJV)

Protection comes in all different manners, friends, families, and even pets. But have you ever thought about God's protection, how even in the smallest things, He will scoop you up into His arms and carry you the rest of the way? Last summer, Rebekah and I went with our Bowman Hills church teen group on a boating trip, and one of the activities they had was tubing.

When it was our turn, we hopped onto the tube and situated ourselves, preparing for a wild ride. Once settled, the boat sped up in attempt to shake us off, swerving left, then right and doing donuts. Meanwhile, back on the tube I was clinging on for dear life trying hard not to fall off. In the process, I forgot Rebekah was there and I started taking up her side of the tube as well, but instead of shoving me over or just letting go of the tube she flung her arm over me and grasped the handle across the tube, securing herself and me to the tube.

This reminded me of God and how I know that He will never leave me. Often times, the thrill of the world distracts many of us. We throw ourselves into what we think is innocent fun, but when we get sucked up into the never-ending murky water of sin we realize that we could or will actually get hurt. We forget that God is there and can help us. We push Him away and just focus on ourselves, but God doesn't leave us alone. He secures us to Him and tells us to keep going, that this obstacle is nearly over, and to trust Him for He is with us and is our refuge through the bad times in our life. Everyone has a downfall or a problem in life that jerks us around trying to shake us from our faith, but we don't have to be afraid. Just ask Him to save you and trust that he will surely "deliver you from the snare of the fowler and from the perilous pestilence."

— Katie Lassiter, Class of 2017

No Matter Where You Are
To Love

He lifted me out of the slimy pit, out of the mud and mire; he set my feet on a rock and gave me a firm place to stand.
(Psalm 40:2, NIV)

When I was five years old, I lived on the campus of Blue Mountain Academy in Pennsylvania. Like most states up north, we had an annual delivery of white, sparkling snow. One year in particular, the snowfall stacked up inch by inch until we had a whopping five feet. As you can imagine, school was cancelled that day and everyone within a fifty-mile radius was experiencing the same productivity-paralyzing problem; being snowed in. Have you ever tried to open a door with five feet of frozen water crystals packed up against it? It's basically impossible. Since I obviously did not have a job or attend school, I certainly did not have a problem with the current climate. I was enthralled with the idea of playing in such a copious amount of snow and excitedly began scribbling out the blueprints for the three-story ninja turtle headquarters I was going to build.

I bundled up, grabbed my incredibly professional blueprints drawn in Crayola® magic markers, and climbed up the couch to exit the non-snow-blocked window. Before I could leave, a hand grasped the strap of my bright blue snowsuit.

"You'll get stuck out there!" my mom exclaimed. I made a face of discontent and plopped myself down on the couch to begin a pouting session. Instead of taking my mother's warning, I decided to interpret it as a casual suggestion and proceeded to make my exit.

What do you think happened? You got it, I got stuck waist deep. After only two minutes of intense waiting, my mom made her heroic appearance whilst carrying a shovel. I could tell she was trying not to laugh as she came and literally dug me out. She didn't say one harsh word or punish me for going against her word, even though I totally deserved it.

My mother's love and willingness to dig me out of the snow is the same as how God is towards us. The only difference is that God's grace and love is so much stronger than anything we could ever imagine. Whatever we do, whatever we are going through, whatever mistakes we make, God will reach down and pull us out of slimy pit, the mud, and the mire. Even if we deliberately go against His Word, once we repent and ask for His help, He is readily there to pull us right back up and loves us just as much every time.

— Shelby Lewellen, Class of 2017

Service Outlet
To Serve

Whoever welcomes one of these little children in my name welcomes me. (Mark 9:37, NIV)

For the past four summers, I have volunteered at my church's Vacation Bible School program, or VBS. I am one of the music people. I sing the songs and do the motions and generally make a fool of myself up front, but it's worth it. I play a very large part in how the kids see Christ during the week. I don't have the option to have a bad day or to be grumpy for any one of our sing and play sessions. If I slack in my job by acting like I would rather be somewhere else, one of those kids could decide that they don't want to try to get to know God, or that VBS is stupid, or that they're too old for VBS. But when I get up there as a teenager, and show them that I want to be there, I show them that VBS is still cool, God is still cool, and it's cool to be silly every once in a while.

This verse doesn't just apply to literal children. It applies to everyone, as we are all children in Christ. We are called to be servants, to witness to these children. I have found my "Service Outlet" in my church's VBS program, and I hope to continue helping with it.

So I'm giving you a challenge. Find your "Service Outlet." Find a way that you can serve the people around you. It doesn't have to be a spiritual gathering; it doesn't even have to be a planned gathering. The amazing thing about service is that you don't even have to say a word to change someone's life (brings a whole new meaning to the saying, "Actions speak louder than words," doesn't it?). Find your outlet, and "plug in" to it as soon as possible. I promise you won't regret it.

— Caitlin Lopez, Class of 2016

Shadows
To Know

But let all who take refuge in you be glad; let them ever sing for joy. Spread your protection over them that those who love your name may rejoice in you. (Psalm 5:11 NIV)

There was a blade of grass that loved to dance in the sun and sway in the breeze. It had seen the flowers bloom in spring and the new life of the earth. Then one day the sun did not reach the blade of grass. The blade was standing in the shadow of something great. A tree stood taller and stronger than the blade of grass. The blade felt inferior and no longer danced in the sun or swayed in the breeze.

There was a tree that loved to stretch its branches and reach for the sun. It had survived the bitter winters and scorching summers. Then one day the sun did not reach the tree. The tree was rooted in the shadow of something great. A mountain towered over it with age and beauty evident. The tree felt inferior and no longer stretched its branches and reached for the sun.

There was a mountain that loved to watch the seasons change the gown that it wore and show it off in the light of the sun. It had watched as the earth around it came and went, throughout the ages. Then one day the sun did not reach the mountain. The mountain was based in the shadow of something great. An enormous cloud traveling on its way passed over the mountain. The mountain felt inferior and no longer watched the changing of its gown or showed it off in the sun.

Sometimes there are shadows in our lives that seem to block out God. Those shadows can be as sturdy as a tree or as old as a mountain or as ever changing and ever moving as a cloud. When we find ourselves caught up in these shadows we forget about God's love shining down on us, and without us knowing it we can bring a shadow upon someone else.

Like a blade of grass, a new Christian finds the faith beautiful and alluring, but as soon as a shadow falls on them they may find it difficult to remember God is still there. Not only have the babies in the faith had these issues with shadows. Even the strongest in the faith have shadows of their own that can cause doubt to grow, and it can spread like a weed. There are also people who have grown up in a Christian home that are fifth or sixth generation Christians who find themselves with shadows, too.

God allows these shadows to cover us for a while to test us. Will we turn to Him? God loves us and He wants us to know Him, but it has to start with a little faith. We need to trust in Him, especially when shadows cover us, He can lift us above them. What shadows do you have in your life? Are you willing to give them to God?

— Noelle Lucas, Class of 2019

Lost?
To Know

> *For we do not wrestle against flesh and blood, but against the rulers, against the authorities, against the cosmic powers over this present darkness, against the spiritual forces of evil in the heavenly places. (Ephesians 2:12, ESV)*

In this present darkness, our world is shadowed with horrors and evil that were unimaginable a few centuries ago. Pastors preach that we are in the last days before Jesus' second coming and the only way to go to heaven is to be saved. I used to have many issues with those teachings. I asked myself questions like "Can we hear God"? or "Is God real in our lives"? I've dueled with those polarizing questions for years but I never really was able to answer them until I came to GCA.

My life was a big mess before I went to boarding school. I was previously in public school and my spiritual life had sunk so low that I was almost to the point of completely abandoning God and religion altogether. My first few weeks at GCA were extremely hard, but I grew to love it. I was shocked with the friendliness and amiability of the students and staff. Another thing that helped me grow spiritually was Mr. Leeper's religion class. It made me think critically about my spiritual life and my religious beliefs entirely. I realized that one of the biggest issues in my relationship with God was my selfishness. I constantly asked God for things to happen and I put all my blame upon God. In reality, I was so selfish that I never realized that in the connecting ends between God and me, I was the one doing wrong. I started to read the Bible again, and by the end of my sophomore year I essentially rekindled my connection with God.

Throughout the year I found out more about God than I ever would have at any secular school. I learned how to get to know God through personal devotion and reading the Bible more often. I learned that God doesn't ignore us or abandon us when we cry and pray at our lowest. We just have to be selfless and humble and God will answer our prayers.

— John Macedo, Class of 2017

Masterpiece
To Love

So God created man in His own image: in the image of God He created him; male and female He created them.
(Genesis 1:27 NKJV)

We have all looked at another individual and thought, "Wow that person really isn't a very attractive person." Some of us might have felt bad after thinking, or maybe even saying something like that. In the same way most of us have been called ugly or some other insulting term, and it's not the best feeling. Why do we all forget that when we insult another person, we insult God by telling Him His masterpiece is not the way it should be? Is He not the master? Is He not the Creator, the all-powerful, the all-knowing God we are to fear? Thinking things like, "Wow she is ugly, she'd probably look better without that big forehead," is absolutely the same as telling God, "Oh, this person that you made is kind of ugly, maybe if you made her forehead smaller she would look better."

If being His masterpiece wasn't enough, He made us in His own perfect image as well. When I was little, I was constantly teased and bullied for many things. I grew up hating myself. I hated everything I saw when I looked in the mirror. I would ask God everyday why He made me the way He did, and I'd ask why I didn't have features other people had, until one morning in my family's worship, as we were reading through Genesis. When we read Genesis 1:27, it made me feel really guilty, because for a long time I had been telling God He made some mistakes in His work. I finally accepted myself as flawless, because God doesn't make any mistakes. Not only was I able to love myself for the person God made me, but I could also love everyone else regardless of how they were made.

Get rid of all your self-hate, accept yourself as the beautiful masterpiece that God made you to be. Equally, love everyone around you for the person God made them. Apologize for telling God He made some mistakes, ask Him to help you find the beauty He put into all His work, including the beauty He put into you.

— Amber Maddox, Class of 2018

Fear vs God
To Know

Be still, and know that I am God. I will be exalted among the nations, I will be exalted in the earth! (Psalm 46:10, NKJV)

Do you remember running to your parents as a child when you were scared? Can you count how many times you have? I remember when I was around the age of five, my grandmother died. Watching my mother break out into tears during her speech affected the way I thought for the following weeks. Every night after my grandmother's funeral I would repeat in my mind: *Grandma was mom's mom. Mom is my mom. Grandma died, so does that mean mom is going to die? Mom is going to die? Is Dad going to die too?*

Being just a little five-year-old, I was never actually introduced to death nor had I ever actually had to think about those things. It scared me to the verge of tears, it left me broken. Sometimes I even had nightmares. Those nights that I did, which was often, I would start to bawl, and then do what every child does, I would walk through the hall and knock on my parents' door and explain through broken, trembling tears. My dad would then pray for me and reassure me that all I needed to do was to trust in God and everything would be all right.

That was a long time ago, but I honestly still have not learned. Just a couple of months ago I was bawling to my dad on the phone because I was terrified over something that had been troubling me for a while.

He said the same thing, "Everything is ok, why are you scared? You have nothing to be worried about."

Why did I forget? Why do we forget? Shouldn't we automatically know that God is our protector and provider? Being human, it is natural to forget. Pop Quiz: who knows God's full power, but wants us to forget in order to lead us astray? The answer is obvious. Satan knows about God's full power, if we knew what he knew we wouldn't forget. What is there to forget?

Fear is very real and it's OK to be scared, but we have to remember and know that God can handle it. The Bible says in Psalm 46:10 (NKJV), "Be still, and know that I am God. I will be exalted among the nations, I will be exalted in the earth!" Pray that we may know God for what He truly is and not limit Him down to our understandings.

— Taylor Maddox, Class of 2016

Part of the Family
To Serve

But in humility count others more significant than yourselves. Let each of you look not only to his own interests, but also to the interest of others. (Philippians 2:3-4, ESV)

When Mrs. Britt, the work coordinator for GCA, told me that I was going to be working at the Gordon Health Nursing Home during the summer, I was not upset, but I most certainly was not happy. During the last weeks of my junior year, I realized that this would be my last summer as a high school student. Therefore, I wanted to make this last one count and working at the nursing home was not going to get me there. I honestly wanted to use every second I could get my hands on for myself.

Though our years are numbered and our time is always mysteriously falling from our hands, we have to remember who gave us that time in the first place. Have you noticed that when we spend time on ourselves, hours seem to slip away faster than it would have if we had been doing an act like community service? That brings up the question, what does God really want us to do with our time? In the nursing home a simple smile brightened the residents' day, which could be counted as a service. Could we possibly serve someone with everything we do? Yes, but it is not going to be done staying in our rooms all day.

The nursing home was a blessing in my life. The memories that I have received from my time there will forever stay with me. The residents made the other GCA students and myself feel as if we were part of their family. Goodness can come out of being a servant for Christ. I am not saying that it is easy, but life-changing experiences always come in the aftermath. Pray that you will be a servant for Christ and change someone's life as well as yours.

— Taylor Maddox, Class of 2016

Why Do Bad Things Happen to Good People?

To Know

> *Now we see things imperfectly, like puzzling reflections in a mirror, but then we will see everything with perfect clarity. All that I know now is partial and incomplete, but then I will know everything completely, just as God now knows me completely.*
> (1 Corinthians 13:12, NLT)

Right now in this sinful, imperfect world we do not understand why a lot of things happen, but when we get to heaven we will understand everything. I'm really excited to find out why things in my life happen, whether it is good or bad.

April 9, 2013, the date of my father's death, is a day I'll never forget. It all started when I woke up one morning and was alarmed to see my mother frantically running around the house. I was confused so I asked my mom what was wrong. She told me that my dad had a heart attack and had collapsed on the bathroom floor. A few minutes later an ambulance came and four men rushed into my house and put my father on a gurney.

As they passed me, taking him away, I called out to my father and said, "I love you, Daddy" with tears streaming out of my eyes. I didn't know at the time that those words would be the last words I would ever speak to him.

My friend's family came to pick my sister and me up to take us to school. When I got there, I could barely focus on my schoolwork. I was in a haze all day and I didn't like it at all. The next day my friend's mom told me my father's diagnosis, he had a blood clot in his groin down his left leg. The next few nights I spent the night at my friend's house. A few days later during lunch my "aunt" came to my school. I was excited because I thought she might have news about my father. She told my teacher that she was taking me home, and I was happy as we got in her car because I thought I would get to see my dad. My "aunt" was driving me to my house and she also was talking about a bunch of random stuff, which I thought was odd.

When we pulled into my driveway, I could hardly contain myself. I ran up the stairs to my front door and barged into my house. I scanned my living room and saw my mother sitting on our couch, many of her friends from work surrounding her. I slowed my pace and got a weird feeling in my stomach. I walked up to my mother and placed my hands in hers, smiled and then I asked my mother where my dad was. Her eyes started to water as I repeatedly said "no." I started to cry a river as I sat beside her and buried my face into the crook of her neck.

Her friends started to come around and comfort us. After most of my tears had left, I asked where my sister was and she told me that she was in her room, because she doesn't like to mourn in front of other people. Many people came to my house that day: the pastor, old friends, and family. I was out of it for the rest of the day. Everything went by really slow. I didn't go to school for the next week. My friends and family distracted me from bad thoughts for that time.

To this day, two years later, I still don't understand why God would let my father die, but I know it was probably for a good reason, and I accept that.

— Darrby Marshall, Class of 2019

Lost One but Gained Another
To Know

I have told you these things, so that in me you may have peace. In this world you will have trouble. But take heart! I have overcome the world. (John 16:33, NIV)

My freshman year, in 2013, was the craziest year of my life. I was that kid who grew up in a sheltered Adventist home where nothing typically went wrong. Until that year, of course. I wasn't interested in the church and my dad and I weren't on the best of terms. He and my mom had been arguing a lot and I tended to side with her. It got to the point where I would not really talk to him unless I had to.

On the morning of April 8 around 6:30 a.m., my dad had a heart attack. When he was taken to the hospital they found a blood clot from his knee to his groin. Due to the severity of his condition he was sent to a bigger hospital in the city. Once there, they went into surgery on the clot. In the middle of the procedure, he had another heart attack. When they went to check his heart, they made a slight mistake. They may have checked one area but not where the heart pumps blood through the body, and by this time it had stopped functioning and was overlooked. Thinking that everything was fine, the doctors went back into surgery on the clot.

Around 3:00 a.m. on April 9, my dad passed away. It happened so fast. The sad thing was, at the time I didn't care. We had been fighting and I thought that he would be okay. God had a different plan, and in the long run, it happened for my benefit. If he hadn't died, I wouldn't be where I am today. I would still be in public school fading away and blocking out God. My dad didn't want me at GCA, but my mom did.

During the summer after his death, my mother was informed that I would be attending GCA that fall for my sophomore year. It was then that I began to have devotionals every morning. I remember one in particular. It was on the day of the one-year anniversary of his passing. The verse with it was John 16:33 (NIV) which says, "I have told you these things, so that in me you may have peace. In this world you will have trouble. But take heart! I have overcome the world." This verse has stuck with me ever since and has kept me believing that God is in control. If my dad hadn't died I wouldn't be at GCA and I wouldn't have the relationship I do with God. Because I lost him, I was put in a place where I truly met my heavenly Father.

— Sydney Marshall, Class of 2016

The Power of Just One
To Serve

You are the salt of the earth, but if salt has lost its taste, how shall its saltiness be restored? It is no longer good for anything except to be thrown out and trampled under people's feet. You are the light of the world. A city set on a hill cannot be hidden. Nor do people light a lamp and put it under a basket, but on a stand, and it gives light to all in the house. In the same way, let your light shine before others, so that they may see your good works and give glory to your Father who is in heaven. (Matthew 5:13–16, ESV)

There is a story called "The Starfish Story" and it goes like this:

One day a man was walking along the beach when he noticed a boy picking something up and gently throwing it into the ocean.

Approaching the boy, he asked, "What are you doing?"

The boy replied, "Throwing starfish back into the ocean. The surf is up and the tide is going out. If I don't throw them back, they'll die."

"Son," the man said, "don't you realize there are miles and miles of beach and hundreds of starfish? You can't make a difference!"

After listening politely, the boy bent down, picked up another starfish, and threw it back into the surf. Then smiling at the man, he said, "I made a difference for that one."

Some of us may approach life like the man in the story. When we think about everything there is to do for God, the mountaintop seems so far away, and it is easy to become weary. Where to start?

Try starting with the Bible and with prayer. God often starts with just one: one person to be changed, one task to accomplish, one day at a time to consider. And in pretty much every case, change begins with you, and not another person. Too many of us feel like we know God and have "been there, done that" without seeing our actions make a difference. But God can and wants to use you for His purpose of changing lives through the Gospel and through your actions.

There are so many people who need to know God's love in their life, and if you can make a difference for just one of them, then it will be worth it.

— Sydney Marshall, Class of 2016

Spread Love
To Love

By this all will know that you are My disciples, if you have love for one another. (John 13:35, NKJV)

If we want to truly be lights in this world, we must manifest the loving, compassionate spirit of Christ. To love as Christ loved means that we must practice self-control, showing unselfishness at all times and in all places. God desires His children to remember that in order to glorify Him, they must love those who are in need of it most, and nobody should be neglected. We are not to confine our love to only one or two people.

Those who gather the love of Christ, and refuse to share it with others, will lose God's grace. Love should not only be for a selected few. Our love is not to be sealed up for special ones, break the bottle of love, and the fragrance will fill the world.

— Kami Martin, Class of 2017

Forgiveness That Heals
To Love

But Jesus was saying "Father, forgive them; for they do not know what they are doing." (Luke 23:34, NASB)

A loud crack as my head meets the ground, there's a concussion; a swift slip of a blade, and there goes a slice of my skin; a bright light as my hand and arm ignites into blistering flames; a loud crash as my body is entwined in a tangle of flesh and metal. These incidents have all been events in my life that have left me reminders, scars that paint my body as a painter skillfully moves his brush across a canvas. With each mistake, with each accident that I went through, I had just another friendly reminder of "Woooow, I'm an idiot, why do I keep hurting myself?" Clumsy, quite forgetful, and overall filled with dumb ideas that always end badly, I can do nothing but wonder why I'm always hurt.

As intelligence begins, we can always pick ourselves up and learn from our mistakes, but unfortunately I don't have that quality. Through my life I have been faced with the consequences of the mistakes I have made. Though most of them have resulted in the painting of my body with scars of various sizes, each one is a reminder of forgiveness. Each scar, painful and nasty, has healed and I have become new again. This forgiveness is given by the ultimate sacrifice of Jesus on the cross. His scars, the consequences of our mistakes as a human race. His forgiveness to us all as we make mistakes in our daily lives, is forgiveness that heals our pain, that makes new the covenant we have with the Most High. With all that is done, with what may be painful and dreadful, we have the security that we have the ultimate gift, the forgiveness through the death of Christ on the cross.

— Landon Martin, Class of 2015

To Know Humility
To Know

Be still, and know that I am God. (Psalm 46:10 NIV)

I love the heat of Georgia in the summer, and I especially love laying out in the sun and soaking it in. I usually grab the same things every time I go out: a towel, book, water, sunscreen, my phone, and earphones. One day, in late spring when the temperatures started rising, I decided to spend a day in the sun. I grabbed my usual necessities and lay down on my towel. At that time, I was stressed and just needed a break from everything.

Putting in my earphones, I tried to listen to some relaxing music that might ease my mind. That didn't help. I tried opening my book and reading, that didn't work either, because I forgot my sunglasses and the sun was glaring in my eyes. So I sat there, tossing and turning in my thoughts, when all of a sudden my thoughts shut off and I heard the songs of what sounded like hundreds of birds chirping and singing all around me. At that moment, I felt an overwhelming feeling that my problems weren't even problems at all, and that there are bigger issues in the world. I was so engrossed in my thoughts and my worries that I failed to hear and experience God's creation. It was as if God abruptly stopped the unnecessary worrying and told me to just be quiet and listen.

Too often we get stuck in our own agendas and daily routines. We forget to stop, put our phones, books, and distractions down, and actually listen to what God is saying to us. By getting stuck in our agendas, we forget how blessed we are and that we are actually taking a lot of what we've got for granted. We begin to think that we are the center of our universe, when God should be the center. Take time to stop and look around God's nature. There could be something as simple as a bird chirping to shake you out of your rut.

"When I consider Your heavens, the work of Your fingers, the moon and the stars, which You have ordained, what is man that You are mindful of him, and the son of man that You visit him?" (Ps. 8:3, NKJV)

— McKenzie Martin,
Class of 2016

Serving God
To Serve

For God is not unjust. He will not forget how hard you have worked for him and how you have shown your love to him by caring for other believers, as you still do. (Hebrews 6:10, NLT)

I come from a Cuban family, and part of the Cuban culture/government enforces classes and school on Saturdays, but my mother, being raised a Seventh-day Adventist, didn't attend. There are certain tests that the government sends out to all the schools in the district and that test determines if a student can pass a grade or needs to retake it. One catch though is that those tests are on the Sabbath, and if my mother didn't take the tests she would fail her grade and would have to retake the whole year all over again. What the government does to keep people from cheating is that after students take the test it is sealed and the seal cannot be broken at all. If a teacher does anything to it at all, they are punished by either losing their license and/or even going to jail.

So while that Saturday was ahead, her heart told her that taking the test was against what God wanted, and what her family had helped her learn over the years. She didn't go. And when school started that day she went to church instead. She prayed to God, trusting, serving, and believing in Him and releasing her worries to Him. She didn't think about it the rest of the day. After sundown a tentative knock came at the door and her teacher was there with a nervous look and with a test in her hand.

She told my mother, "You have 60 minutes to complete the test. I know you are a Sabbath keeper and couldn't come, but something in my heart told me today that I should see you and give you this test." My mother was overjoyed and was so glad she served God when He asked her.

This whole story speaks to me about serving. Serving can be hard and difficult at times, but with God anything is possible. Serving, trusting, and believing in Him is so rewarding and God doesn't forget what we do for Him. The sacrifices we make are important to Him, just like the teacher who helped my mother. The service and love we do for others is never worth nothing, but is everything.

— Elysse Mastrapa, Class of 2019

True Control Comes from Giving Freedom
To Serve

And a man of understanding is of a calm spirit.
(Proverbs 17:27, NKJV)

God designed us to resist efforts by others to control us. It was built in to give us the ability to resist temptation. The curious thing is that we use this feature to resist and break free from those who would like us to do things their way, and to think like they think.

Strong messages are sent that communicate a lack of acceptance or disapproval if we don't think or behave the way the other person wants. Fear of anger, threats of physical or emotional pain, or withdrawal of love pollutes the joy God has in store for us.

When we comply, and do what another person urges us to do, we are no longer motivated by love, but by fear. We fear losing relationship or connection with another person. Feeling trapped or stuck, resentment begins to deteriorate our relationships.

God's design is that true control comes only when freedom of choice is available. Only then can joy replace fear. Intimacy can't be forced or coerced, and yet, intimacy is what all humans most desire.

How different would life be if, instead of trying to be in control of others, we simply give others the freedom we value so deeply? Stress and frustration would evaporate were we to implement the principles of God in our intimate relationships with family and friends. All the wasted energy of trying to control and resist that control would be free to generate enthusiasm, attachment and love. Imagine a world full of the wonderful creations we were designed to be? What a privilege!

How different would our world be if we simply expressed how we feel and declared our opinions in calm, kind and loving tones? What if we could all have the privilege of being ourselves? Control only begets control. Only when a human is given the freedom of choice to give love and respect, can love and respectful behaviors really be reciprocated.

What a paradox–to have control, we must be willing to give freedom!

— Arlene McFarland, Class of 1966

Fear? Or Love?
To Love

Fear and love just don't go together. Love dispels fear because fear focuses on punishment and won't let love mature.
(I John 4:18, Clear Word)

Many lives have interfaced with mine as I serve our community as a Family Therapist. Each one entering my door contributes a new situation that illustrates the principles of God that determine the outcomes of our interactions. Conflict, addictions, anxiety, depression, anorexia, parenting challenges, grief, phobias, and hopelessness all have a central thread—fear. Our text presents the best formula for the challenges of living with other human beings.

As life teaches principles to guide our choices and behaviors, one principle seems to be at the core. All behavior arises out of either fear or love. Like a seesaw, we may alternate between the two with frustrating regularity.

Children operate out of fear because they don't want to lose the relationship of security they experience from loving consistent parents. Punishments, threats, being ignored, criticisms, deprivations and abuse torture the child with hopelessness, helplessness, and fear. Living with thoughts of possible abandonment, humans begin to act in scary ways. We become resistant, disobedient, defiant, and infect those around us with the poison of fear.

God's love is a perfect model for our dealings with each other. Our understanding of another's fear generates love. Fear is aborted. Behaviors of those around us begin to reflect love. It is that simple! The love of God is transforming!

If we want to be surrounded with loving people, we simply seek to understand the fear underneath their actions and words. Expressing our understanding begins to fill them with the love and confidence God offers. They find it easier to comprehend that God can love them. While this concept is so simple, it is at the center of God's plan of salvation. He understands our fear of separation from Him for eternity. He has provided a way of salvation for each of us. Our job is to "get it"—to sense His complete understanding and acceptance of us. Allowing God's love to make fear impossible to reside in our hearts allows us to experience the taste of heaven here on earth!

My prayer for you is that you may experience the peace and joy that come from knowing with assurance that you are understood and loved supremely. Wouldn't it be wonderful to infect the world with love and understanding, eliminating fear?

— Arlene McFarland, Class of 1966

Dishonoring God
To Love

The Lord GOD helps me, so I will not be ashamed. I will be determined, and I know I will not be disgraced.
(Isaiah 50:7 NCV)

I had just started my freshman year in high school. I had never gone to a dance, prom, or anything like that my entire life, and the school year's first banquet was coming up fast. I had asked one of the prettiest, nicest girls in our class, and I was terrified of messing up somehow. The day came soon, and I found myself escorting a girl in a gorgeous white dress. We sat down in the café where our banquet was taking place. I did my best to make conversation without giving away my actual feelings of pure fear. I noticed that she was running low on juice in her glass. Trying to be a gentleman, I offered to refill her glass. While standing up to go over to the juice station, I knocked over the glass right onto her pure white dress. It was a direct hit, a huge apple colored streak right down to her shoes. I was done for. There was no way she would ever talk to me again, or even finish out the night with me. To my unbelief she began to laugh, forgiving me immediately. Three years later I received a picture message from her. It was that dress from that night, stain still completely viewable. She didn't hate me for ruining her dress. She actually loved it for the memories it gave her. To her it represented all the fun we had together and the friendship that grew from that night.

Sometimes I get scared that I will dishonor God. Every time I do something wrong, I feel like I have stained His name. But God doesn't work that way. We are far from perfect and will spill our apple juice over and over again, but God forgives us every time. He loves us with a passion that overlooks our downfalls. Next time you feel like you can't face God in your sin, remember He will always forgive you. There is nothing you can do that will make Him love you less.

— Allen McKinney, Class of 2015

Love Your Enemies
To Love

Love your enemies, do good to those who hate you, bless those who curse you, pray for those who abuse you. But love your enemies, and do good, and lend, expecting nothing in return, and your reward will be great, and you will be sons of the Most High, for He is kind to the ungrateful and the evil. Be merciful, even as your Father is merciful. (Luke 6:27–28, 35–36, ESV)

Love is easy to give to those who love us. It flows naturally and liberally, it's fun and rewarding, but it seems so very hard to love those who don't like us or want us around! Jesus came to this world to love us, knowing we would break His heart and reject and abuse Him, and yet He chose and still chooses to love us with an everlasting love. Jesus came to win His bride (the church, you and me), a bride who had other lovers and didn't want Him, and yet He has treated us with tender, forgiving love! Now that's real love, a love that can transform the hardest heart, a love that keeps on loving in the face of mind-blowing rejection and heartbreak. This is the love God wants us to experience, and it is the love He wants us to have for our enemies and those who break our hearts. As we receive His love and forgiveness, His love fills us and enables us to love our enemies and pray for those who abuse us.

GCA in so many ways was a wonderful experience for me, but like life, all was not roses. There was a particular girl that did not like me, and seemed to go out of her way to mistreat me. The three years I was at GCA, she would slam doors in my face as well as slinging profanities at me. She was quick to say mean things if I got within earshot, but refused to talk with me. She seemed very unhappy and it made me wonder what she was going through. She was often in my prayers and though it was not easy, I tried to be as kind to her as possible, hoping somehow it would make a difference in her life, but nothing seemed to change.

At the end of my senior year we had a special service in the girl's dorm. White roses were supplied so each of us could give a rose to someone in the room that had impacted our lives in a special way. When she headed my way, I couldn't believe it. She came and gave me her rose. She shared a little of her struggles and her difficult family life and how my kindness through the years had touched her life in a significant way. I was blown away and have treasured that memory ever since.

God loves you, my friend, and I encourage you to think of how kind and forgiving God has been toward you. Let His love fill your heart and heal your soul, and ask Him to help you be kind and loving to those in your life who don't love you. God's love and forgiveness is the vaccine for the virus of sin and misery. God wants to fill you with His love and use you to reach someone who is in the darkness and misery of sin with the light and joy of His love. I pray God will use you to touch a life for Him.

— Sherry McNiel Boettcher, Class of 1990

Self-Confidence
To Know

For you formed my inward parts; you knitted me together in my mother's womb. I praise you, for I am fearfully and wonderfully made. Wonderful are your works; my soul knows it very well.
(Psalm 139:13-14, ESV)

There I was, a twelve-year-old with an innocent heart and silver Harry Potter glasses with black duct tape around the center. I regret those years deeply, but remembering how it molded me as a person, I wouldn't change a thing. Because of my appearance, it wasn't everyone's first desire to be my friend. But the people who got to know me and became my friend loved me for who I was as a person and not my appearance.

While I was bullied, I had this friend whose name will remain anonymous. Behind her back our other friends would make fun of her weight, and I always defended her as she did me. We were best friends throughout that time in our lives, but as we aged we drifted apart. My senior year of high school I went to Prayer Conference at Camp Kulaqua, and as I tried to get God, past experiences tried to get me. I saw her again, and I was quite excited because it had been a while since I'd seen her last. Unfortunately, though, she wasn't excited to see me. Some of my so-called friends had started untrue rumors about me and she believed them.

I tried to speak to her about the situation, but she didn't even want to speak to me. She was so immature that she didn't even want to state the problem, even though I had already known from someone else. I cried that day because I valued her so much! She's the very person who taught me what self-confidence was. That night the pastor spoke about how we must find value in God and not in others. I let the words resonate. God puts so much value in us, so much that we can't even imagine it. That's kind of weird to think about, but it's so true. In Psalm 139:13–14 it says that we are fearfully and wonderfully made by God. Which means we are all special no matter what others may say about us, even if we value them.

— Amaris Medina, Class of 2015

Destined by Time
To Know

Watch therefore, for ye know neither the day nor the hour wherein the Son of man cometh. (Matthew 25:13, KJV)

Have you ever been late to something? I know I have. I will admit that I am not the most punctual person. I find it very difficult to consistently arrive at places on time. Every now and then I will be late to an event or meeting. I have a bad habit of procrastinating and leaving things to be done at the last minute. There was even one time, back when I was in public school, that I got detention for being late to school too many times. And countless times I have been stressed with beating deadlines just for waiting too long for accomplish tasks.

One busy, hectic day, I remembered what Jesus said in Matthew, and the hymn inspired by that Scripture, "We Know Not the Hour." I realized that, in this world, it does not matter whether people are punctual or they are always late. The world may evaluate us by the latter, but in the end, our ultimate goal is to be ready for the second advent of Jesus, or for the end of our lives (whichever comes first). Our decision to accept Jesus beforehand is the determining factor for our eternity, which is our ultimate priority.

Having stated all this, I have learned that I should never push God aside in my daily life, no matter how busy it might be. I want to make sure I choose Jesus while I have time before it is too late. Even to this day, I struggle to put God first every day, but it is all a process, not a one-time choice. No matter how hard life can be, I will never give up Jesus, and I will be ready for His soon return. We should be ready to accept Jesus and put Him first today.

— Grayson Mejia, Class of 2015

The Greatest Blessing from God
To Know

For I know the plans I have for you," declares the Lord "Plans to prosper you and not to harm you, plans to give you hope and a future. (Jeremiah 29:11 ESV)

Our family isn't rich or poor. We live in house that has three small rooms and two bathrooms. I am amazed how God has blessed my family and me throughout my entire life. Out of all the blessings there is one that I'll never forget.

The year 2011–2012, our family was going through economic and family problems. We lived in a different house that year. I remember listening to my parents complaining that they didn't have enough money for rent, water bills, etc. They were really frustrated because they had to pay for my sister's and my education also. My parents are very faithful with their tithes and offerings. They always give to God before everything else. I remember sitting there with a sad face looking at them. I couldn't comprehend what type of pain they were in, but their faces said it all.

The next day I woke up and went to school. My elementary school years were very interesting. I was constantly in trouble. My parents dropped me off at school at 7:40 a.m., and I would purposely stay in the bathroom forever. Class started at 8:00 a.m., and I would come at 8:20 constantly, sometimes it was on purpose, other times it wasn't. I remember my mom yelling at me in the face, with an angry expression. Every day when I came back from school I had a routine. I would come in through the garage, throw my backpack in my room, change into comfortable clothes, and eat dinner. One particular day I was eating popusas (a Salvadorian dish) and remember listening to my parents complain over rent again. I was multitasking, both eating and listening.

Then I heard my dad say, "We're moving. We can't afford to pay this much money for rent."

I was really shocked because the house we lived in was amazing. It wasn't a two-story house, but it was still big.

My parents made up their minds and started searching. I can't remember how long they searched but it was a long time and they found nothing. I remember seeing my parents with desperate faces searching online house by house. Then my dad came across one. It was small and needed a lot of work and dedication to fix it. I went with my dad to go check it out. When we got there the house was surrounded by tall pine trees. We got in the house through the back window. I remember just gazing around the house with my mouth open. It had three small rooms and two bathrooms and needed a lot of work.

When we were through inspecting the house, my dad said, "This is the one." My dad asked me to help him fix the house. I had to accept because there wasn't a choice. Day by day I went with my father to fix the house.

Finally, the day came when the house was finished. My dad bought the house, and our family started packing the same day. I started packing my belongings with mixed feelings. I was sad because we were leaving the best house I had ever lived in, but I felt happy for my parents because they moved to a house that they could afford.

The day came when we said good-bye and moved to our new house. As the years progressed our family felt happier in our new house. As of today, I have never heard my parents complain for rent or bills. We give thanks to God because in mysterious ways our budget stretches to pay rent, bills, and school tuition. I saw God work things out for my family. He planned everything for us and guided my father to find the house. The house is now marvelous on the inside. It's so beautiful and filled with happiness. Every day I walk in I always remember how great our God is and how He has a plan for everything.

— Anthony Melgar, Class of 2018

Don't Rush
To Know

Being excited about something is not enough. You must also know what you are doing. Don't rush into something, or you might do it wrong. (Proverbs 19:2, ERV)

I'm the kind of person who likes to rush into things. I often do things without thinking, which gets me into trouble. When taking tests, depending on the class, I'm done with it in fifteen minutes at the most, and it reflects on my test scores. Sometimes when I'm driving, I go over the speed limit because I feel the need to get to wherever I'm going as soon as I can, even when I really don't need to.

One time I was running in the gym at my middle school. The floor was cement and was slippery. I wanted to be the first one done, so naturally, I ran as fast as I could. I was on one of my last laps, and I was running fast as I turned a corner, and then I fell. My arm was broken, and I was in a cast for a couple of weeks.

If I hadn't have rushed myself, then I wouldn't have broken my arm. God talks about taking things slowly and taking your time. He says that when we rush into things, we're likely to mess up more than if we were to take our time. I fell and broke my arm because I didn't take my time. If we're trying to rush everything before we think about it, then we're going to slip up big time. But God says that when we trust Him and His timing, He guides us in paths that are straight and won't cause us to stumble.

— Allison Melton, Class of 2015

Maria
To Know

Trust in the Lord with all your heart, and lean not on your own understanding; in all your ways acknowledge Him, and He shall direct your paths. (Proverbs 3:5–6)

To know God is to know that He always has your back no matter how deep you are in trouble, how badly you've been exposed to the world, or how horribly you have sinned. God has a plan for us and knows exactly how to carry it out. We have to know this to understand that the bad things that happen to us are just going to better equip us to carry out God's plan.

There was once a small village in Africa. In that village there was a hut. In that hut there was a twelve-year-old girl named Maria. Maria worked as a goat herder along with her father. One day, while Maria was herding, her friends came up to her explaining that there was a new teacher in town talking about a man named Jesus who died to save them. Maria wanted to go so badly. So she mustered up the courage to ask her dad if she could attend the meeting.

He screamed at her saying," Maria, you better not go to that place! If you go, you will be in trouble."

She took little heed to this warning the next day. As she was herding, the goats kept getting closer to where the teacher was holding his meetings. She ignored her father's warning and went up to the place where they were meeting. She lost track of time and was home late. Her father knew that she had attended the meeting. When she walked in, her father beat her. She was beaten so severely, she could not walk the next day.

A while later, she heard her friends singing and having fun, and again she joined them. She did this for a while without her dad finding out about it. Then one day, while they were having worship, her dad busted through the door, picked her up, and took her to their house. He was so infuriated that he met with the village elders to decide a punishment for her. They decided to tie her to the ant tree. The tree was in the center of the village and was infested with flesh picking ants.

Later on, they strapped her up to the tree and set two rows of guards around her. The ants began going up her body, biting as they scurried along her skin. Maria was screaming and praying to the Lord to help her, but it seemed like nothing was happening. The ants had now reached her face and were taking chunks of skin from her cheeks. In the midst of all of her screaming and praying the teacher ran through the men, got her, and ran back out without being touched by the guards. She was then nursed back to health and went on to live a healthy life for God.

This shows that we need to know that God always has our back. Like Maria, we can find ourselves in difficult situations. We have to trust that God will have our backs.

— Miles Mitchell, Class of 2017

Changes
To Know

Be strong and courageous. Do not be afraid or terrified because of them, for the LORD your God goes with you; he will never leave you nor forsake you. (Deuteronomy 31:6 NIV)

Change can be a very hard thing to deal with. Starting at a new school in my junior year was not something I planned way back in my freshman year. Most likely the kids at school would know each other already. Wouldn't there already be cliques? People would only talk to me if they had to. What if I wasn't as smart as everyone else? These were some of the fears that ran through my head the first day of school.

If these fears weren't enough, my mom told me a week later that I would be moving into the dorm. I nearly screamed. Hadn't there been enough changes? New school. New people. The teachers had different teaching styles than I was used to. My grades weren't like what they used to be in my previous years of high school. So now I would have to move in with someone I didn't really know and live there for the rest of the school year?

I nearly went frantic with the changes that were whirling around in my head. Then it was a whisper imprinted into my mind. "Be strong and courageous. Do not be afraid or terrified because of them, for the LORD your God goes with you; he will never leave you nor forsake you." (Deut. 31:6, NIV). Even though I would be somewhere completely different than what I was used to, and things would be completely different, God would still be with me, wherever I went and no matter what I did, and that was all that really mattered. There was no reason to feel terrified because God would be with me.

— Brianna Moore, Class of 2017

He Knows What He Is Doing
To Know

I know what I'm doing. I have it all planned out—plans to take care of you, not abandon you, plans to give you the future you hope for. (Jeremiah 29:11, MSG)

I woke up that morning to the incredibly annoying alarm I set the night before and already knew it was going to be a rough day. My throat burned with pain when I tried to swallow, and I couldn't breathe out of my nose. I had a PreCal test that afternoon, a memory verse quiz to study for, a rough draft research paper due, and a big Spanish quiz later that week. To top it all off, my dad was having heart surgery that day as well. I remember getting out of bed extremely slowly and just wanting that day to be over already so I could crawl right back into bed.

A lot of times we get caught up in every little thing that life throws at us. We consume our lives with stressing about school and complaining about how we never have free time.

"I just need to get this review done for class" or "I stayed up late last night studying and today I'm just too sleepy to care about anything else." Bad days come and go for everyone, it's just something you have to get through, but little do we know as humans that there is a really easy way to turn that day into something wonderful, even if we feel like it is the end of the world.

God promises us in Jeremiah 29:11 that He knows what He is doing. Every test. Every paper. Every quiz. Even if we mess up or do poorly on a test, His goal could be to take the information you studied and help make you more intelligent in that area so later it isn't so hard to understand. Or it could even be to make sure that your dad never faces another heart problem again. Always keep an open mind and willing heart to the things God has in your everyday life, because you never know where they might lead you.

— Brooklyn Moore, Class of 2015

Having a Relationship
To Love

Dear friends, let us love one another, for love comes from God. Everyone who loves has been born of God and knows God. Whoever does not love does not know God, because God is love.
(1 John 4:7–8, NIV)

Love is patient, love is kind. It does not envy, it does not boast, it is not proud. It does not dishonor others, it is not self-seeking, it is not easily angered, it keeps no records of wrongs. Love does not delight in evil but rejoices with the truth. It always protects, always trusts, always hopes, always perseveres. (1 Corinthians 13:4–7, NIV)

As teenagers, we struggle to fully understand love. We were taught from a very young age that love is finding our prince or princess and riding away into the sunset, and then everything is great. From that moment on, we strive for that mythical love. It confuses us, because once we step into reality, we quickly realize that love is not all rainbows and sunshine. It's confusing and frustrating sometimes. Love is not just between a boyfriend and girlfriend or husband and wife, it's in all relationships and it takes understanding and patience, which we fail to recognize sometimes.

Most importantly, besides our relationships with others, we also need to love ourselves which is probably the hardest type of love for us all, especially teenagers. Without the love for ourselves, it makes it extremely difficult to love others the way they deserve to be loved and how God wants us to love them. We get so focused on receiving love from others that it distracts us from what we should really be striving for; showing love to others.

In high school, it's easy to get caught up with the idea of having a relationship and being in love with somebody. Our minds get warped into thinking that the only way to love ourselves is to receive love from somebody else, which it beyond not true.

God intended for us to love ourselves and others, and to look to Him as an example to learn how to love. Having love within our lives and showing it, shows we know God and that we love God.

— Phoebe Morgan, Class of 2016

To Know God Is to Love God
To Know

If you love me, keep my commands. (John 14:15 NIV)

Joe was a regular guy who had just enlisted in the army. As he was sleeping in his hard, dirty bed, the sergeant started knocking on his door.

"What do you want?" questioned the private.

"Get out of your bed and run outside now!" screamed the sergeant.

"But why?" the private questioned back.

"Do not talk back to someone whose rank is higher than you. Now you will suffer punishment! On the floor and give me a hundred pushups!" He screamed. "If we were in a battle you could have been killed."

Often people view God just like an angry army sergeant. They view Him as a mean tyrant who will punish harshly if we merely ask Him a question. But is this how God desires us to follow Him? Does He punish us when we question Him? Romans 12:2 (NIV) says, "Do not conform to the pattern of this world, but be transformed by the renewing of your mind. Then you will be able to test and approve what God's will is—his good, pleasing and perfect will." From this verse we learn that God allows us to investigate His orders so that we understand why those orders should be followed. The more we question and learn about Him, the more we understand Him. The more we understand that He is not a harsh and punishing God, but instead a God of love and forgiveness, the easier it is for us to love and follow Him. To know God is to love God. The more we know Him and the more we are filled with His Spirit, the more we love not only Him but others. As we are filled with His love, we are then enabled with the desire to enter into faithful service.

— Peyton Morrison, Class of 2019

Love of Brotherhood
To Love

A new command I give you: Love one another. As I have loved you, so you must love one another. By this everyone will know that you are my disciples, if you love one another. (John 13:34–35, NIV)

It was my sophomore year when one of my best friends and I lost our friendship. Losing someone is something that I highly despise in life. My dear friend and I didn't talk for about seven out of nine months. It was honestly one of the worst seven months of my life. I had never held so much hate in my heart as I did at the time. Just seeing him talk to one of my other friends made me upset. I tried to ignore him as much as possible but it was hard because we had been through so much together.

One day my friend, Hudson, and I wanted to try a group activity but we knew we would need someone else's assistance in order to achieve our goal. We both instantly knew that we had to ask my dear old friend for help. We all sat down and talked about our past and current dilemmas. It took about five minutes until we were friends again. We both loved each other as brothers so much that we barely even had to think about forgiving one another.

Sometimes you can feel the Holy Spirit in your heart, telling you to do the right thing. Until this day my dear friend and I are very close. Even though we may not see each other every day, we are constantly communicating with each other by phone. Losing a friendship is heartbreaking, but gaining it back is gratifying. I can only thank God for the friendships I have in my life. God has filled my life with love and given me the opportunity to share that love with others.

— Bruno Moura, Class of 2016

To Love Even the Annoying People
To Love

Be humble and gentle. Be patient with each other, making allowance for each other's faults because of your love.
(Ephesians 4:2, TLB)

I can't even begin to count how many times I've been annoyed by someone. Growing up it was always my siblings that bothered me. We would get into petty fights, and sometimes my siblings didn't receive the punishment I thought they deserved. As I grew up my pet peeve list got bigger and there were more things, insignificant things, that bothered me.

My junior year at GCA was probably its peak. I had become a harsh person and believed everyone needed to just grow up and do better. I would judge people with a snap of the finger and it usually wasn't something nice. In my praise and worship class I became a bossy dictator, and my band members started to not enjoy the class. In class I would snap at people that weren't acting the way I thought high school students should act. It had come to the point that I let every little detail around me irritate me, even though I might have had nothing to do with the situation. Life was one big complaint about how other people needed to do better, and meanwhile I forgot to focus on my own actions.

During the summer before my senior year at GCA I was searching for help in the Bible on how I could conquer my harshness and irritation. I found the verse Ephesians 4:2. When I read it, the words slapped me in the face, and I finally realized that I needed to be a kind and patient person.

God calls each one of us to love each other as we love ourselves. If you think about it, you have probably messed up just as much as everyone else. No one is perfect and we all have our quirks. Yes, there are always going to be those people in your life that drive you crazy. But before you start to say something harsh or think negatively about that person, remember what the Bible says: we are called to be patient. We need to remember we mess up too, and we are no better than the next person. Despite another person's faults, we are called to love them like Jesus loves them.

— Cassidy Munson, Class of 2016

There Is a Rainbow in the Midst
To Know

I have set my rainbow in the clouds, and it will be the sign of the covenant between me and the earth. (Genesis 9:13, NIV)

Have you ever seen a really distinct rainbow in the sky? Scientists will tell you that rainbows are just light reacting with water, but I believe there is something more.

October of my junior year at Georgia-Cumberland Academy something happened that changed my life forever. My dad passed away. He had been through a twelve-year battle with cancer and had suffered five months bed-ridden in a hospital because of complications in surgery. About three days after my dad was admitted into hospice, I received the call that he had died overnight. Right then and there I fell on my knees in my dorm room. I prayed for peace and comfort, but most of all I prayed for a promise that everything was going to be all right in the end.

I kept that promise in my heart, and when I got home for the funeral, my mom showed me a picture taken the day of my dad's death that brought tears to my eyes. The picture was of my house and right above it was a bright, full rainbow. A promise. A wave of relief rushed over me and peace filled my heart. At that very moment I knew that no matter what, everything was going to be all right.

There's a story similar to this in the book of Genesis. Noah and his family had spent a little over a year in the ark. Their hope of ever reaching dry land was probably fading. But when they emerged from the ark onto dry land, God gave Noah and his family a rainbow to symbolize a promise: a promise to never flood the earth again. Noah's promise was different than mine, but I believe it was given for the same purpose.

God gives us rainbows in our lives that come with the storms or trials we go through on a daily basis. God has placed so many promises in His word that can apply to anyone and their struggles. He promises that He holds the plans for our future. He promises to give rest to the tired and stressed. What does the rainbow mean to you? What promise that God has given in the Bible comforts you? Spend some time in His word and maybe, just maybe, you might find your rainbow.

— Cassie Munson, Class of 2016

God My Savior
To Know

Guide me in your truth and teach me, for you are God my Savior, and my hope is in you all day long. (Psalm 25:5, NIV)

The year was 1940 when the Germans invaded Europe. You could hear the sounds of gunshots and explosions going off in the distance. Johanna, a seven-year-old girl, was hiding in a wooden barrel with nowhere to go. She had just lost her parents when German forces invaded her home and killed her parents right in front of her. She barely escaped alive. For hours she hid in a little barrel, waiting for someone to save her.

She prayed to the Lord, saying "Dear heavenly Father, please help me through this time, Amen."

She then heard a faint voice coming from outside her temporary refuge, "You can come out now, you're safe with me." Johanna was scared wondering if it was just her imagination, but then she heard it again, but louder.

"You can come out now, I won't hurt you." She was slightly frightened, but she came out of the barrel and saw a tall, skinny man in a uniform with an American flag. She was so happy because God had answered her prayer. She then hugged the man and thanked him for saving her. And then she prayed to God, thanking Him for saving her.

This story may not be true, but it is still very powerful, showing that God loves us and will do anything to save us from this sinful world. He wants us be with Him in heaven forever and ever. Psalm 25:5 can relate to this story because it says, "for you are God my Savior." In the story, God had saved little Johanna. Just like in the story when Jesus died on the cross. He came down from being a God to becoming a perfect human, so that we can be with Him in heaven.

God will always hear our prayers. Sometimes He will answer with yes, and sometimes He will answer with no. If you are in trouble or scared, just know God is there to protect you and provide for you. And don't ever doubt Him, because He has your back and will never fail you.

— Ephraim Mura, Class of 2019

The Least of Them All
To Serve

The King will reply, "Truly I tell you, whatever you did for one of the least of these brothers and sisters of mine, you did for me." (Matthew 25:40, NIV)

My family and I were leaving the house to go to town one day. As we were passing by an empty house, we saw a dog lying on the front porch. We had seen him earlier that day but thought nothing of the dog until now. With curiosity, we got out of the car and approached the dog with caution. As my family and I stepped onto the porch steps, the dog began to howl painfully loud. After inspecting the inside of the house, it was clear to us that no one lived in the house and that this dog was an abandoned dog, left to fend for himself.

Seeing that the dog wasn't coming to us anytime soon, my parents called our neighbor to help us get ahold of the dog. After about thirty minutes of waiting, we finally lured the dog out to us. The dog was very thin, sported many scars, had a torn ear, and carried himself on three and half legs.

Before we had gotten out to see him, I had wanted nothing to do with the dog, thinking he was perfectly fine and that we would only waste our time. If we had decided to keep going, that dog would have either died from lack of food or from the condition that he was in.

We need to serve people from the neediest to the ones that just need a simple task done. Even if you serve the greatest, the least are worth just as much, even if it's just a simple, small dog.

— Sassy Mura, Class of 2019

When in Danger
To Serve

The angel of the Lord encamps around those who fear Him, and rescues them. O taste and see that the Lord is good, how blessed is the man who takes refuge in Him. (Psalm 34:7–8, NASB)

One hot summer day, I was in Seattle, Washington. I was not there for vacation, but instead for my job. I was working there as a colporteur. I was selling Christian-themed books, such as Steps to Christ and other Ellen White books. I came upon this one house that had a gate and many bushes surrounding the gate. I couldn't really tell what was inside of the yard. So I opened the gate and started to go on to knock on the door. Suddenly out of the corner of my eye, I spot an enormous mangy-looking dog glaring menacingly at me.

Next thing I knew, my palms were sweaty, knees weak, arms were heavy. There was sweat falling on my sweater and I thought, God please help me. I was nervous, but on the surface I looked calm and was ready to drop everything. But I kept forgetting everything. What did I read about in my Bible this very morning? Yes, I remembered. "The angel of the Lord encampeth around those who fear Him." So I turned around and continued on my way to the door and finished my job. The dog just stood there as if it was incapacitated, and I walked away safely from the house. In life when something unexpected turns your way and you are in danger, just remember that Jesus is always near you, and if you trust Him, He will protect you no matter what happens.

— Mathew Nanbu, Class of 2016

Trust
To Know

Trust in the LORD with all thine heart; and lean not unto thine own understanding. In all thy ways acknowledge him, and he shall direct thy paths. (Proverbs 3:5–6, KJV)

The last summer before I came to GCA, I went canvassing on a hot scorching day in San Diego, California. I was roasting, walking in the middle of a street and having a really bad day. Everyone was rejecting me and I was getting $0 and I was thinking malicious thoughts about leaving the program. I had to sit down from the depression of the thought of doing badly.

Then we changed territories and I met the worst people ever. They were constantly saying, "no soliciting" and I was so depressed. So I thought that perhaps, if I trusted God, I would end up having a good day.

Nevertheless, I was very depressed when I knocked on a door where some old guy said out of the window, "What are you doing?"

I responded, "I'm working."

So he said, "Hold on, I'm coming down."

So I waited and waited, and he eventually came out the door. At first I expected nothing from this old guy, but he came out with a checkbook and wrote it out for a Benji [$100 bill]. I was so astonished and shocked because that whole day it had been so slow, but then at the end I had fought the good fight and ended up having a good day. Throughout the day I was trusting God and at the end of the day, God blessed me very much. So no matter what happens, you have to trust the Lord with all your heart and God will direct your path.

— Mathew Nanbu, Class of 2016

Love
To Love

He answered, "Love the Lord your God with all your heart and with all your soul and with all your strength and with all your mind; and, 'Love your neighbor as yourself.'" (Luke 10:27, NIV)

We should all love God like this because of what He did for us. He died on a cross for our sins just so that we can live. The Father chose His only Son to die on the cross for our sins. Some of us don't even give God five minutes of our time. We just go along with our day and forget what He has done. He calls on us and tries to grab our attention, but we continue to ignore Him as if He doesn't exist in our lives. Everybody should be giving Him at least five minutes of our time. We call ourselves followers of God, yet half of us aren't even taking the time to listen to God. How can we call ourselves disciples or Christians as we go along with our lives, when we are ignorant of what He has done for us?

God, our Lord and Savior, has given us the most beautiful thing in the world, which is eternal life. There are many things in this world that can take our attention away from us, when He is trying His hardest to enter our hearts. Examples of distractions that can lead us away from God are the Internet, video games, movies, and shopping. All of us should accept Him into our hearts by starting our day off with a morning devotional. Before we go to bed we should pray to God, and thank Him for another day of life. God is our Savior, Deliverer, and our Leader; He is the Alpha and the Omega. Give God at least a bit of your time each day. Can you do that for Someone who has done so much for you?

— Michael Nanbu, Class of 2019

To Know Peace
To Know

Don't worry about anything; instead, pray about everything. Tell God what you need, and thank him for all he has done. Then you will experience God's peace, which exceeds anything we can understand. His peace will guard your hearts and minds as you live in Christ Jesus. (Philippians 4:6–7, NLT)

When I was young I was the cutest, most adorable child ever. My opinion may be slightly biased. Growing up I don't remember having the normal toys most kids would have today or even many toys at all. I played mostly outside in the large pasture we had for our horse and the stream that ran next to it. The only toys I really remember playing with were my Matchbox® cars and my toy train set.

Let me give you some background on my train set: When I was about three years old, I loved to sing. So my dad proposed a deal. If I sang "Jesus Loves Me" for special music at our church, he would surprise me with something big. I had no fear of being up front and gladly accepted. The something big was my train set.

Everything had to be in its place. I was a very OCD child. I even had a picture so that I wouldn't forget where every train, every tree, and every person went. If something was out of place, I would fix it. It wasn't a problem. Until …

When my little cousins came over, my room was the designated play area. Of course these kids didn't care about tidiness. Legos everywhere, Matchbox® cars in my bed, and my train set … my train set was demolished. I was so mad. I would go and cry to my mother about how long it would take to clean everything up and put it back in its place. How could I do it all? My mom, calm and loving, would encourage me to just take things one at a time, and it would all be ok. Of course I didn't think so, but we would stop and pray and ask God to help me clean up everything. Giving it to God seemed to make things better. Going back to my room

I'd start with the Legos, and then lastly I would put my train set back together. Mom was right. It wasn't that bad and didn't take that long at all. I just had to take things one at a time.

A lot of times we forget to put our lives in God's hands. We stress and stress but nothing seems to get done. It's not until we plop our busy schedules and emotional stresses in God's hands that we can truly experience His peace, the peace that no one can understand.

— Caleb Neal, Class of 2017

To Know
To Serve

The heart of the discerning acquires knowledge, for the ears of the wise seek it out. (Proverbs 18:15, NIV)

"Hey, Alex, come here," my friend said, as I was passing his dorm room.

As I hesitated, I noticed the same smile that he had worn the day before. It was exactly like what he was doing now, luring me into a trap, most likely involving a pillow to the face. Even though he was my friend, I approached with caution.

"Alex, hurry up, do you want some food?" He added. This piece of information only added to my caution. As I slowly, and carefully edged closer and closer to the ominous shape of the doorway, I carefully peeked into all the corners of the room, ready to flee at a moment's notice.

My friend noticed and asked "Alex, what are you so nervous about?"

I easily replied, "Just checking to make sure your friend behind the doorway is all right," and then sprinted like there was no tomorrow.

It was Christmas banquet, 2015. This was the banquet where we were allowed to roam the streets of Atlanta, unchecked, unsupervised, and utterly free. I was bouncing from group to group like a pinball, when, as I was making my way to another group of my friends, I heard somebody shout. I froze, not knowing if I should fight or flee. Then I heard the shout again, coming from down the alley I was passing.

"Hey you!"

Staring up the alley, every muscle in my body quivering with anticipation of either my first inner city brawl, or the fastest speed record about to be broken, I tentatively called back, "Hello?"

As the smog cleared, I could slowly make out the figure of a woman, who was just not right. As the smog cleared you see that her eyes were just a little too wide, her gait was a little too trippy, and her look was just a little too glazed.

As she tried to stumble back to a trashcan, she called, "I need you to get over here right now." Seeing that she was no longer focusing on me, I quickly edged out of view, and rejoined my friends.

Every now and then my mom asks me to do something for her. Over the years I have gotten some strange questions, ranging from, "Have you brushed yet?" to "Is your homework finished?" Every day my mom will ask me to do something. And every day I do whatever she needs me to do. She could be outside, and I could be on the far side of the house when the request is made, but whatever it is, it will be done.

I know my Mom, I know my friends, but I didn't know the woman in the alley. I love my Mom, I love my friends, but it's not easy to love random people in alleys. I serve my Mom, and sometimes serve my friends, but I rarely serve strangers. It's amazing how much easier it is to love and serve somebody, if you know them first. It works the same way with God, it's much easier to serve Him, if we love Him first.

— Alex Nesmith, Class of 2018

Lord, Give Me Strength
To Love

For the Lord takes delight in his people ... Let his faithful people rejoice in his honor and sing for joy on their beds.
(Psalm 149:4, NIV)

Well done, good and faithful servant ... Come and share your master's happiness. (Matthew 25:21 (& 23), NIV)

"Lord, give me strength." This is the prayer of my Grandpa Myers each evening to end family worship. He suffered from multiple sclerosis, a degenerative muscular disease, which confined him to his bed or wheelchair, but his prayers kept him, and me, strong. He died two evenings ago, and in passing gave up this prayer. Because of his condition he couldn't walk or feed himself and had difficulty speaking, but the twinkle in his eye when he smiled made up for any lack of physical motion.

When he stayed with our family something changed. Having Grandpa in the house made God seem nearer, as if a tangible part of God's wisdom and understanding was embedded in Grandpa's very being. He sat next to a window listening to music we would play by the hour, including a recent original hit by Angelina and Calvin, my younger siblings, "Grandpa is Eating a Banana," accompanied by a ukulele. Each time he visited he became an integral part of our daily lives, from the little ones singing, to Alexander talking with him about his day, to us all listening to him tease Momma, calling her a "codfish."

Grandpa was a brilliant man who completed several degrees including nursing, preaching, and education, as well as being awarded first in an international oration contest.

He kept his bearing and his posture, which led to Momma's saying, "There are three things that can never be taken from you that you don't allow to be taken: your faith, your dignity and your posture." Most days he spoke very little, as the effort was great, but I know he prayed, all day, every day. On good days he sang at worship with us, and his deep, rumbling voice reminded me of my dad's hugs. I will not see him again in this life, but because of his prayers I have faith, and I continue to have the faith bestowed upon me at birth. I will see my grandpa again on the last day. His prayer was, "Lord, give me strength," Now this has become my prayer.

— Christianna Nesmith, Class of 2016

Serving Words
To Serve

If anyone speaks, they should do so as one who speaks the very words of God. If anyone serves, they should do so with the strength God provides, so that in all things, God may be praised through Jesus Christ. (1 Peter 4: 11, NIV)

Often times, when people think about serving God, their minds go directly to the action of physically serving. Images of high school students building churches in Panama, and pictures of dirty, white doctors trekking through dangerous jungle terrain, dressing natives with clean bandages materialize in our heads. These are both incredible ways to serve God, but have you ever sincerely considered the power of serving God through the words that you speak?

Near the end of my sophomore year, my sister, close friend, and I were accepted to work at a camp, taking the role of kitchen crew.

Upon arriving, we met our co-workers and boss. All of us co-workers developed an immediate camaraderie, and we had a skilled boss. As a team, we formed a strong, productive workforce, eliminating most avoidable, stressful situations. Unfortunately, our boss was a stress-aholic. For her, life was not worth living if she was not stressed, and she needed to pass her stress on to other people.

Normally on a Sunday, supper prep started at 4:45 pm, but one week our boss panicked because two of our crew became sick. She decided that the rest of us needed a whole extra hour of prep time. Unmercifully, my sister and I were wrenched from our fun registration jobs and dragged into the cold grip of the kitchen.

Irritated, I snapped, "What would you like me to start, *before* 4:00?"

She didn't even need to turn around for me to know that I had surprised and hurt her with the unbridled comment.

Winston Churchill once said, "We are masters of the unsaid words, but slaves of the ones we let slip out." Looking back, my boss most likely did not want to start early either. It was not fair for me to take out my exasperation on her. I could have taken that moment to serve God by saying, "What can I do to give you time to take a small break?" How much better could I have served God if I had guarded the words that I spoke, or simply not spoken at all?

We need to remember that we can serve God in our daily interactions with other people. One of the biggest ways we interact is through speaking. Always guard what you say to others. By serving others through your words, you are serving God as well.

— Danyelle Nesmith, Class of 2017

Understanding God
To Know

Where were you when I laid the earth's foundation? Tell me, if you understand. (Job 38:4, NIV)

When I was still living in Florida I attended an Adventist school that I had gone to since pre-k. I had grown up with almost everyone there. My parents decided to move me to another school for eighth grade. When I first got to the school, I was amazed by all the new people, and how big the school was. There were over one hundred kids in my grade versus only nine at my previous school. As I continued to go there, I realized the difficulty of finding new friends in a school where everyone had already decided their friend groups from previous years. I struggled to fit in with people but was always excluded. I joined the football team and was always picked on. I would pray and pray at night for something to change, but nothing happened and I didn't understand why. This continued for nearly the whole year.

One day in Bible class, the teacher read Job 34:8. In this verse God is speaking to Job. Job's story is of a man whose faith was tested to the limits. His family died, all of his cattle, servants, and houses were somehow destroyed. He even became covered with sores. He had done nothing wrong, and people were telling him that it was all just a punishment.

He questioned God and asked why all this had happened to him. God's response paints a very clear and vivid picture of the difference between God and man. It shows that God is not man and never was, and no matter how hard we try we will never have the power to understand God. I believe that at the core of trusting God and His plan for our lives is knowing that He is the One who created us. If we think there is someone or something on earth that is more worthy of our trust than the Creator of everything, then we have bigger problems in our life than being picked on. Take this verse and let it teach you that some things are beyond our understanding but nothing is beyond the Creator of the universe.

— Jordan Nioso, Class of 2017

Twice Saved
To Love

"Because he loves me," says the LORD, "I will rescue him; I will protect him, for he acknowledges my name. (Psalm 91:14, NIV)

When I was younger, I almost died twice. The first time, I was sitting on my bed, doing my work peacefully, when all of a sudden, I got nauseous and ran to the bathroom. When I got there, I was hit with dizziness and faintness. I sat down, and the next thing I knew, I was in the hospital. My doctor, Dr. Shotunsa had put me on a drip, and he was talking to my parents solemnly about what was going on with me. Seeing as how I was young and clueless as to all the medical terms being used, I assumed I had a cold that took a horrible turn.

I was hospitalized for a month or two, and as I was there, I thought to myself, *I hope I don't die because I want to fulfill my dream of coming to America and living the rest of my life there.* As I sat there, my thoughts shifted to God. Deciding that I was near death anyways, and maybe God could either put me out of my misery or heal me, I prayed. The result was almost instantaneous. The next day, my health started to get better, and I thanked God for it and thanked my parents for letting me know God. The second near death experience happened a year or two after the previous incident. It was late at night, and prayer meeting had just ended. I was walking back to my house with my uncle and his sister, talking to myself.

My aunt said that she wanted to make a quick stop at Mama Bolu's shop, so we did. When we came out, I was sporting my newly-bought Agege bread (a type of white bread) in my hands. As we walked, I noticed that my uncle and aunt had started walking ahead of me, so I decided to walk in a zigzag line to catch up with them. As I started down the road in a slant, I walked too far, and the next thing I knew, I was falling down a deep wide gutter that got shorter the farther you walked up it. I must have screamed or something because my aunt and uncle rushed back and instructed me to walk further so they could pull me up.

As I walked, I felt lightheaded, but blew it off as an aftereffect of the fall. When I was pulled out, my aunt screamed, and told my uncle to call my mom, their sister. My aunt held her white handkerchief to my forehead, and brought it back two seconds later for me to see that it was covered in blood. My whole forehead was busted open. My uncle ran back to my house, got the car, and drove me to the hospital where my mom worked. When I got there, I was on the verge of passing out because of loss of blood. My mother had to stitch my forehead back together, and while she did that, my aunt prayed for God to help me heal and not die, which brings me to the passage at the top.

Because we love God, He will rescue us and protect us, for we acknowledge His name. Because my aunt and uncle and I love God and put our full trust in Him, He protected me and kept me alive from my near death experiences. God is willing to help us as long as we acknowledge His name. Because I trusted and acknowledged His name, he fulfilled my seven-year-old dream of coming to America. He is faithful and just and deserving of praise for all He has done for us. Amen!!!

— Gift Nnakwu, Class of 2019

God Finishes What He Started
To Know

And we know that for those who love God all things work together for good, for those who are called according to his purpose. (Romans 8:28, ESV)

About four years ago, my grandparents moved in with my family. It wasn't something to take lightly. My grandmother had just been diagnosed with lung cancer. After going through many medical procedures, having her left lung removed, and going through chemotherapy, the tumor still insisted on staying. It wasn't long until the cancer spread to other parts of her body, and eventually it made its way to her brain. To all of our great sadness, she passed away shortly after.

My mentality had always been a bit of, "It can never happen to anyone in my family, God wouldn't allow that to happen." However, it did. Why? I'm not exactly sure there was a specific reason. God didn't do it directly, but why did He allow it to happen?

I'm sure many of you have struggled with very similar questions around the same topic. Why does God allow bad things to happen to people who never really deserved it? We, as humans, don't exactly have the right to know, and God is not required to explain to us, exactly why some things happen the way they do. All He asks us to do is to *know* that He will never leave anything unfinished. He will always turn out everything for good or according to His will.

Granted, it is easier said than done when it comes to trusting God. Due to our human nature, it's difficult, sometimes, to fully trust someone we can't physically see. I find myself in this rut more often than I wish. However, I believe that the more time we spend with God, the more we begin to see God working in ways we only took for granted before. The boundary between God and us slowly dissipates, until we don't really notice a separation in our relationship at all. It's not impossible, it just takes time, and that's all our heavenly Father asks of us. Find time today to start growing a personal relationship with Jesus by spending time in the Word. If you already have a strong personal relationship with Him, pray and ask for complete trust in Him. Ask Him to show you His plan, according to His will.

TALKING TO GOD +
SPENDING TIME IN HIS WORD ⟹ CLOSER RELATIONSHIP

A CLOSER RELATIONSHIP ⟹ TRUST

Question/Response: Think of a time where something hasn't exactly gone the way you wanted it to. How did God turn it around for good? What blessings or lessons came out of that trial?

— Ken Norton, Class of 2017

Miracles Do Happen
To Know

And we know that all things work together for good to those who love God, to those who are the called according to His purpose.
Romans 8:28, NJKV

It was a normal Tuesday school morning, or at least it was supposed to be. My nanny, Ms. Michele, was driving me to school on a chilly autumn morning. I was in the passenger seat, and while she was driving on the interstate, she passed out behind the wheel. When that happened it felt as though my life would end there. By God's grace she bounced off the interstate guard rail and the jolt of that woke her up. She regained her control of the wheel, and we continued on to school.

Providentially, her doctor was behind us on the interstate and followed us to check up on her. She was admitted into the hospital that day. We later found out she had a ventricular tachycardia, something like a heart attack where the heartbeat is not in rhythm. She almost died. That wasn't the end of it.

My nanny had been with me all of my life because both of my parents worked full time jobs and were not able to be there to take care of my two brothers and me. I called her "Sho" from a very young age because I was unable to pronounce Ms. Michele. Sho has had heart problems for as long as I can remember. Having this problem on the road was neither her first, nor her last. She later had to become a steady visitor to the hospital.

Even though this happened over and over, she still tried to help us as much as possible. She would even help out with the fruit program at school. Despite being sick with a dire heart condition, she still wanted to help. I asked her why she loved helping so much, she replied with the Bible verse Romans 8:28 (NKJV), "And we know that all things work together for good to those who love God, to those who are the called according to His purpose." I didn't understand at all what this meant because her condition continued to worsen.

It got so bad that she had to be put in the ICU, and doctors said they might have to put her on life-support. They asked her how many days she would like to be on it before they turned off the machine. I was there witnessing the whole conversation, and I couldn't help but break down in tears. I was angry with God and asked why. Every time I asked God for an answer I came back to Romans 8:28 over and over again. Despite this, Sho always called home to check up on me. Thankfully her condition got better, but they said to survive much longer, she would need a heart transplant.

Sho made a marvelous recovery after that, but her heart was still deteriorating. She had finally been put on the heart transplant list, but the surgery was too expensive for us to afford. Then Sho reminded me of Romans 8:28, once again. A couple days later, the hospital called her to say that they had a heart.

When I heard this, there was so much joy in my heart. It was ironic because we were hosting an event to raise money for her heart transplant on the same day she got called in for the surgery. All those who donated were people that she had helped while being sick. I laughed and cried at the same time because God had been telling me the whole time with Romans 8:28. I thank God because now she is better than ever.

I challenge you to serve others even in time of need.

Prayer: Pray that God will give you a selfless heart to abide by.

— David Nwadike, Class of 2017

Always Have Fun
To Serve

A joyful heart is good medicine, but a crushed spirit dries up the bones. (Proverbs 17:22, ESV)

This year in February, I went on a mission trip to Guyana, South America for a month. We arrived in Georgetown, the capital city of Guyana. We had to take a ship for nine hours, and the ship did not have anything on it.

When I heard that, I was annoyed, and I really had to go to the restroom. My other friends did, too, but we could not, so when we arrived in the jungle we just ran to the restroom. It was really hot. I was sweating even just standing. Even though I was not doing anything, the weather made me sweat a lot, and that annoyed me. Every night, when we took a shower, we did not have clean water, unlike here. The water was brown colored and sandy. After four days, I started to complain about everything that we were facing. I complained about why they did not have enough food, and why they did not have clean water, even why the weather was so hot.

One day, I talked to one of my friends, complaining to her about this mission trip.

After I talked to her, she told me, "You have to change your mind first. Try to have fun, have a joyful heart, and try to think positive. You came here for God's work, not your own life. God led you to come here and be a missionary. But you are just complaining about everything."

After she talked to me, I was shocked and I remembered why I was there. Then I changed my mind, and I tried to have fun with the people who lived there. I talked with the children, taught them Korean and Japanese, and I tried to do many things with them.

One day I realized I was not complaining anymore, and that I even liked the hot weather. When I came back to school, I prayed to God that I could do well and thanked Him that He gave me a good friend. When you are having a hard time, and when bad things happen, try to change your mind, then you can do well with whatever you want.

— Olivia Ok, Class of 2017

What it Means to Know God
To Know

And we know that God causes everything to work together for the good of those who love God and are called according to his purpose for them. (Romans 8:28, NLT)

In this day and age nothing is more important than knowing God. But there is more than one definition to the phrase "Knowing God." Many people know of God, and know who He is. Even most atheists believe that Jesus was a historical figure and lived in the first century. It is whether His teachings were true and if He actually rose from the dead that people argue over.

In the grand scheme of life, it doesn't matter what you know, but that you apply those things and teachings to your life. For example: It doesn't matter if you know that cheating on a test is wrong, but that you make the personal choice not to cheat. It is summed up in the verse James 2:20 (ESV), "Do you want to be shown, you foolish person, that faith apart from works is useless?" In this case belief without actions is useless.

In my opinion to know God means to believe in the works He has done for us. Not only that, but to act on the knowledge we have and try to help other people believe in Him, too. We cannot love God if we do not know Him, and we cannot love others if we do not love God. Without knowledge of God we cannot love or serve God properly. It is rightfully the first part of "To Know, To Love, and To Serve".

In conclusion, God loves us and the most important thing in our lives is to know that. We need to know that God will work out everything to the best of our benefit, and that through His love we are saved. That is what it means to know God.

— Nnamdi Onyeije, Class of 2018

To Know, To Love, ...
To Serve

Be sure to fear the Lord and serve Him faithfully with all your heart, consider what great things He has done for you.
(1 Samuel 12:24, NIV)

Serving God, what does that truly mean to you? To many people, serving God means going to church and obeying His rules and commandments. This is true, but there is so much more to it than just that. If you don't have the want in your heart to do this, then why should you do it at all? "Each one of us must give as he has decided in his heart, not reluctantly or under compulsion, for God loves a cheerful giver" (2 Cor. 9:7, ESV)

Sadly, many people go to church and try to obey God but don't really want to. If this is true for you, then maybe you should start trying to find the reasons why you should want to. Some reasons you might want to think about could be the fact that God is a magnificent being, and He actually cares for you and loves you. You may also want to think about how He sent His only Son, Jesus, to die for your sins so that if you choose to, you may go to heaven. You should want to serve Him because He serves you every day, all the time. God doesn't need our help, He doesn't need us to serve Him, but He wants us to because He loves us and wants us to be in heaven with Him. "And he is not served by human hands, as if he needed anything. Rather, he himself gives everyone life and breath and everything else" (Acts 17:25, NIV).

Now you might be wondering, how can I serve Him? There are many answers to that question and here is mine. You can serve God with your talents and abilities. If you are artistic, then you can serve Him with your drawings or paintings. If you like to sing, then you can serve Him with your voice. If you like to write, then you can serve Him by writing about Him or the things He created. And even if you are good at sports, you can serve Him by thanking Him for giving you the ability to play.

"You're the proud owner of a special set of talents that can be nurtured or ignored totally. The challenge, of course, is to use your abilities to the greatest extent possible. Your talents are priceless gifts from the Creator, and the way to say thank you for God's gifts is to use them." (Swanberg, *Man Does Not Live by Sports Alone*)

Another way to serve God is by serving others. Matthew 25:14–30 talks about how serving the poor and needy is equal to personally serving God. It is very important to God that His people want to help each other. There are many different ways to serve God. I encourage you to find your special abilities, if you haven't already, and learn how to praise God with them. I also encourage you to find the reasons why you want to serve God, instead of just doing it because it's right. I challenge you to find out how God serves you all the time and realize how important it is to want to serve Him back.

— By Allison Ormes, Class of 2019

Off the Deep End
To Know

For all have sinned and fall short of the glory of God, and all are justified freely by his grace through the redemption that came by Christ Jesus. (Romans 3: 23–24, NIV)

It was over ninety degrees that day, and my friend and I were dying of heat. That weekend we were at a spiritual retreat with our church, and the days were long and hot. We needed to cool off somehow. At that moment, we both had the same idea … jump into the lake! We ran back to our cabin to change into our bathing suits, and there we met our other friends and my mom. My mom asked us where we were going, and I told her down to the lake. She warned us not to use the rope because it was very dangerous but, like the children we were, we didn't listen. We ran down to the lake, in a hurry to get wet. When we arrived, we ran to the rope, dying to jump in. I went in first, and nothing went wrong. Then one by one we all jumped in and everything ran smoothly. Then Tommy, the last one to try, got on the rope. He swung down towards the water and let go. He plummeted down and hit his back on a rock hidden under the water. We ran up to our cabin where my mother was, and, even though she was disappointed, she helped us.

Sometimes we are just like that with God. He warns against us doing certain things, but a lot of the time we ignore Him. Even though it might feel good at first, one day it will hurt you badly. But when you get hurt, God will be there to pick you up and bandage you. As the verse says, we all have sinned and come short of the glory of God, but because of Jesus' death on the cross, we can be saved by God's grace and love, which is unconditional no matter what we do.

— Andrew Ouro-Rodrigues, Class of 2017

The Heavens Declare
To Know

The heavens declare the glory of God; and the firmament shows His handiwork. (Psalm 19:1, NKJV.)

For sixteen years I have had trouble getting to know God on a personal level. I always thought it was something that would one day just happen to me like the snap of a finger. I had heard so many stories about how angels have saved people, and how great it was, but I had never experienced anything like that. For a while I questioned God and asked Him why He wasn't revealing Himself to me. Was He even there? Could He even hear me? These were all questions that I struggled with for quite a while.

This summer I chose to volunteer my time at a summer camp in Texas where I hoped God would have a purpose for me. I kept praying to God that He would show me what purpose He had for me; that everything would just be spelled out for me. I tried to stay faithful and trust that His timing was the best, but I began to grow impatient. As the weeks went on, I wasn't feeling anything and it began to worry me. It angered me that I had made the decision to do this for God, because it was as if He didn't acknowledge it. I wanted so badly to know God and to experience who He really is. But it wasn't until the very last week of summer camp that God finally showed me what I was waiting for.

One night they gave the opportunity to sleep outside under the stars for anyone who wanted to do it. My friends and I decided it was something that we were interested in doing. That night we all bundled up next to the campfire, told scary stories, and made s'mores. The night air had a cool breeze to it and everything felt calm. When we were lying in bed we started to discuss our relationships with God, and I was finally able to vent my feelings. We stared in awe as the dome of stars just engulfed us. There was this feeling that I got that is hard to describe. It was unlike anything I had ever experienced. During this time a verse popped into my head and I heard, "The heavens declare the glory of God." As that night went on and the silence grew, I fell asleep, just taking in the incredible scenery that shone right above me.

The next morning, I felt somewhat different. God had renewed my faith and brought me to the realization that I already have everything I need to know Him. Just take the time to look at all the marvelous things that He has crafted. It doesn't necessarily have to be the stars, but anything in nature that God is able to speak through, to get to you. By just waiting and having faith, God is faithful to show us His majestic works. I challenge you to take the time to look at the little things so that you are able to know Him on a personal level.

— Isaac Overfield, Class of 2017

The Apple
To Know

Your word is a lamp for my feet, a light on my path.
(Psalm 119:105, NIV)

I had just come home from school, and already I could tell that it was going to be a quiet and rather uneventful evening. Looking around, I saw my parents were getting ready for dinner, both chopping up some vegetables. I took off my favorite light-up sneakers and plopped my lunch box on the counter. Sitting down at our kitchen table, and trying to ignore my hungry stomach, I took out my very hard kindergarten homework, and got started.

"Hey, Becca," my dad called right on cue, "You want an apple?" The biggest smile appeared on my face, as I threw my crayons on the table and ran to go get my prize. But, as I drew closer, I began to get confused. This most definitely didn't look like a normal apple. It was round, just like an apple, but its color wasn't right, and it had a terrible smell.

"Daddy, what is that?" my five-year-old self asked.

"It's a special apple, Becca. Go ahead and try it!" my dad coaxed, a mischievous smile plastered on his face.

My tiny hands reached out and took it from his. Bravely, I brought it to my face and took a huge bite. Immediately I spit it out of my mouth and ran to the sink, drinking water from the faucet. My dad's laugh was louder than the roar of a lion. What he had given me was not an apple, but a reeking, nasty onion.

Because of my loving, yet playful father, from a young age I've learned that you not only must be cautious of people's intentions, but also be aware that there are people out there who are ready and willing to lie to you and lead you astray without thinking twice about it. The only thing that we know for sure is true, is God's Word. Because of that, we have to use God's Word for direction in our lives. God gave us the Bible so we have something ready to help us in times of trouble, and to make sure we know that we need to trust in Him, and not be deceived by the people who give us onions instead of apples.

— Becca Overstreet, Class of 2017

Never Give Up Faith
To Serve

Their responsibility is to equip God's people to do his work and build up the church, the body of Christ (Ephesians 4:12, NLT)

As part of my GCA high school experience, I was fortunate enough to participate and travel with the school to Panama to do mission work alongside with Maranatha Volunteers International. We were assigned to build a church, assist with teaching English at schools, and host a free and non-profit medical clinic. Over the course of the eleven days we were there, we worked on a tight schedule. The current church members had never had a real church building to meet in. The piece of land that the church was being built on had been sitting empty for a while, and Maranatha took up the responsibility of finding supplies and workers for the church project. The medical clinic was moved to a different location every day, and you didn't know who might walk in. Dr. Remy came along with us to help diagnose those who were sick or not feeling well. When we helped in the local schools, we were assigned in pairs so that each classroom duo consisted of one English speaking GCA student and one bilingual GCA student who spoke Spanish and could translate.

Over the eleven-day mission trip, we were primarily proud of the accomplishment of building the church. Although the church members had been without a building to worship in, they did not lose confidence and give up. They did not beg and beg for someone to help them. They waited and waited and trusted God to provide for them in the best way possible. This shows us that no matter what they had, they never gave up faith in God. Today we can complain about problems and issues with our churches without realizing that somewhere else in the world, there are others who are struggling just to keep their church running. Be thankful today for what you have, and don't let go of what you are fortunate to have been blessed with.

— Brennan Paderanga, Class of 2016

Gods Existence
To Serve

And without faith it is impossible to please God, because anyone who comes to him must believe that he exists and that he rewards those who earnestly seek him. (Hebrews 11:6 NIV)

Stumbling upon God's miracles is an everlasting memory. You just can't get them out of your head. There is a valid reason for this. God made us so that we can never forget Him and what He does for us. The more good we do in this world, the more He will save us from danger and Satan. We should all be thankful for what He has done for us. The little things we do in life can put us on a dangerous path to death, but there are times when He has changed our path to avoid danger in an instant.

One breathtaking miracle has happened to me recently. My dad was following his usual work schedule. He would sit at the breakfast table and finish all his work for the day. He would usually finish and go to bed around 1:30 each morning. No matter how good or bad his day was, or if he had an important meeting the next morning, he would still finish his work and end at the same exact time every night.

But for some reason, my mom told him to go to bed early. When she tells him to go to bed, he usually leaves the table thirty minutes later. But this time, he left the table right away and went straight to bed. Approximately twenty or thirty minutes later, there was a loud bang. It sounded like someone had set off a bomb in the house. Both of my parents woke up scared and confused. They thought someone had broken in, so they crawled out the window and saw a large hole in the side of our house. Someone had driven their car through our house. They looked through the large hole in the wall and saw a black Cadillac. There was smoke coming from inside the house. Massive amounts of bricks and debris were visible. The car had completely obliterated the breakfast table and kitchen countertops. There was nothing but bricks and destruction. All cabinets, tables, sofas, lamps, and televisions were broken into lots of pieces. The police report said that a woman was driving drunk and was going about seventy or eighty miles per hour upon impact, based on debris and tire marks. The woman was going so fast that bricks from that end of the house broke through the other side of our house.

You can probably see where this story is going. God guided my father out of danger through my mother. There is no way that this happened by chance. It is a miracle that both of my parents are alive today to tell this amazing story to others. There are many Christians in this world that doubt God's existence. The stress of what happens in your life is based on your faith in God. Without God, there would be no stable control in humans. God is the reason humanity has not fallen and died. If you are having a bad day or week, just turn to God because He is looking over us each and every day. People need to know that He really is there, protecting us. God's existence can only be acknowledged by those who believe in His Word and serve Him. We need to be fishers of men to others that do not know Him, so He can lead them on a safe path through life without suffering.

— Caleb Paderanga, Class of 2018

The Beauty of Serving Others
To Serve

For even the Son of Man came not to be served but to serve, and to give his life as a ransom for many. (Mark 10:45, ESV)

Earlier in the year I was asked to help out with a VBS for some kids on my friend's street. We were having a great time with the crafts, activities, swimming, and games. It was perfect Florida weather.

At one point in time, we were told that the neighbor's family had something happen to them. Their yard had been left unkempt, and was in desperate need of raking. We all decided that the next morning we would show up a little earlier than normal and rake their yard without them knowing, as a surprise for them for the weekend.

We had cleaned everything up, put the tools back in the garage, and were about to go inside to get changed for a swim, when the owner of the house came outside. She began to thank us profusely. It meant so much to her that we would be willing to do that for her. Every one of us looked at each other with big grins on our faces, happy that we had done something to contribute to making someone's life easier.

As high school students, we often think of service as doing things just so we can get our community service hours in for the semester. A synonym for service is kindness. By serving others we are giving out of our hearts, where we have to love to be kind. In reality that's what it comes down to: love. Without love we can do nothing. Everything good we do is based on love for someone or something, propelling us to make a change in the world. By serving each other, we can be sure that the love God has shown us is being spread around to those who are most in need of His promises. Sometimes that's the best way we can show people we love them. I can guarantee that when you do something for another person, not only will they be happy, but you'll feel good as well.

— Jessica Paradis, Class of 2019

A Month South of the Border
To Serve

And the word of the Lord was being spread throughout all the region. (Acts 13:49, NKJV)

When I was twelve my Pathfinder group decided to travel to Anconcito, Ecuador. We wanted to go on a mission trip somewhere, and after much deliberation we decided to travel to Anconcito, which is a small fishing town that doesn't get very much tourism. We chose to go there because of Mark 16:15 (ERV) which says, "He said to them, "Go everywhere in the world. Tell the Good News to everyone."

We wanted to take the news of the gospel to a very remote place where they may not have heard about God. While in Ecuador we built a church, held a health fair, and did nightly sermons at twelve churches. In Ecuador, I helped my grandfather preach the nightly sermon at his assigned church. His church was in the worst neighborhood out of all of the churches!

The first night was very difficult because no one showed up until one hour after the arranged starting time. Once inside I help my grandfather prepare, then he would speak for about an hour. The next night everything started on time and there were even more people there. By the last night the church was filled with people standing in the back and out the door!

Our mission while in Ecuador was to spread the news of Jesus' second coming and to spread the gospel to whomever we could. We heard stories of people coming to hurt us, and people that wished to delay us by cutting off our power. We had great fun in Ecuador, but most importantly we helped spread the good news of the second coming, and baptized one hundred people on the last Sabbath. We had completed our mission, and at the end of the trip I felt as blessed as those we had served. After the trip I returned to the United States and told others about the good news we had shared.

— Isaac Patterson, Class of 2018

Is God Really There?
To Know

The heart is deceitful above all things, and desperately sick; who can understand it? (Jeremiah 17:9, ESV)

Whenever there is a catastrophe in the world or there are problems and situations in my life, I always ask if God is real or not. This question is the barrier between God and me, and if I should have a relationship with God. I always ask myself, if God is there, why is there still sin in the world? Why hasn't He stopped all the hatred, killing, and sadness in the world? Why hasn't He even shown His face or body to the modern world? These are just some of the questions that make me wonder if God is really here for us or not.

I have always been raised in the church, and have always been told that God is always there for us and will never stop loving us. He will always protect us from evil and will only give us the best if we believe in Him. That always stuck with me, and I always believed that God is there for us.

As I got older, and saw the world more and more, I noticed many tragic events in the world that we live in. I also noticed the stuff that was going on in my family as well. With the type of situations I had in my life, it was very challenging for me to have full trust and love for God. It felt to me like having a best friend that I knew and loved for my whole life, and then one day He didn't want to be my friend anymore.

Experiencing one tragedy after another, I decided that if God didn't want to be there for me and help the situations in my life, then I didn't need Him at all. I started hanging out with the wrong crowd, getting into trouble and doing things I never did before. I was lost and I thought that I had no one to turn to in my life. I thought I was all by myself and had no one to help me.

No one, except one person—God. Even when I did terrible things to myself and other people, even when I cursed His name, He was still there for me and cared for me. This is what the Lord has said, "Cursed is the one who trusts in man, who depends on flesh for his strength and whose heart turns away from the Lord" (Jer. 17:5, NIV).

My relationship with God is still not one hundred percent, and I sometimes struggle to believe if He's there. I still don't understand parts of His plan or ideas. Maybe I'm not supposed to know for my own good. Sometimes I think it would be easier if He just showed Himself. I also believe that people should have faith and trust in God just like you have faith that there is oxygen in your lungs. I think God is here and loves and cares for us, but I sometimes feel He's not really there when I need Him. When I have those feelings, I need to remember what faith in God is—trusting that He is there for me even when I don't sense His presence.

— Justin Patterson, Class of 2018

Feeling Bleak
To Know

I have made the earth, the men and the beasts which are on the face of the earth by My great power and by My outstretched arm, and I will give it to the one who is pleasing in My sight.
(Jeremiah 27:5, NASB)

My experience with God is in His nature.

Often as I take a leisure stroll in the woods, whether it is in my back yard or a national park, I am always amazed at its beauty. Many things cross my mind as I go on but one thing that comes to my mind the most is, "How can something so pure and intricate come to be?", and "Why is it here?" You can get caught up in all sorts of reasoning and ideas about what it's for and why it's there.

Whether you're looking at the stars at night, or the complexity of an ant pile in the summer, always know there is a Creator who created the stars and the ants and the most perplexing things of all: you and I. That very Creator who loves you more than the stars, sent His Son down to die for ants like you and I. Every time I look to nature I think of that. So the next time you question it, look to the Book before you jump to any conclusions.

I found my answer in Jeremiah, where it tells us that God created nature for us to enjoy and to have. This is such an uplifting gift to have. It always helps me when I'm feeling down. So next time you are feeling bleak in the spiritual part of your life, just look to Jeremiah 27:5.

— Justin Peel, Class of 2016

Knowing Your Boundaries
To Know

In their hearts humans plan their course, but the Lord establishes their steps. (Proverbs 16:9, NIV)

Knowing your Father and Ruler is very important, but knowing your limits is also important. On a summer day during a vacation down on the Florida coast, I saw the beauty of the ocean, smelled the salty sea air, and felt the sultry southern heat. I loved watching the seagulls and sitting in the shade of the umbrella my dad provided me. I usually built sand castles with my dad, because I couldn't lift the heavy buckets on my own. Everything was good and safe, until I saw the other, much older, kids running to the sea and swimming.

I asked my dad if I could go and swim, and he said, "No son it's not safe for you to be out there without me." I wasn't satisfied with that answer so I sat on my beach chair mad. I just loathed the kids having fun out there.

Pretty soon my dad was lulled to sleep. I thought about asking him again, but a new idea formed in my head. I thought, *I should just go by myself without my father.* So I quietly got up and slinked off. I was in up to my knees and was having fun, but the others were deeper. I inched out farther and farther and it wasn't long before I was so deep that I couldn't touch the bottom.

I began to panic, but I didn't want to call out to my dad because I thought for sure I would be in a ton of trouble. I swam as hard as my legs would kick, but the current was sweeping me out farther and farther away. I knew I was a goner. But just as my last sliver of hope went away, I screamed out for my father to help me.

He awoke and waded out to me. He picked me up and carried me to the safety of the beach. He sat me down and I awaited a punishment. Instead, he smiled and handed me an ice-cream sandwich, and said that when I want to swim I just needed to take him with me.

In life we seem to forget that we cannot do anything without our loving Father. At times we get fed up with having restrictions and go out into the world by ourselves. But pretty soon we get so caught up in the world that we can't get out on our own. We must always remember to keep a loving relationship with God and call out to Him when we need Him.

— Justin Peel, Class of 2016

Kidnapped by Mom
To Know

Peter replied, "Man, I don't know what you're talking about!" Just as he was speaking, the rooster crowed. The Lord turned and looked straight at Peter. Then Peter remembered the word the Lord had spoken to him: "Before the rooster crows today, you will disown me three times." (Luke 22:60–61, NIV)

When I was around five or six, my parents sat my brother and me down and had the "stranger danger" talk. As a very trusting child, I saw no real need for this, but soon became an expert on the proper phrases that would get people's attention if I were to be in actual trouble.

The following day, I was wandering down the cereal aisle in the grocery store, amazed by all the colorful boxes filled with sugary goodness. Grabbing a box of Lucky Charms, I walked over to the shopping cart and placed it inside. My mother, already in a foul mood, commanded that I put it back. Appalled that my mother would speak to me in such a way, I naturally became enraged.

With hot tears streaming down my face, I began to scream, "This woman is not my mother!" "Fire," and all the other phrases that I had learned so well the previous night. I was like a screeching siren, shrill and obnoxious. In the mist of one of my well-rehearsed alarms, I heard a loud and authoritative voice, "Elizabeth. Paige. Peltier." I turned around slowly to see my mother, very red in the face, and knew at that moment that my life was over.

Just as I declared that my mother was not my mother, how often do we cry out this God is not our God? It happens on a daily basis, whether we try to or not. As teenagers, sometimes we try to hide our Christianity to fit in. I have certainly done it. We do it with the way we act, what we watch, and sometimes even the clothes we wear. If we are not proclaiming God's name in our everyday actions, we aren't claiming Him to be our God. Maybe it is time that we start living our lives claiming God in everything we do instead of crying out that this God is not our God.

— Paige Peltier, Class of 2015

God's Plan
To Know

For I know the plans I have for you, declares the Lord, plans for welfare and not for evil, to give you a future and a hope. Then you will call upon me and come and pray to me, and I will hear you. You will seek me and find me, when you seek me with all your heart. (Jeremiah 29:11–13, ESV)

When I was thirteen years old, I had to leave my home in the Tri-cities, Washington* to move across the U.S. to Ohio. I went from a small Adventist school to a huge public middle school. I had to leave my friends behind, my eldest brother, and my dad. This was a horrible time for my family because my stepdad, whom I had in my life for seven years, had just committed suicide because of depression. I was upset with God and I didn't understand His plan for me, and at that time I felt as though God had left me.

For three years I didn't attend church. I was depressed, I had friends that were bad influences, and I needed family whom I didn't have in Ohio. My freshman year in high school I wanted something more to do with God, so I started to pray and came back to God. I prayed for family, and when I was sixteen years old I got the news that we were moving to Dalton, Georgia, where a lot of my family lives. I was so excited at the time and was already looking at Georgia-Cumberland Academy. So when I got asked whether I wanted to go to public school or academy, I chose GCA, knowing it was God's plan for me.

I have now almost finished two years at GCA, and I definitely see God's plan for me. My spiritual life has grown tremendously with the help of teachers and friends that all believe in God and His plan. In the end it wasn't God who left me, it was me who left God and His plan that I couldn't yet understand.

So whenever you feel lost or left behind, just remember that God does have a plan for you. Instead of leaving God behind, seek Him with all your heart and you will find Him. Call upon the Lord and pray to Him because He is always there to hear you even when you don't think He is.

*The area in south-central Washington known as the Tri-cities includes the towns of Pasco, Kennewick, and Richland.

— Haylee Peterson, Class of 2016

Setting an Example
To Serve

Don't let anyone look down on you because you are young, but set an example for the believers in speech, in conduct, in love, in faith and in purity. (1 Timothy 4:12, NIV)

The third chapel meeting of my senior year, Dean Janet, AKA DJ, asked all the seniors to stay afterward. She gave us a talk about how we need to be leaders, because we were seniors and the classes below us looked up to us. I didn't take this to heart until she told us to think about the seniors during the year we were freshmen. That was a scary thought to me, thinking that there was someone looking up to me, and that I needed to be a good influence on them.

I want to be a great leader and influence people. I want the freshmen to remember me when they are seniors and think, "Wow, I want to be like her." I may not be president of SA or a girls' dorm RA, but that means nothing to God. We are all called to be leaders and leave a good influence behind.

God wants us to reach out to people to guide them on the right path. It may be someone who is really struggling, or even a brand new GCA student, for example. They may need help in making friends, finding their classes, or maybe even growing a closer relationship with God. It's not just our senior year—God wants us to be influences for the rest of our lives. Just because we are young does not mean we can't set an example for people who are older than us. Just the way we act can show people what we are all about. God shows us that it comes with great reward.

God says to devote ourselves to public preaching and teaching Scripture until He comes. God doesn't want us neglecting our gift that He has clearly given to each and every one of us. God wants us to give ourselves wholly to Him so that everyone will see our progress. We need to remember this as we go through our daily walk. We don't want people to look down on us because we are young, but we need to set examples by the way we talk, the way we act, and the way we love.

— Haylee Peterson, Class of 2016

The Haircut
To Know

Whoever conceals their sins does not prosper, but the one who confesses and renounces them finds mercy. (Proverbs 28:13, NIV)

Growing up I always found myself getting into trouble. One day, when I was about 5 years old, I was playing alone in the living room. Part of my game consisted of opening drawers and looking at their contents, and in one of them I happened to find a pair of shiny red scissors. At that moment, I decided that I was going to become a hairdresser, and I knew who the perfect person to practice on would be: myself. A part of me knew that cutting my own hair was a bad idea, but the other part of me still wanted to do it. So I crawled behind the couch, grabbed a chunk of hair directly in the middle of my forehead, and snipped it off. Thinking no one would notice I happily went off to enjoy the rest of my day. Of course, my world quickly fell to pieces once my mom saw the strands of hair poking up from my head. Once I realized that what I did was a huge mistake, I completely confessed to my mom.

In the same way I thought I could get away with cutting my hair because I was hiding, we sometimes think that we can hide our sins from God. Proverbs 28:13 says, "He who conceals his transgressions will not prosper, but he who confesses and forsakes them will find compassion."

Sometimes when we sin, we think no one is watching. However, God is always watching us and like my mom, our sins are very obvious to him. It's better to confess your sins to God, because the moment you confess them, all your burdens will be taken away and you will be made new.

— Kelly Quintiana, Class of 2017

Traveling Dogs
To Know

"Therefore do not worry about tomorrow, for tomorrow will worry about itself." Matthew 6:34, NIV

"Baxter come here," I motioned for my dog to come to me, "come and get inside your kennel." We were moving from Guam back to the United States, and we had to send my dog separately back home. He would be in a kennel, all by himself, for eight straight hours until he reached the mainland. He looked at me with his puppy dog eyes as we locked him inside his kennel. He looked at me asking, "Why would you do this to me? Can't you see that I'm scared?" All I could do was tell him that everything was going to be alright. Then came the day when we had to send him off. We got up at the unruly hour of 4:00 a.m. and my dad and I drove him to the airport cargo pickup. He was scared and confused. As they loaded him onto the cargo truck's trailer, he was watching us as if asking, "Why would you leave me?" I tried to tell him that everything was alright. I tried to communicate to him that we weren't leaving him for good. I guaranteed him that everything would be alright in the end, but he just didn't understand me.

Sometimes we as Christians are like dogs. We don't fully understand God's plan for us until it has happened. We can't see ahead of time and witness how the situation ends up. We have just to trust and know God will take care of all our problems. Sometimes we ask Him, "Why are you allowing this to happen to me? Can't you see that I'm scared and hurting? Why can't you help me?" God only looks down on us and assures us that it will all be alright in the end. We must trust and obey. We don't always understand His plan, but we can know Him and obey Him until we see the final result of His better plan. Just like the verse says, don't worry about tomorrow, for tomorrow will worry about itself. Know God more by leaving your problems in His hands with the assurance that He will take care of everything.

— Cameron Reel, Class of 2017

Out of the Darkness
Knowing God

Whoever does not love does not know God, because God is love.
(1 John 4:8, NIV)

Most of my life I didn't really know God. I went to church, sang songs, gave tithe, and even sat through the sermons. I thought I knew God, but I was just living a lie. I was going through all of the motions of being a Christian, but my mind was always somewhere else. It usually would be videogames or TV that I constantly thought about in church. It became irritating to me to even go to church.

I didn't understand that Sabbath was a special day made for us to relax and enjoy God's creation. I didn't know God until I went to GCA. My first day I was terrified, living in a dormitory five hours away from home without any friends. That didn't last long, because as soon as I entered the door I was welcomed with friendly smiles and kind greetings. I was instantly friends with a group of people who were hanging out in the chapel. They weren't talking about the normal things teenagers talk about like videogames, TV, or fashion. They were talking about God and how He has shown Himself in their lives.

I eventually was eventually brought into the conversation, but I really didn't know what to say. They didn't laugh or make fun of me, but instead took it upon themselves to help me know God and to love Him. They had worship with me and would give me verses in the Bible to read. Slowly but surely it came into focus that God was real, and He loved me. It came into focus that I was supposed to worship and love Him and enjoy His creation.

I stopped watching TV on Sabbath, and instead read the Bible with my new friends. They brought me out of the darkness and put me into the beautiful world of God. All it takes is a few good people to show you the way. All it takes are a few friends to show you the truth.

— Jordan Reid, Class of 2017

Newborns
To Serve

You are witnesses, and so is God, of how holy, righteous and blameless we were among you who believed.
(1 Thessalonians 2:10 NIV)

Think about your earliest memories. Whatever they were, whether you were at a birthday party or playing with your favorite toy, you probably can't remember all the way back to infancy. Babies need so much care. If they don't have someone to feed them and care for them twenty-four hours a day, they wouldn't be able to survive on their own.

New believers in Jesus are like newborns. Someone who is just joining God's family needs a spiritual parent to care for and protect them, especially in the first weeks and months of their new Christian life. If you are a person who has helped bring someone to a spiritual birth in Christ, it makes sense to fill the role of a spiritual parent. But what does a spiritual parent do?

First, check their vital signs. In the first few days of becoming a Christian, spiritual babies might be tempted to doubt that they are truly different. They need to be reminded that even though they may feel like their life hasn't changed at all, it has. It has changed tremendously for the better, and they need to know and remember that.

Second, supply nourishment. Like a baby needs food to survive, a new Christian needs God's Word to mature (see 1 Peter 2:2). One of the first things new believers need is assurance about what happened to them when they trusted Christ. Go over the facts about their new life in Christ on your first visit together:

When you trusted Christ, you became a child of God (John 1:12).
Your sins were forgiven (1 John 1:9).
He will never leave you (Hebrews 13:5-8).
You have received eternal life. (John 5:24; 1 John 5: 12-13)

Third, throw in some bonding time. Newborns need to bond with their parents just like new Christians need to get involved with other believers. Introduce them to your Christian friends and pastor. Invite them to events such as Bible studies and prayer meetings. These are only three of the many ways that we can help bring a new believer, a newborn in Christ, even closer to Jesus. We are able to make a difference and serve Jesus Christ.

— Taylor Reid, Class of 2016

Finding the Berries in the Briar Patch
To Know

Trust in the Lord with all your heart and lean not on your own understanding; in all your ways submit to him, and he will make your paths straight. (Proverbs 3:5-6, NIV)

Everyone has gone through times that have been rough and stressful. Throughout those times, we look for something that we can look up to whether it's a relative, close friend, or music. Most importantly, God is there for us to look up to, literally. There is nothing too big or too small for Him to help us with. There are things that happen in our lives that we can't understand or find the meaning of, and it stresses us out. We don't have the ability, but God does. He can see everything. He has a plan, and we only need to trust in Him. God is trying to help, although it may not seem like it at that very moment. God is always working to help each and every one of us.

A couple years ago my dad became sick and for a few days we believed that it was just a stomach bug, but he wasn't getting better. Eventually, he went to the doctor. They ran tests and X-rays. The X-ray of his abdomen showed that he had appendicitis, but that wasn't the end of it. They also found a mass in his kidney. Testing was postponed until his appendix was removed. After he was well enough, the tests continued: cancer. Finding out that my dad had cancer hit me like a ton of bricks. I was so scared and worried. Would my dad live, or would the cancer overpower him? This question ran through my mind until I realized that he wasn't going to fight this battle alone. We had God on our side. My prayers began to include, "Please help my daddy to live. Please save him."

The cancerous mass had not spread outside his kidney; it was contained. The surgeons were able to take the whole kidney out. The cancer has not come back. When this was going on in my life I was stressed and worried, but I didn't need to be. God was there through it all.

Who knows how long he could have had the cancer if God hadn't allowed my dad to have appendicitis. We should find the berries in the briar bush. A prick can be painful, but God can use the things that we go through to help us rely on Him more, and build our character to be more Christ-like. There are tests in life, I know. The briars and thorns are there, but so are the sweet berries.

— Taylor Reid, Class of 2016

Grandpa
To Love

And God shall wipe away all tears from their eyes; and there shall be no more death, neither sorrow, nor crying, neither shall there be any more pain; for the former things are passed away.
(Revelation 21:4, KJV)

My father-in-law (I called him Grandpa) recently died. He was my friend and spiritual mentor. Below is a tribute to him giving some examples of how he impacted my life.

He would send me Bible studies by e-mail. I would study them, and then e-mail him back my thoughts. He always listened to me and encouraged me with my studies, to dig deeper, to pray more for the Holy Spirit to impress upon me what I should learn. A few years ago I was looking through one of his Bibles and asked him could I have it when he died. He gave it to me right then. It is highlighted in many different colors, many notes are written in the margins and some of the pages are worn and falling out from numerous hours of study by a man who coveted a closer walk with His Lord. I cherish that Bible.

One time I was lamenting the fact that this world is in terrible shape and the end times are upon us and what if this happened, or that happened. Would I be able to be true to my Lord?

He simply and calmly told me, "Trust, just trust. The Lord will take care of you."

I told him once that I like to have my devotions early in the morning, and he sent me this text, Psalm 143:8: "Cause me to hear your loving kindness in the morning for in you do I trust; cause me to know the way in which I should walk, for I lift up my soul to you." Every morning I look up out my window to the heavens and repeat that verse.

One morning he called me out of the blue and said that he had been thinking about the people he felt the closest to. He had counted ten people, and he told me I was one of them. I said, "Wow, Grandpa, I made the top ten!"

Not long ago my husband and I were visiting Grandpa and Grandma in their home at Pisgah. I couldn't get Grandpa to show a lot of affection but sometimes he surprised me and did. We were leaving and I usually would hug him and tell him I loved him. Sometimes he would respond, sometimes not.

But this particular time before I could say I loved him, he looked me in the eyes and said, "I love you so much, Pam."

Grandpa was a good man. I will miss him so much. But hopefully, Jesus is coming soon, and I will see him again. Until then I will trust, just trust.

— Pam Byrd Reifsnyder, Class of 1967

Sisters
To Love

Ask and it will be given to you; seek, and you will find; knock and it will be opened to you. For everyone who asks receives, and he who seeks finds, and to him who knocks it will be opened. (Matthew 7:7, 8, NASB.)

My two sisters and I get together at least once a year, and if we are fortunate, twice a year for a "sister retreat." We share memories, laughter, and sometimes tears as we strengthen our bond. We go shopping and out to eat, and this particular time, we enjoyed the awesome wildlife of coastal birds and graceful dolphins in my sister Kay's backyard overlooking the river.

All of this is fun and renewing, but the most enjoyable part to me is the time we spend in our worships together. We read, sing, and pray together. On our knees we plead with our Lord to fill us with the Holy Spirit. We long to live according to the principles of the kingdom and to be a blessing to others. We desire to perfect our characters so we will be worthy of heaven. Each of us has our struggles and heartaches. We know for a fact that our heavenly Father hears our prayers, because we can feel the Holy Spirit in our circle of three.

The Lord is calling us all to seek a closer relationship with Him. Heed His call. He opens the door and accepts us just as we are. Our God is gracious and merciful! He loves us to the "drop edge of yonder."

— Pam Byrd Reifsnyder, Class of 1967

Probability of Impossibility
To Know

And so we have the prophetic word confirmed, which you do well to heed as a light that shines in a dark place, until the day dawns and the morning star rises in your hearts.
(2 Peter 1:19, NKJV)

Peter Stoner, Professor Emeritus of Science at Westmount College, and approximately 600 of his students calculated the probability of one man fulfilling the forty-eight major prophecies regarding the Messiah. After much debate and calculation, they submitted their conclusions to a committee of the American Scientific Affiliation. Their calculations were determined to be dependable and accurate based on statistical methods.

First, Professor Stoner and his students determined the probability of any man fulfilling only eight of the prophecies as approximately 1 in 10^{17} or 1 in 100,000,000,000,000,000. To illustrate how large this number is, Stoner gave the following example. Mark a silver dollar. Mix it in with 10^{17} silver dollars and spread them across the state of Texas. The silver dollars would cover the state two feet deep. Finally, ask a blind man to find the marked silver dollar. What would his chances be?

Then they increased the number of prophecies to forty-eight. The chances of any man fulfilling forty-eight of the prophecies is approximately 1 in 10^{157} or 1 in 10 unquinqaugintillion! If the chance goes past 1 in 10^{50}, it is considered a statistical impossibility.

Peter Stoner and his students used the science of statistics to arrive at their conclusions. Statistics is the science that deals with the collection, classification, analysis, and interpretation of numerical facts or data. It imposes order and regularity on contrasting elements. Probability is the relative possibility that an event will occur. It is expressed by the ratio of the number of actual occurrences to the total number of possible occurrences. The accuracy of probability has been so well established that even insurance companies fix their rates according to statistical probabilities.

The Old Testament contains 1,239 prophecies. 456 of those prophecies pertain to the Messiah. Based on the laws of statistics, what is the probability that one man could fulfill all 456 prophecies? We know from the New Testament accounts of the life of Jesus of Nazareth, He did not just fulfill forty-eight prophecies, He fulfilled 456, a statistical impossibility.

Mathematicians and statisticians agree that it is statistically impossible to deny that Jesus is the Messiah of the Old Testament. As the verse above states, the prophetic word has been confirmed through Jesus Christ. We would do well to heed this light that is shining so brightly in our dark world.

— Dane Rhodes, Class of 2019

Love with a Price
To Love

For God so loved the world that He gave His only Begotten Son, that whoever believes in Him shall not perish, but have eternal life. (John 3:16, NASB)

Gymnastics is a very big sport at Georgia-Cumberland Academy, and at the time of this story, I was a very new gymnast. I was T-ing in a tossing group, which meant I was supposed to catch the head and shoulders of whomever we were tossing. One of the other new gymnasts, who was a flyer, got ready for us to toss her and we set … "5, 6, 7, 8." She jumped into the basket and we tossed, but something went horribly wrong.

She, instead of flying straight up, went about ten feet forward. The other two bases for this tossing group were very experienced bases, and they could read what was happening. I, being the new guy, stood there, frozen, not knowing what to do. But they ran and dove underneath her, making the unexpected flight end without any injury to the flyer. However, these two guys didn't get out unscathed. The base on my right was hit in the face and his tooth bit through his lip. The other guy on my left was hit in the lower abdomen, ending in a very painful experience for him.

God paid a great price so that we could be saved from ourselves. That is because He loves us. The above story reminds me of God's love for us. The two bases who got under the flyer and caught her, paid a price for breaking her fall. However, the price that these two guys paid is not anything close to what Jesus had to pay. If these two guys cared so much for this girl to put forth the huge amount of effort required to quickly move under and catch her, and get hurt in the process, how much infinitely more must Jesus love us to give His life on the cross for us?

God is a God of love, mercy, and power. He uses His power and wisdom to protect us from the evil one because He loves us. All we need to do is believe and put our faith in Him and He will be faithful to us.

— Indy Rhodes, Class of 2016

Taking Care of the Bees
To Love

Come to me, all who labor and are heavy laden, and I will give you rest. Take my yoke upon you, and learn from me, for I am gentle and lowly in heart, and you will find rest for your souls. For my yoke is easy, and my burden is light.
(Matthew 11:28–30, ESV)

In the summer of 2014, I went on an ADRA* mission trip to Tanzania with twenty or thirty other Georgia-Cumberland Academy students. We were tasked with building a large rainwater retention tank for a small village—so small in fact that just to get out there, we had to drive for about an hour on an old dirt road after leaving the city where we stayed. The people in this village had previously needed to walk about a mile to get water from a creek that flowed by.

The cylinder-shaped slab of concrete and metal, by the end of the week, was about eight feet in diameter and eight feet tall. We, obviously, had lunch breaks and throughout the week, our lunch breaks got longer and longer. Close to the end of the week, twenty or so of us Americans decided to take a stroll to the village's previous water provision center, the creek. The walk was only about ten minutes and shortly after arriving, we began exploring.

There was a small trail of rocks about a foot wide, elevated to about fifteen feet above the water and running between the creek and a large rock face. Most of us followed this little trail for a good while before we heard screaming from the front of the pack. At first, I couldn't distinguish what they were saying over the noise of the current.

Quickly though, I heard people around us start saying a word you don't want to hear in Africa— bees. Almost immediately I understood that the high-pitched, male screams were most definitely yelling, "BEES, BEES!"

Hearing this we all booked it back to the clearing where we had first met with the flowing water, and some of the hoard followed. Many of our group had not returned with us. Unfortunately, our teacher, one of the heads of the trip, was still back at the part of the rock trail where they had found the bees, and was standing in the water trying to defend himself from the swarming mass of African killers.

Eventually, our guide was able to get to our teacher, who had sustained about thirty stings, and direct him away to a safe place, the bus. In the process, he was stung himself, including once on the lip, swelling part of his lip to the size of a grape. We had to go the hospital after that, because the sheer number of stings our leader had gotten was beginning to take its toll. There were also two guys who are allergic to bees that had been stung.

The next day, we figured out that our teacher had left his hat at the creek. So, being the brave men that we were, four guys, including myself, returned to the place where the tragedy occurred. On the way there, I noticed something that wasn't there on the first trip—bees. Instead of actually attacking us, though, the bees were pollinating the flowers around us.

God takes care of His creatures. Yes, we will have some dangerous and painful experiences in His labor, but everything works for good. Though we had to go through a scary time of being attacked by an angry swarm of bees, we, without knowing, were helping God. The bees that had followed us, trying to attack us, had found a new source of food. God was using us to take care of His creation, as He says He will.

We are a people of worry and doubt. Maybe it isn't something like the African people of that village, who don't know where their next meal will come from, but we still worry about many things: grades, test scores, appearances. Doubt and worry are the very things that God asks us to bring to Him. When you are hauling bags of concrete, usually the bigger people take the bigger loads, so why not let God's enormous shoulders bear our heavy burdens? When we give everything to God, we receive the peace that surpasses all understanding and are able to grow in our relationship with the Lord. That doesn't mean we can give everything to God and think, "Here God, do my homework." No, we must still do our part. Though why do it with the burden of life on our shoulders when we can work with peace and love in our hearts? We can live with the understanding that even as He takes care of the bees, He will take care of us.

*Adventist Development and Relief Agency

— Indy Rhodes, Class of 2016

How to Lead
To Serve

Remember your leaders who taught you the word of God. Think of all the good that has come from their lives, and follow the example of their faith. (Hebrews 13:7, NLT)

This school year, I went to Leadership Conference in Florida. I wrote a poem about basically everything we were taught. This verse spoke to me that weekend.

As a natural-born leader, I've learned. "Jump first, fear last."
Don't let the world put you in its mold, its cast!
Example is key for the way to lead.
I'm the only Jesus some people will ever see.
Listening, as well really works.
Getting along with others has its perks.
If you want to be great, you need to be small.
It's not necessary to always stand tall.
You see your pride? It's something you should swallow.
Because to lead, you need to know how to follow
Leaders don't make themselves look good
Though the world says we should.
God says, "I will forever be with you."
Don't be nervous, just know His word is true.
God is I AM therefore I am not,
But I know I AM whom I've always sought.
Just know that Christ must increase,
And just like John we must decrease.
We need to get ready for Jesus' return,
Not just for the jewels on the crown you'll earn.
This has been a poem on how to lead,
I pray we reach out to the world, and plant the seed.

— Tova Robinson, Class of 2016

My Tunnel
To Love

Thy word is a lamp unto my feet and a light unto my path.
(Psalm 119:105, KJV)

Growing up this was my favorite verse. By the time I got to seventh grade, I had been asked the question, "Why is this your favorite verse?" multiple times. It took me awhile to really understand why it was still my favorite Bible text.

I remember to this day, sitting at my desk in seventh grade, contemplating what to write down for that assignment, and I came up with a reason that I still strongly believe to this day. My reasoning was that I had been through a lot in my short life, and I knew what it felt like to be alone. How it feels if you're walking down a never-ending tunnel. When I actually started reading my Bible, this verse became so real to me. I realized that there was a light at the end of that tunnel, and I was able to reach it with Christ's help, because He is the main light.

As a senior at GCA this year I feel bogged down at times, and confused. It feels like the tunnel all over again. But I met this new junior, and every morning we try to meet in the hallway in the dorm to have worship. There is a sophomore that likes to eat lunch in my room with me each day. I tell her about the worship we had that morning. She says it usually makes her feel better.

I know by sharing this small tidbit each day, I am reaching out and blessing her. I don't ever want to have another student feel that "tunnel" feeling. They need to know that Christ loves them and there is always a light at the end of the tunnel.

— Tova Robinson, Class of 2016

Big White Cards
To Love

Though your sins are like scarlet, they shall be as white as snow;
though they are red like crimson, they shall be like wool.
(Isaiah 1:18, NKJV)

Charlie couldn't fall asleep. You couldn't guess why. It was the sound of his father yelling as his mother would cry. It was like this every night. You might guess that yelling wasn't the only abuse Charlie's mother got. It got even worse that one time she fought back. This happened as Charlie grew up, though he'd say it didn't bother him or wouldn't wake him up.

I wish it got better, but instead it got worse. So worse, so violent, his mother never woke up from sleeping one day. Maybe you could guess what Charlie's father had done. Then, when Charlie grew up more, he went to see his father in jail. He didn't want to see him, yet there he was. He came up to the glass, but didn't pick up the phone. Charlie just watched as his father sat there alone. The look on his face was that of a stone, while Charlie returned the favor.

Behind Charlie's back were some big, white cards. It was hard, but he pulled them out to show his dad. The first one read, "You never cared." The look on dad's face looked like he was scared. The second, "You were always drunk." Both their shoulders joined in a slunk before Charlie revealed the third saying, "You yelled at me and Mom."

The air was calm, though the beating of their hearts stayed strong. The fourth, "You abused your wife." Charlie's father began to feel the closure, hating his life, knowing that he had ended a life. The fifth, "And killed my mother." Seeing his demon made the tears flow like none other. Both of their eyes flooded with tears. I guess you could say that was it. Revenge.

Seeing the brokenness of the man who killed his mother, you would guess Charlie was done, but there was one more card. What else? What could it be? Was there something else that there was left to see. As the fourth card dropped, and it didn't fall fast, the words shown broke them both as the grown boy revealed the last.

Before Charlie left there, still tearing a tad, leaving the shattered heart of a long lost father, the last card read, "I forgive you, Dad." Then he left there in the jail, those big white cards, piecing together two hearts in shards. So I guess you could say, Charlie did the right thing, to see his dad like the cards, forgiven and clean.

— Cristian Rodriguez, Class of 2015

A Promise to Serve
To Serve

For even the Son of Man came not to be served but to serve, and to give his life as a ransom for many. (Mark 10:45, ESV)

A couple years ago I made a big promise—a promise that I am eager to fulfill. A risky promise, some would say. In a way some would say I was testing God, and of course, there is room to think that. In my opinion it was a simple way to say thank you. Of course there is no way I could pay Him back for it, but by simply serving Him and spreading His gospel to people who have no resources. To go to people in other places where religion does not come as easy as we have it in the United States. If you have not figured it out, I'm talking about a mission trip.

In return for what He did for me, I would go on a mission trip. Some prefer colportering because you get the money you make. A mission trip is more of an inner reward within yourself. The satisfaction you get from serving others is like none other. I have not had the opportunity to go on one, but I'm hoping to go on one soon. Mark 10:45 states, "For even the Son of Man came not to be served but to serve, and to give his life as a ransom for many."

Of course my service will not be as extreme as the one Jesus did for me and for all humanity. Serving others is the ultimate way of being happy and it is so rewarding. I have heard many stories about my classmates going on mission trips, and the things they have said about them is all good. Giving up the luxury of our homes and going to a different country where you have no idea what to expect sounds terrifying. The whole experience is all together humbling.

— Nicole Rodriguez, Class of 2017

Joy in the Midst of Pain
To Know

And everyone who calls on the name of the Lord will be saved. (Acts 2:21, NIV)

It feels like just yesterday that I was being pushed around in a wheelchair. I had to be fed, bathed, and clothed, with minimal ability to walk. I had never really thought about how such a thing could happen to me. My eight-year-old mind didn't wrap around the situation. All I knew was that I couldn't walk. In fact, I couldn't really do anything for myself. I felt hopeless. I was a hopeless third grader with immense amounts of confusion.

After much prayer, and hundreds of doctor's appointments and tests later, they diagnosed me. I had dermatomyositis. I felt a bit of relief, but even more scared of these big medical terms I couldn't comprehend. My only option was to trust. Trust God, trust my parents, and trust the doctors. This was not the regular life of a little girl. I knew that. But I had nothing left. I had to get over this.

With God's help, I slowly progressed until everything was back to normal. I could walk. I could feed myself. I could shower on my own. It was a miracle. There was no doubt about it. I did, in small ways, *think* it was the medicine, but I *knew* that it was definitely an answer to prayer from an all-powerful God. It is because of this struggle that I came to know God. I learned who He *truly* is. I learned that He does care, that He does help His children. He puts trials in our way only to make us stronger and draw us closer to Him.

Sometimes we feel the same way in our lives. Maybe not medically, but maybe mentally, physically, or emotionally. We feel lost, confused, scared, or maybe all of them together, but we simply have to call to Him. Regardless of what we have done in the past, He will always be there to hear you when you call His name. Come to Him with anything, whether big or little, He's willing to help you through anything and everything. He will never fail you. All because He loves you so much.

— Jesmalis Rosales, Class of 2016

Hold to the Light
To Know

She gives no thought to the way of life; her paths wander aimlessly, but she does not know it. (Proverbs 5:6, NIV)

One night I walked through my peaceful, quiet house, and got something to eat for myself. When walking back to my room, my clumsy self happened to trip over an open dishwasher. I got back up acting like nothing happened, and kept going to my room. As I was walking, I touched my arm, feeling that something was there. I thought it was a fork that got bent, and I shook my arm, making it wiggle around. It started to hurt. A little farther was the door to my cousin's room, and there was a light underneath. I brought my arm up to the light, and saw a bloody knife stuck in my arm. Of course, I screamed and freaked out, my cousin ran out of his room to me. He grabbed my arm, counted to three, and pulled it out of my arm. Later on my mom took me to the hospital, and we were there for hours waiting to get a few little stiches.

Out of this horrific story, I wanted to show how when we walk in the dark, in the path of the devil doing wrong, you're really hurting yourself or others. While walking in that path, sin will get stuck on you. You may think that it's not that bad or not a big deal, but all sin is bad. God will still judge all sin the same. At first you may not see the sin, but if you hold it up to the light, you will see how it affects you and your life. You just have to ask God to take the sin away from you and He will

— Ashley Roxas, Class of 2019

The Beautiful Cat
To Love

But I say unto you which hear, Love your enemies, do good to them which hate you. (Luke 6:27, KJV)

This story is about a cat. An ugly cat. He had only one eye, and where the other should've been, there was a big hole. He was also missing one ear, his left foot appeared to have been badly broken, and had healed at a strange angle. The cat's tail was gone, and the only thing there was a stub where his tail should've been.

Every time someone saw Ugly they always said, "That's one ugly cat!" All the children were warned not to touch him. The adults threw rocks at him and sprayed him until he left. Ugly always had the same reaction. If you turned the hose on him, he would stand there soaked until you gave up. Whenever he saw children, he would come running, meowing and bump his head against their hands, begging to be petted. If you ever picked him up, he would begin sucking on your shirt.

One day Ugly went to visit the neighbor's dogs. Ugly was badly hurt. From a man's apartment he could hear the cat's screams, and he tried to rush to his aid. By the time he got to where Ugly was, Ugly's sad life was almost at an end.

While the man was taking Ugly back to his apartment, he felt Ugly, in so much pain and suffering, sucking on the man's ear. Ugly, purring, bumped his head against the man's palm. Then, he turned his one golden eye towards the man. Even in the greatest pain that ugly battle-scarred cat was asking only for a little love, perhaps some compassion.

Ugly was a beautiful, loving creature. Never once did he try to bite or scratch anybody or struggle in any way. Ugly just looked at him, completely trusting in him to relieve his pain. Ugly died before the man could do anything to help him.

I think about how that cat showed Jesus' love. Ugly showed those people in the neighborhood what it means to have true pureness of spirit, to love so totally, truly, and unconditionally. Ugly taught me more about giving and compassion than books, lectures, or talk shows ever could, and for that I will always be thankful. Ugly was like a mini Jesus. Jesus was hated by many, but He still loved them; He was mistreated, but still loved those who hurt Him. They killed Jesus, but He still asked God to forgive them. On the outside Ugly was hideous, but on the inside his heart was gold, he at least taught me to love truly and deeply.

— Ashley Roxas, Class of 2019

My Life
To Know

Hatred stirs up dissension, but love covers all transgressions.
(Proverbs 10:12, NET)

When I was growing up, I was always a crazy kid, always wanting or craving violence, or was always angry. I grew up listening to rap, and started playing "Call of Duty" games around age twelve or so, and that's when things started getting bad. I started failing in my classes, I started being disrespectful to my friends, family, and teachers, and was always having fallouts with God. I blamed everything wrong in my life on God, questioned why He made me, why He turned me into who I am, and how I act today.

A couple of months after that, things started getting rough. I stopped hanging out with my best friends, and my family. I isolated myself from the world. The only thing I wanted to see was my journal. Writing how I felt in that journal made me feel better, and got anxiety off my chest. So I started jotting tons of things down in it. I began drawing pictures of things I wanted in life, started writing poems and encouraging words to help me become a better, more efficient writer. I soon started to hang out with people again, and things seemed to be getting better. Then my mother told me what every kid hates to hear: "Honey, we're moving!"

I hated her for saying those words. I hated her so much I ran away, and I ran about seven miles straight to my aunt's house, straight up hill. I didn't tell my mom or anyone that I was leaving, I just left. Things seemed to be getting awful and horrible. I started cussing, started yelling, punching walls, cursing everyone's name that "claimed" they just wanted what was best for me. I was so distraught.

Sometime after that I decided to visit a counselor/ pastor because I knew there was no way I was going to get better on my own. After long hours and many days of debates and arguments, he read a text, Proverbs 10:12 which states, "Hatred stirs dissension, but love covers all wrong." After just reading that text, I got chills and started crying, which led to sobbing.

I was baptized after that and stopped arguing and feeling hatred towards people and things. I now had a sudden motivation to learn to love things, even when things seem impossible or hopeless for me. I still loved journaling and writing poems, even though I was learning to deal with the hate I still sometimes felt. I am learning how to let go and see the bigger, better picture in life, and learning to love everything.

— Bruce Roxas, Class of 2017

Love Is Stronger
To Love

And I am convinced that neither death nor life, neither angels nor demons, neither the present nor the future, nor any powers, neither height nor depth, nor anything else in all creation, will be able to separate us from the love of God that is in Christ Jesus our Lord. (Romans 8:38–39, NIV)

"Now that I've (insert sin here) what if God doesn't love me?" I'm sure many people at some point in their life think this. Humans are always plagued with doubt. There is a fear that no one is going to love us if we aren't perfect. But God loves us no matter what.

Last year our neighbor's dog chased my cat, Chin, up one of our trees in the front yard. I didn't notice until later that evening, and I tried to coax him down. Chin started to come down, but he became scared and climbed back up, spending the entire night in the tree. Finally, I decided to take drastic measures. I called my dad over and got a ladder. My dad climbed up the ladder and tried to pick Chin up, but the poor kitty started pushing him away for fear of being dropped. Sometimes we're like Chin, if we try to push God away, He's still going to love us.

Nothing can separate us from God's love. Life can be very busy and sometimes we get so caught up in worldly things we forget about Him. Even though we may feel like He isn't there, or we don't deserve His love, He is there and loving us always.

We will face many trials and be stressed, but God is going to love us through all of it. We might even get mad at God if things aren't going how we want them to, but His love is stronger than all the anger we could possibly have towards Him.

I think of God's love for us like the love I have for my cats. Obviously I don't have kids, so they're basically my children. When I try to hug and kiss them, they pin back their ears and sometimes scratch me. I still love them even when they hurt me. God is trying to love us but sometimes we just push Him away. Often when I come home I can't find my cats, so I search for them. Sometimes they come when I call, but other times they are off exploring. God is out there searching for us, and while we are exploring, He is waiting for us with open arms and willing to forgive us when we ask. To ask forgiveness shows our sincerity and belief that He'll always love us.

God's love for us and for the world is so big we can't even begin to understand it. Just know nothing in this universe can stop God from loving you.

— MariRuth Runyon, Class of 2019

Fearing No Evil
To Love

Yea, though I walk through the valley of the shadow of death, I will fear no evil: for thou art with me; thy rod and thy staff they comfort me. (Psalm 23:4, KJV)

Have you ever lost a loved one? Someone whom was dear to your heart? Someone so important in your life that you thought you'd never lose? Well I have, I lost my father in 2012. I was about twelve, going into the seventh grade, when he was diagnosed. I didn't know much about brain cancer, but all I knew that a lot of people die from it, so I was basically panicking. On top of that, I was going to a new school, a private one, and it's a first time experience. I was freaking out, because I was a shy kid, and the year before I was home-schooled.

As the year went by, my dad was doing great. He trained with me for soccer since I was going to high school, and I had to step up my game. But once my freshman year started, he became worse and worse to a point where he was unable to feel or move the right side of his body. Then later he wasn't able to walk.

Since my mom had to work a lot now, I took care of him on top of studying and homework, which brought my grades down very low. I was watching my own father slowly die right in front of me, and I couldn't do anything but pray. The problem was that I was always praying and everything kept getting worse. My faith in God was literally pouring out of me when I cried out to God to help my father.

So then it was time, the last time I would see my dad alive. He was sitting in a hospital bed that we ordered, and he was on oxygen trying to keep him alive. At the time he was responsive and that was a great sign, so I didn't expect him to die. But I guess my mom knew, since she sent me to my friend's house for the night. When I came back home, my sister was crying, my mom was crying, just everybody was crying. In my head I was thinking, *thanks, God, for making my life a thousand times worse than it can be.*

After the funeral and I went back to school, everyone comforted me, and I was thankful, but it just didn't change how I felt. My close friends and my mom noticed I'd changed, and so did I. I was emotionally broken, and I was never the same again. I was just mad at the world and at God, especially Him. I don't know why, but more and more people came to talk to me. I never opened up until I went to a new school and had a devotional assignment. I felt so good letting most of it out, and I thank God so much because He showed me a way that I can let out my frustrations rather than bottling them.

This brought me back to my father's and my favorite verse, Psalm 23:4. It helped me to love God again, because He was always with me and comforted me through so many people. To love God, you must always trust in Him, and He will comfort you in tough times.

— Laurhenz Saint-Aime, Class of 2017

Stuck in a Rut
To Love

But when the goodness and loving kindness of God our Savior appeared, 5 he saved us, not because of works done by us in righteousness, but according to his own mercy, by the washing of regeneration and renewal of the Holy Spirit. (Titus 3:4–5, ESV)

"You mean to tell me you spent a whole day in the fourth grade and didn't do anything but play? Man, it must be fun to be a kid."

I laughed, "Well that's not all I did, see I was SUPER good today!" I yelled with reckless abandon, "I raised my hand to answer questions, I helped pick up trash when we went to recess, and I even said excuse me when I wanted to get in line. I got a gold star to prove it!" I beamed with a proud smile on my face.

My dad glanced at me through the rearview mirror. "You know son, it's not always about what you do that makes you good. One day it might not matter how brightly the gold star on your chest shines, what really matters is what shines in your heart."

We are all sinners. It's bad, but the truth is, no matter what we do we're stuck in a rut. Everything we do to get to Jesus will not work unless we call on Him to help us out. I thought that by working hard and earning myself a gold star I had proved myself, but in reality I just showed how much I didn't yet understand. God wants to show us what we're missing out on if only we would stop focusing on how much our gold star shines, and instead focus on how much He could shine in our lives.

— Frantz Saint-Val, Class of 2016

Serving with a Purpose
To Serve

God is not unjust; he will not forget your work and the love you have shown him as you have helped his people and continue to help them. (Hebrews 6:10, NIV)

Working at the nursing home I believed was going to be a pain. The idea of having to smell human waste and work with elderly people every day really bothered me. I saw myself as a much better person, undeserving of having to work at a place like a nursing home. I viewed having to work every day as a punishment. That is until I started noticing the things around me. How everyone's face would lighten up when a group of students would walk through the doors. How the residents would become so interested in playing bingo and coloring worksheets when we were there. How they wanted to spend as much time talking to us as they could. All they wanted was an ear that would listen to what they had to say.

Before I knew it, I had created friendships at the nursing home. I looked forward to visiting with some people. The card games they would struggle so hard to remember, the interesting stories they had to tell about their childhood. It all started to interest me, and I started to see things differently.

There was one lady in particular that I grew very attached to. She was around ninety-five, but could still hear and see perfectly. I would go into her room and listen to all that she had to say, including stories of her brother during World War II, stories of her mother, and more. What she greatly enjoyed the most was reading the Bible. She would have me read to her and stop me after every verse to add a comment or clarify if she thought I didn't understand. There was one time when she asked me to summarize what I had just read so she could make sure I wasn't just reading, but paying attention as well.

I honestly thought I was going to strongly dislike working at the nursing home, but I began to somewhat enjoy it, and I got to serve others. I think all of us should strive to serve others with a joyful heart, the way Christ did. God will not forget our work and in the end we will have a great reward.

— Jonathan Samaniego, Class of 2018

The Life of Serving
To Serve

For even the Son of Man came not to be served but to serve, and to give his life as a ransom for many. (Mark 10:45, ESV)

In the past three years of my life, I've had life changing experiences at GCA. Two of those years I had the privilege of serving others through mission trips. I enjoy being useful to others and using the talents that I have in changing the lives of others.

Since I was a kid my mom has always had the dream and devotion for me to serve Jesus in my life and preach to others. I come from a hard working family. My father is a hardworking construction worker who works hard enough to pay for two kids to come to GCA. I love to work, and it gives me a life changing feeling. There are no words to describe how it feels when you have accomplished your goals and see the results it has had on the people you worked for.

I have been lucky enough to have traveled to Nicaragua and Panama and helped build two churches for people to worship God in their everyday lives. I am one of the gifted people that speak Spanish. I began to preach for the people in evangelistic meetings and for little kids in schools. My mom had tears in her eyes when she heard the things I did for God by working and preaching for God.

God gave me the privilege to be a member of the Acroflyers gymnastics team, which gave me the opportunity to share my talents with kids from third-world countries. When my team and I do a gymnastics show for little kids and see the life changing smiles, it brings happiness to our lives knowing that we cause a smile. I am grateful to be a student at GCA in which I am able to serve others my talents to others. I am proud to be a student at GCA in which I follow the motto to serve.

— Luis Samaniego, Class of 2016

God's Plans
To Serve

For I know the plans I have for you, declares the LORD, plans to prosper you and not to harm you, plans to give you hope and a future. (Jeremiah 29:11, NIV)

Over the time that I have been here at GCA I have really been blessed because of the fact that GCA isn't for everyone, and not everyone is allowed to be at GCA. I went to public school my whole life and was getting used to the bad lifestyle of the school. Many kids were getting expelled and on drugs on my eighth grade year. I was so excited for high school and all the fights and parties that were coming. My world was about to dramatically change when I learned that private school would be my new home. My parents planned a Mexico trip for me over the summer and applied for me to go to GCA without my knowledge. When I arrived at GCA, just by looking at where it was located and how small it was I said, "Oh, no."

As I look at what my middle school friends have become, many have become parents at my young age, bodies full of tattoos and literally most of them are locked up in jail. Most of my friends have already set how they want to live the rest of their lives—working at Burger King or doing construction in the sun. My past friends serve as an example to me that without GCA, that would've have been the path I would've taken, for a fact. GCA has led me in a good path to Christ, helping me become a generous person, which is not normal in today's society. GCA is a life changing experience that I am glad to be a part of.

I am proud to be called a four-year senior at an institution where drugs and fighting are not allowed, where I can find friends just like me and not be the only Seventh-day Adventist in the whole school. I gave my parents a hard time, but now I don't regret anything. GCA has taught me to be generous in a way that I give my time and efforts to serve the community, and go out in outreach out of the country. Without GCA, it would've never crossed my mind.

GCA has made me a better person in the eyes of my parents and my church. I have been on three mission trips out of the country to build a church for God and an outreach to the people who don't know God. I enjoy serving God at GCA. In the future I hope to be an international civil engineer, by which I can have the pleasure to go out and serve the third-world countries that don't have the same accommodations we have. And be a person of Christ.

It is important for us to know that whenever the plans are not going as we plan them, God has a plan set for us. God had a plan for us before we were born.

— Luis Samaniego, Class of 2016

We Don't Have to Worry About Mistakes
To Know

In my trouble I cried to the LORD, and He answered me.
(Psalm 120:1, NASB)

The summer of my fourth grade year, my father was leading out in some youth summer activities when he discovered tubing. For those of you who do not know this redneck sport, it is when you take a donut tube and ride it down a mountain river. After about an hour or so of a smooth ride down the river we came to a fork. We were told that the left side of the river had large rapids and that we should stay toward the right. I wanted to be cool and go down the left path. I got half way down the rapids and my tube flipped over. While under my knee scraped against a concrete rock. When I came back up, I called out for my dad. In a split second my dad was there. He had never left me even when I made a bad decision.

I wanted to be cool so I went down the path that I thought would make me cool. I chose the path I was told was a bad decision for me. From my mistake I received consequences. Just like in our spiritual walk with God we are told what is good and bad for us. It is sometimes clearly laid out for us in the Bible. But sometimes we want to be cool and chose what is bad. We don't have to worry though.

In Palm 120:1 it says, "In my trouble I cried to the LORD, And He answered me." Just like when I called out for my father we also can call out for our heavenly Father. My father saw my bad decision and followed close behind me. When I got hurt my father was right there for me when

I called out for him because he never left me. Our heavenly Father is the same way. If we just call out for Him when we are in trouble, He is always there when we need Him because He never leaves us.

"Fear not, for I am with you; be not dismayed, for I am your God; I will strengthen you, I will help you, I will uphold you with my righteous right hand" (Isa 41:10, NKJV). We are not perfect. We are always going to be making bad decisions. But we don't have to worry because God will never leave us no matter what mistake we make.

— Rachel Santana, Class of 2016

Always with Us
To Know

For I know the thoughts that I think toward you, says the Lord, thoughts of peace and not of evil, to give you a future and a hope.
(Jeremiah 29:11, NKJV)

Let your conduct be without covetousness; be content with such things as you have. For He Himself has said, "I will never leave you nor forsake you." (Hebrews 13:5, NKJV)

When I was in fourth grade, my father was offered a job in a different state. When he told my sisters and me that we were moving to Tennessee, I was mortified. I was a very shy child and hated meeting new people and going to new places. That wasn't even the worst part. I would have to go to a new school in the middle of the year. I didn't know any one and was terrified to try and make friends. My first day of school I hid behind my father's back, trying to convince him to take me back home. Sooner than I thought was right, I was left alone in a strange place. I had heard my parents tell me to trust in God when I am scared, and I did just that. Soon a girl about my age came up to me and started to talk to me. To this day we are the best of friends. I thank God every day for sending my friend Cassie to me that day. God never left me alone when I was in a strange place even though I could not feel Him.

The Bible says in Jeremiah that God has plans that can only create happiness in my life. I wasn't able to see the good in moving ten hours from my friends at that time. Now I see the wisdom in God's plan. If

I hadn't moved, I would have never met Cassie and the several other friends I made there.

Also in Hebrews 13:5 God says that He will never leave us nor forsake us. Even though I prayed for God's help, I couldn't feel His presence until I meet Cassie. The devil will always try to make us think that God does not care for us, but He will never break the promise He made.

— Rachel Santana, Class of 2016

Give Me Patience
To Know

Do not be quickly provoked in your spirit, for anger resides in the lap of fools. (Ecclesiastes 7:9, NIV)

My sophomore year of high school, to many faculty members, was quite interesting and even humorous. It all began with an *allegation* of me cheating on an assignment. The assignment I submitted was similar to another student, we had both used the same resources online. No matter what was said, I couldn't change their perspectives of things, because the facts showed otherwise. The decision came—I received a massive stump.

As a city boy, I had never worked on such things, so I was completely lost. Fortunately, Mr. Short came and showed how it should be done. Although that wasn't enough, because it was the biggest stump ever found on GCA's campus. The faculty members would drive by and laugh hysterically as I would work on it. After a week of hard work and getting nowhere near done, Dr. Gerard being the wise man he is, felt I had learned my lesson. Finally, I was done with the stump, although it didn't take long for another problem to arise when my father found out—it felt like it was the beginning of everything all over again.

In life we constantly face situations in which we will be provoked. That's where we have to ask God for patience. When we allow anger to get the best of us nothing good comes from that. We will do things without properly thinking of it, and every single time we do that, we've committed a mistake. That anger is going to want revenge and God doesn't want us seeking revenge. Sometimes we will just have to swallow our pride and take the consequence.

Throughout my sophomore year, I constantly felt angry with the way things happened. However, I prayed about it and God gave me patience, so that I could best handle the situation. If I had allowed the anger to get the best of me, I could have made things even worse. It would have escalated, so I took the consequence as is and had to live with the mistakes I made.

— Lucas Santos, Class of 2016

God Is Greater Than Your Fear
To Know

The Lord is my shepherd, I lack nothing. He makes me lie down in green pastures, he leads me beside quiet waters, and he refreshes my soul. He guides me along the right paths for his name's sake. Even though I walk through the darkest valley, I will fear no evil, for you are with me; your rod and your staff, they comfort me. You prepare a table before me in the presence of my enemies. You anoint my head with oil; my cup overflows. Surely your goodness and love will follow me all the days of my life, and I will dwell in the house of the Lord forever. (Psalm 23, NIV)

Have you ever felt as if God wasn't in your life? As if He didn't exist? That all of these things that were told to us as children are a bunch of fairytales? At one point I lived a life believing in all of these things. As a child, I was fearful of things. Literally, every single thing frightened me, and that I greatly disliked.

When I was ten years old I went with my friends and their parents to Six Flags. I was never fond of rollercoasters but enjoyed going to spend the day with friends. All my friends were excited but I wasn't. I was dreading the thought of going on a rollercoaster, but I decided it was time to face my fear. Everyone knew of my fear, so they were cheering me on because they all wanted me to get through this fear. As we approached the roller coaster, my desire to just run away grew deeper. Suddenly, I heard a voice in my head that told me to pray. I prayed and spoke to God like a friend, and asked Him to remove this from my fears. After I prayed, I felt so relaxed and knew that God was with me. God wants us to seek Him as a friend and tell Him of our problems. He wants us to seek Him because He is always there for us during our troubles. As He states in Psalm 23, "The Lord is my Shepherd." He is the Shepherd that is there to comfort us in times of need. We are the sheep of His flock. He cares for us no matter the circumstances. Nothing is too big for God. He cares for you so much. Ask God to take control of your fears today.

— Lucas Santos, Class of 2016

Who Are You
To Serve

For who is the greater, one who reclines at table or one who serves? Is it not the one who reclines at table? But I am among you as the one who serves. (Luke 22:27, ESV)

When you're taking part in something, do you want to be in charge or be doing all the hard work? I've always liked to be in charge and not have to do too much work. But if we look at the story of the life of Jesus, we see that Jesus didn't try to be over everybody else. He was always right there with the common people, doing the work with them. Jesus didn't go around proclaiming that He was master over the rest of us.

When He had the Last Supper with the disciples, there was no servant to wash their feet, which meant one of them had to wash the others' feet. Each man was hesitant because he didn't want to do the work of a servant. Jesus took the water, knelt by each of their feet, and washed away the dirt. By doing this He was showing the disciples that being humble isn't wrong. His example showed that everyone's job is important, and no one is to be looked down upon.

From this example, I learn that I am no better than anyone else, nor should it think so. I want to make it a goal to hold everyone as equals. What do you think? Where do you fall in this situation? Are you the one that reclines at the table or the one who serves? Is that who you want to be?

— Toni Sargeant, Class of 2019

Self-Worth
To Know

Who can find a worthy woman? For her price is far above rubies. (Proverbs 31:10, WEB)

Worth? I have always struggled with this, and I still do. Always feeling as though no one in the entire world cares for me, and that they just thought that I wasn't worth caring about. These feelings came from being bullied as a child. It was so bad that I had started saying, "What if it's true? What if no one really cares and thinks I'm worthless?"

As I grew up I started to think more on this, taking it into serious consideration. It bugged me so much that I became seriously depressed and needed help. One day I had been crying in bed asking God why people were saying these terrible things about me. I had all the intention of hurting myself, so I went to go get a razor and started scarring the Temple of God. Then I asked myself, "Why am I doing this?"

It was then that I prayed more than I had ever done in my whole life, asking God to come into my life to help me through whatever was eating at my mind, heart, and body. I was telling Him that I needed help, asking Him what I should do, asking Him if He could just send me a message, or give me a little bit of hope that I was worth something, and that I was loved and cared for.

After I'd gotten myself back on track, I went into my room, picked up my Bible, and flipped to a random page. As I read, I found this one verse in Proverbs 31:10 that says, "Who can find a woman of worth? For her price is far above rubies." I struggle to feel worthy of the things in my life but I know that God does amazing things in people's lives to make them understand how much they are worth to Him.

There is a song that is called *Gold* by Britt Nicole that says, "You are worth more than gold." I live by this song when I'm feeling depressed or hopeless. I turn this song on and pray to God, saying that I know He has a plan for me, and ask Him to guide me in whatever that direction is.

I hope that you pray about this and ask God to give you that little sliver of hope to get you through, and to never think that you aren't worth it. You were made by the hands of God, and you were made special. I also want to let you know you are not alone. There are thousands of people struggling with the same thing you are. I encourage you to talk to someone. That's what I did. I got the help I should have a long time ago, but you can get it now. I pray that you will understand that you mean *everything* to God.

— Alexx Schlapa, Class of 2019

My Grandpa Taught to Serve
To Serve

We all, like sheep, have gone astray, each of us has turned to our own way; and the Lord has laid on him the iniquity of us all.
(Isaiah 53:6, NIV)

Growing up, my grandfather would always tell us that the lamb is the most important symbol in the Bible. I remember him saying that Jesus was the Lamb of God, and that He is the only reason why we are living today. He always stressed that the lamb was important, and every Christmas each of the eleven grandchildren was given a stuffed animal lamb. As we all sat around the fireplace, he told us the story of Jesus.

My grandpa died when I was ten years old, yet I can still clearly remember his face and the seriousness, yet gentle kindness in his voice when he told us the story every Christmas night. When he died, my grandma took all of the grandchildren into the living room and brought out about five or six boxes. My dad, along with his brother and sister, opened the boxes to reveal many of the stuffed sheep that my grandpa had collected and saved all his life.

Each one of us took turns picking out our favorite two and when the boxes were empty, my grandma took the seat my grandpa always sat in and explained why he had saved these sheep for so many years. My grandpa was always a lover of sheep, and God and he wanted all of us to be able to have a relationship with Jesus. He wanted to make sure we always had a symbol nearby to help us remember that God is always with us, and also to remember the story we had heard so many times the night of Christmas.

My grandfather's favorite chapter in the Bible was Isaiah 53, but the verse that stood out to me the most was Isaiah 53:6 (NIV) which says, "We all, like sheep, have gone astray, each of us has turned to our own way; and the Lord has laid on him the iniquity of us all."

Although it was extremely sad when he died, my grandpa embedded the story of Jesus into my and my cousin's heads so firmly in hopes to help us become closer to Jesus. I know now why my grandpa did this, and to be honest, I have not thought about it in a while. God was calling him to be a part of my and my cousin's spiritual journeys and my grandfather took that calling seriously. Although he was usually a strong but quiet man, he jumped at the chance of helping us.

God is always calling people to be a part of someone's spiritual journey. It may be family, just a friend, or even a stranger. Either way, God asks us to help spread His ministry. I don't know about you, but I want to strive to be like my grandfather and influence others in God's name.

— Ashtin Schlisner, Class of 2016

He's Always There
To Know

Our God is a God who saves; from the Sovereign Lord comes escape from death. (Psalm 68:20, NIV)

When my family first moved to Dalton, Georgia, we went swimming at a nearby lake frequently. My three siblings and I loved going there. The oldest, Ashtin, was thirteen. I'm the second oldest and was twelve at the time. The middle child, Devin, was ten, and the youngest, Corbin, was nine. All of us could swim except for Corbin. Whenever we would go to the lake he would have to use a circular, blue tube.

One bright and sunny day my parents decided to take us down to swim at the lake. We finished getting dressed and piled into the car. When we got to the lake there was an immense sign in front that said to be careful because there was *no lifeguard on duty*. Without noticing the sign we parked and ran down to the lake. My parents stayed and laid on the towels on the warm sand, while we ran and bounded into the water.

At the deep end of the lake there was a long yellow plastic marker. We climbed on it and jumped off several times. One time Corbin leaped off into the water. When Devin and I got up, we noticed that Corbin's tube had slipped off, and he was drowning. Without thinking, I dove in and grabbed hold of my brother. Out of fear, Corbin climbed on top of my head trying to get out of the water and pushed me under. I couldn't breathe and had no idea what I was going to do. I was only focused on keeping him out of the water. Finally, I couldn't hold my breath any longer. As I started to lose consciousness, I felt two large arms grab hold of Corbin and me. The next thing I knew, I was on the beach with my family.

When I was in this situation, I had no idea what was going to happen. But somehow I knew no matter what, God would take care of Corbin and me. Throughout this whole occurrence, God was watching out for my brother and me, and He had a plan.

God will never leave you. When you are in trouble, God will always be there to make sure you're safe.

— Jaylyn Schlisner, Class of 2017

Serving, Not Receiving
To Serve

You, my brothers and sisters, were called to be free. But do not use your freedom to indulge the flesh; rather, serve one another humbly in love. (Galatians 5:13, NIV)

People have the natural desire to be selfish and let others serve us, we can't help it. When someone asks for help or we have the opportunity to help someone, we seldom take it. Jesus Himself served as an example for us to serve as well. We need to learn to serve people and fulfill our purpose. God calls us to serve and try to be Christlike.

Every year GCA has a mission trip during spring break, last year they went to Panama. I went on this mission trip and had a great time and life changing experience. We all had different jobs, choices to choose from. My jobs were helping teach at two schools nearby, and helping build their church. I was the only one who played guitar (that brought their guitar) on the trip, so the leaders of the school group asked me to come and play songs for worship services and class. The kids loved it, and they all thought that the guitar was so cool. Right after worship was over, I would be swarmed with kids all wanting to sing more songs. Since I can't speak Spanish very well, the music was helpful to connect with the children. I love ministering to people through music, and I did a lot of that in Panama. At the end of the trip I wanted all of the kids to remember what we sang, and taught them in class, so I wanted to give away guitar picks to the kids so that they would remember when and why we came.

Too often I feel like we forget our purpose. God doesn't want us to do things to glorify, honor and serve ourselves. Jesus was the most righteous person in the world, the only human being without sin, and He still served everyone. If on that trip I was playing my guitar for myself, and I wasn't meaning the words I was singing, I wonder what that would have looked like (not good). We all need to follow Christ's example and serve God and others in all we do and say.

— Laken Scott, Class of 2018

Love One Another
To Love

A new command I give you: Love one another. As I have loved you, so you must love one another. By this everyone will know that you are my disciples, if you love one another. (John 13: 34–35, NIV)

Each summer many kids are excited to spend a week at summer camp. It doesn't often happen, though, that the summer camp experience is life changing. This past summer, mine was.

I attended Cohutta Springs Youth Camp, and I went to a special wakeboard camp. I had coordinated it with my friends, so it was undoubtedly going to be a great week. Our counselor turned out to be a great guy, and we couldn't wait to get out on the water.

We were scheduled to spend the week at a campground on the shores of Carters Lake and our coaches were guys I already knew well: Chris Stiles, Will Green, and Mathias Tenold. It was with high energy that we packed up our stuff and headed off.

We spent the first whole day on the water, and it was one of the best days on the lake that I can remember. After dinner, the coaches decided to put on a show, so we loaded the boat with most of the kids. Chris and Will were best friends and had been riding together for years. Will was a pro and had just recently won the NCAA Nationals. Everything they did looked easy and effortless because of the many times they had done it before.

Their big trick of the day had Will jumping over Chris and Chris doing a front roll under him. It wasn't a new trick for them but it was a hard trick. As they cut in hard toward each other, they miss-timed the jump. In the middle of Chris' front roll, Will's head hit Chris' back with breathtaking force. It knocked Will out. We helped Chris pull him onto the boat. We were very scared and prayed many times. Will struggled to breathe, but Chris' CPR had him breathing some by the time we pulled up to the marina. They put him in an ambulance and then a helicopter to the hospital.

It wasn't until the next day, after we had returned to camp, that we found out Will had died. It was devastating for all of us but even more for the camp staff. Will was like family and each of us had assumed that he would be okay.

Will loved God more than anything and never went anywhere without his Bible. He was so good at wakeboarding, but he would never do it if it interfered with his beliefs. He always said, "God is way cooler than wakeboarding."

I still can't believe Will is gone. His example changed me forever. His love for God showed in everything he did and to everyone he met. He made me want to be like that, too.

— Zain Scott, Class of 2017

Staying Strong
To Know

Now faith is the assurance of things hoped for, the conviction of things not seen. (Hebrews 11:1, ESV)

As a young child, I used to associate with a lot of people that were non-Christian. We had no problems with each other, and religion was not a friendship barrier in the least. However, there were times when our opinions on things tended to differ. There were things that they did that I knew I shouldn't participate in. Every now and then we would get into arguments about the creation of the universe, and it seemed as if no one really cared about what Christianity had to offer.

Even the people I knew that claimed to be Christian wouldn't show devotion when these discussions would come up. They would keep quiet, as if they had nothing to say. It made me feel like I was wasting my time giving my opinion.

I found it hard to be a Christian in a public school environment. Sometimes I would feel alone, but to keep my faith strong I would just remember the principles of Christianity and how God rewarded people that stayed faithful to Him through times of adversity. I believed that God would continue to help me stay strong in what I believed, despite the environment that I was in.

Sometimes in life you will come across things that make you question your beliefs. There are lots of things that I've come across in my life that have made me question the validity of Christianity. However, if you keep faith in God, your relationship with Him will grow. I also believe that the way you respond to the uncomfortable and questionable situations in life determines how successful you will be in life in general. My advice to you is to stay strong and think about the big picture when facing adversity.

— Jay Seaton, Class of 2016

Who Do You Look Like?
To Love

*So now I am giving you a new commandment: Love each other.
Just as I have loved you, you should love each other.
(John 13:34–35, NLT)*

"Oh my, you look just like your mom!" Every time I go somewhere with my mother, I get this response from those around us, although this is untrue. They only say that because they haven't met my dad. I never believed anyone that told me I resemble my mom since I knew that I, in fact, resemble my father. One day as we took some of our guests out to dinner, my dad paused and took a picture of my mom and me, happily enjoying our food. I couldn't believe, but I did in fact look like her. I never noticed the fact that certain facial expressions we share or some ways of handling things made me resemble her a bit.

You see, we don't have to try to look like our parents. Whether it is our mother's hips or our father's nose, we inherit many of their physical features automatically. But how closely do we resemble our heavenly Father? When people look at me do they recognize me as His child? The Bible clearly says that the one thing that can identify us as followers of Christ is love. People will identify us as Christians if our lives reflect our Father's love.

What does this love look like? It is resting in God's peace during times of stress. It is forgiving our enemies and praying for them rather than seeking revenge or harboring anger. It is being kind and patient with others even when they are not. It is putting the needs of others before our own. By doing this, we are serving God Himself.

When we exhibit this heavenly love, people notice these qualities because they are not the world's typical responses. These behaviors do not originate from our sinful natures. On our own, we could never love others as God does. This type of love can only come from the Holy Spirit. It is when we love others, the way that Christ does, that we most look like Him. Do others see Jesus in us? I do not know your stand, but I am willing to try to live my life in such a way that others will say, "You look just like your Father."

— Ailsa Serban, Class of 2019

What Does it Really Mean to Love God?
To Love

Know therefore that the Lord your God is God, the faithful God who keeps covenant and steadfast love with those who love Him and keep His commandments, to a thousand generations. (Deuteronomy 7:9, ESV)

My walk with God has always been troublesome. I was born and raised in an Adventist family and raised in the church, so I always went to church. I never really knew why it was bad to watch TV and play games or sports on the Sabbath. My grandmother is a very strict Adventist who has read the Bible about three times and knows it word for word, but myself—I do not really know anything about God or the Bible.

I was never forced to read and do Bible activities when all the other kids in my primary school did. The only stories I really know, even as of today, would be David and Goliath, or Noah and the Ark. It is very hard for me find God in things, and I have had a really tough time trying to do so. I am not as close to God as I would like to be. I know personally that He is my Lord and personal Savior, but I do not know much about Him.

Recently, I have opened up to my grandmother and my mother and told them that I am having a difficult time finding God and that I was drifting away from Him. They have helped a lot and gave me a devotional book, *The Desire of Ages*, to read every day. I have definitely found God and have had a good connection with Him, as I know He has worked through my mom and grandma to help me. I am still in a struggle with God, and with knowing who He really is. I pray day-in and day-out trying to find Him.

The verse shared at the beginning of this story says that He keeps steadfast love for those who love him. I do love God and that must mean I have His love, which is shared among everyone. Everyone should try and do the same, for our Lord will and does work through us daily.

— Cameron Shatus, Class of 2018

Pure and White as Snow
To Love

God saved you through faith as an act of kindness. ... Being saved is a gift from God. ... God has made us what we are. He has created us in Christ Jesus to live lives filled with good works that he has prepared us to do. (Ephesians 2:8–10, GW)

A miracle recently happened in Georgia—it snowed. And not just a few flurries, but six whole inches! This phenomenon was so out of the ordinary that most of the kids in Georgia-Cumberland Academy—myself included—went out to enjoy the snow. And it was beautiful. The snow nestled lightly, like powdered sugar, on every branch and surface. The ground was so white it blinded you when you looked directly at it. I must have taken at least fifty pictures that day, of my friends and me, of the beautiful scenery, and of people chucking snowballs at each other.

But then in the next two days, something changed. The snow turned into slush, and its pristine white color began to turn shades of brown and gray. I mentioned the slushiness to my co-worker, and he said, "I know, it's disgusting to look at." As people walked by the snow, they no longer stopped to stare in wonder, but kicked it away.

We, as humans, are like the snow. We came into this world, pure and innocent, clean, simple, and beautiful. But as we go through life, we accumulate the "dirt" of our world: all the hate, all the sickness, and all the sinfulness. And in return, those around us don't treat us like new snow, but like dirty slush, pushing us away.

Only God can keep us pure and white as snow, and only God can keep us free from the "slush" of this world. By repenting of our sins and accepting Jesus into our hearts and lives, He makes us like the new snow—pure and simple. That is what everyone wants, to become new in Christ.

— Isabella Showalter, Class of 2016

God's Serendipities
To Know

And we know that God causes everything to work together for the good of those who love God and are called according to his purpose for them. (Romans 8:28, NLT)

Phone numbers, homework assignments, appointment times. We always have something to remember. There is always something pressing at our minds that keeps us from thinking about God. Maybe we remember Him when we're not so busy or when our lives are going well, but how often do we really get a break? So then the question becomes: How do we keep God incorporated into our daily lives? The answer is simply to see coincidences differently.

I remember a time when I had a terrible day. I felt stressed and unmotivated and altogether done with everything. I came back to my dorm room, put my iPod on the speaker, and hit shuffle. The first song that came on was my absolute favorite song ever, and immediately I felt better.

There was another day that had been the first day back from a home leave. I was tired and not really feeling the whole school thing, but for some reason, all day I couldn't stop thinking about wanting corndogs. I kept saying to myself, *All right, you'll be okay if you get some corndogs. You're okay.* When I got to dinner, to my delight, there were corndogs! Everyone was probably super weirded out at how excited I was for dinner, but all the stresses from my day had been completely relieved at the sight of those glorious golden brown corndogs.

Because my stories are somewhat ridiculous, it's easy to write them off as coincidental and move on. But those little victories in life aren't just by chance. Remembering God every day is a lot easier when we can see every tiny detail as His work. Every happy accident is a way to see how God orchestrates every part of our lives. See each green light when you're running late and the penny on the sidewalk as a miracle because God causes *everything* to work together for our good. When we can celebrate the small stuff, we know we are seeing God through it.

— Caroline Smith, Class of 2016

Is Your Glass Half Empty or Full?
To Know

I can do all things through Christ who strengthens me.
(Philippians 4:13, NKJV)

I have always been the small kid, you know the kid that is jumping up and down in the hallway begging for his book back, because some giant is holding it above his head. This is one of the things I hate most, and I can do nothing to change it.

In Psalm 46:1 it says, "God is our refuge and our strength, a very present help in trouble." Maybe there is nothing else you can do to change your situation, but God can do anything. On top of that He says in Proverbs 17:22 (ESV), "A joyful heart is good medicine, but a crushed spirit dries up the bones." Now I know the drying of the bones is a little much, but seriously, He's right. A joyful heart is helpful to your attitude, it's physically healthy to your body, and it's helpful to people around you.

It seems like everything in the world wraps back around to the problem you are dealing with. And it probably does affect some things in your life, but everybody has to have a weakness, that's what humility is for. If you were perfect, you would be living in Heaven.

In the end it comes down to God blessing you in so many other ways that we don't recognize because we are too busy facing the negative. Every once in a while I think we should stop, take a step back, and realize how God has flooded us with blessings and love. You can get angry and focus on the negatives all day, but nothing comes out of that except depression. So keep your head high, step back, evaluate your blessings, and just smile and say, "God, you love me more than I could ever fathom. I owe you."

— Chase Smith, Class of 2017

To Love Him
To Love

Love the Lord your God with all your heart and with all your soul and with all your mind and with all your strength.
(Mark 12:30, NIV)

If you truly love God with all your heart then it will show through your love to others and through your actions. God wants all of us to put Him first in our lives, followed by everyone else. If the love comes first, then the actions will follow. If you love God with all your heart, and your affections lie with Him, then that is what will occupy your time. If you spend your time with God and in worship, then you will develop an intimate relationship with Him. God wants us to be devoted to Him, and devoted to serve Him and everyone around us. We need to love God with everything we have. Do you think you have a true relationship with God?

There is a story that starts out with a woman named Beth. She is sitting at an airport terminal waiting to board a plane. She was there with several other people who were also waiting, whom she did not know. As she waited, she pulled out her Bible and started reading. All of a sudden she felt as if the people sitting around her were looking at her. She looked up, but realized that they were looking just over her head, in the direction right behind her. She turned around to see what everyone was looking at. When she did, she saw a stewardess pushing a wheelchair with the ugliest old man that she had ever seen sitting in it. She said he had long, white hair that was all tangled and such a mess. His face was really, really wrinkled, and he didn't look friendly at all. She said she didn't know why, but she felt drawn to the man, and thought at first that God wanted her to witness to him.

In her mind she said she was thinking, *Oh, God, please not now, not here.* No matter what she did, she couldn't get the man off of her mind, and all of a sudden she knew what God wanted her to do. She was supposed to brush this old man's hair.

She went and knelt down in front of the old man, and said "Sir, may I have the honor of brushing your hair for you?" Everyone was watching to see what his response would be.

The old man just looked at her, confused, and said "Well, I guess if you really want to."

She said, "I don't even have a brush, but I thought I would ask anyway."

He said, "Look in the bag hanging on the back of my chair, there is a brush in there." So she got the brush out and started brushing his hair. She had a little girl with long hair so she had lots of practice getting tangles out, and knew how to be gentle with him. She worked for a long time, until every last tangle was out. Just as she was finishing up, she heard the old man crying.

She went and put her hands on his knees, kneeling in front of him again looking directly into his eyes, and said "Sir, do you know Jesus?"

He answered, "Yes, of course I know Jesus. You see, my bride told me she couldn't marry me unless I knew Jesus, so I learned all about Jesus, and asked Him to come into my heart many years ago, before I married my bride." He continued, "You know, I am on my way home to go and see my wife. I have been in the hospital for a long time, and had to have a special surgery in this town far from my home. My wife couldn't come with me, because she is so frail herself."

He said, "I was so worried about how terrible my hair looked and I didn't want her to see me looking so awful, but I couldn't brush my hair all by myself." Tears were rolling down his cheeks as he thanked Beth for brushing his hair. He thanked her over and over again.

She was crying, people all around witnessing this were crying and, as they were all boarding the plane, the stewardess, who was also crying, stopped her, and asked, "Why did you do that?" Right there was the opportunity, the door that had been opened to share with someone else, the love of God. We don't always understand God's ways, but be ready. He may use us to meet the need of someone else, like He met the need of this old man, and in that moment, also calling out to a lost soul who needed to know about His love.

— Jack Smith, Class of 2019

The Snake
To Serve

It is written, "Man shall not live by bread alone but by every word that proceeds from the mouth of God." (Matthew 4:4, NKJV)

One morning my great uncle was oiling his gun before he went on a walk. Later that day we went to a viewing in town to show respects. When we got back, I went inside and changed into blue jeans and a shirt that said something in Japanese. Then I went outside and sat in a yard swing. Just then I noticed a seven-foot snake between my house and me. It was just sitting there not moving. I called for my great uncle. He came onto the porch and asked what was wrong. I told him there was a snake there, so he went back inside and got his gun, but it wouldn't work. When he was oiling his gun he had left an unfired shell in the chamber and oil got inside of it. Then something came to my mind (prayer). I don't know why I didn't think of it before. When I prayed, I closed my eyes, and when my prayer was over, the snake was gone. God had answered my prayer.

I think this story is interlocked with this verse because it tells me that I can't do some things without God's help. If God didn't help me, that snake would still have been there after my prayer was over.

Anything that you need help with you pray and I know that God can hear you. If you are having troubles in your life or if you need help with anything just pray and God will hear you. He might not always say yes. He might say no or wait.

— Oran Smith, Class of 2019

The Frantz Experience
To Know

Wise people think before they act; fools don't—and even brag about their foolishness. (Proverbs 13:16, NLT)

Headache, backache, and heartache. All pain in which some my friends and I had after an awful mistake. It was near the beginning of my freshman year, and I thought I knew it all. Our school choir was going on a weekend trip to Chase Farms. The farm had a guesthouse with a pool and a diving board. The farm owner, Chase, was an unforgettable man who was very friendly, and hospitable.

Frantz, one of my classmates thought it would be fun to take a couple of us for a ride in Mr. Chase's pickup. The pickup was packed. All seats were full.

Frantz looked back with a mischievous smile and said, "Who wants the Frantz experience?"

Of course we wanted the Frantz experience, so we whooped as confirmation. At that moment, he hit the gas pedal and flying we went. After several rough twists and turns, we drove back to the guesthouse. Some of my friends got off saying it was dangerous, while some of my other friends got on. When the last person got in the pickup, and the door shut, the cheering for the "Frantz experience began."

It started slow, but as we picked up pace, we were going dangerously fast for going off road. We we're driving alongside chicken houses that Chase Farms owned. Out of nowhere, Frantz jerked the car to the left, headed between two chicken houses. The truck drifted nearly thirty feet until we crashed against the chicken house.

Fortunately, no one was seriously injured, except for a few dead chickens. Just as we acted before we thought, Adam and Eve acted before they thought. If we think, pray, and ask for God's council, He will let us know what the right thing to do is. Don't let mistakes hold you down either. God sent His Son to die for us, Adam and Eve, Frantz, you and me. It's true, it's as simple as praying for forgiveness.

— Adriann Stahl, Class of 2018

He Has a Plan
To Know

For I know the thoughts that I think toward you, says the Lord, thoughts of peace and not of evil, to give you a future and a hope.
(Jeremiah 29:11, NKJV)

When I was in my freshman year of high school, I struggled with the existence of God, whether He was really there, and if He was there, why are there so many bad things happening in the world today. I went to church every week, I heard the sermons and they all made sense to me and I could relate them to my personal life, but I still had this problem.

Years passed, and if something had happened in respect to my confidence in God, it was only to lessen it. I was in my junior year, and I had begun to slack on my time with God. The excuse that I gave myself was that I had gotten very busy, which was true, but it was still no reason to lessen the time I spent with God, if anything it should have increased.

Nothing changed for a while until something life changing happened. I was walking in the halls of my school and I saw a girl I knew, not very well, she mostly kept to herself. People called her weird, they did not pick on her, and they just simply left her alone. Well, Sarah was sitting in the back of the cafeteria by herself as always but I noticed something different about her. As she sat a small tear trickled down her cheek. It was not very visible that she was crying, but I could tell something was very wrong.

I approached her and asked her what was wrong. She told me her mother died and she had been sent to foster care, and that there was no point in life anymore, and that it would all be over very soon. My heart fell when I realized that she was talking about taking her own life, but before I could say anything she hurried off in tears. I went home that day with a heavy heart. I knew I needed to do something. That night I prayed heavily, asking God what I could do. Just then a verse came into my mind, Jeremiah 29:11.

Just then I found her on Facebook and I sent her that text; she read it but did not reply. The next day when I saw her, she thanked me for the text I had sent her, and I invited her to my church. She started coming and soon thereafter she gave her life to the Lord and was baptized.

This experience helped her just as much as it changed me. After this experience there was no doubt in my mind that there is a God. The fact that a short text could have a life changing impact on a girl who did not know God—she was not even a Christian. I have no idea what went on that night when she read the text but the Holy Spirit spoke to her, she felt something that made her realize that there was something to live for, and I witnessed the power of God first hand. We are both now new people thanks to the power of God's Word.

— Asa Stephenson, Class of 2017

Serving Through Our Savior
To Know

You, my brothers and sisters, were called to be free. But do not use your freedom to indulge the flesh; rather, serve one another humbly in love. (Galatians 5:13 NIV)

Before coming to GCA, I lived in a small, sunny city in Florida called Saint Augustine. There are not many Seventh-day Adventist churches there, so my family and I went to a small one that was near our house. About once a month, our church would go out to an empty lot near the downtown area, set up a tent, and feed the homeless. Seeing all the smiles on these poor people's faces made me feel happy.

When you serve others, not only are you serving yourself but you are also serving God. When Jesus was put on this earth, He chose to become a servant and perform miracles for the benefit of others instead of making a living like everyone else did. He set a perfect example of what we should try to be. Of course nobody could ever be as perfect as Jesus, but helping those who are less fortunate than us still pleases God.

Also, when we serve others we show the beauty of God through our actions. We could bring the people we serve to God because they like the image of God that they see through us. Here at GCA we are required to give at least ten hours of service per semester. So in total, that's twenty hours every year. That's a lot of time serving for a high school student like me. But it's all for a purpose. The school is trying to prepare us to serve our community when we get into the real world when we have a choice to serve or not. Once you have learned to serve you should use the skill to do so and honor God.

— Jonathan Stover, Class of 2018

Easy as Pie
To Know

Then they cried out to the LORD in their trouble, And He brought them out of their distresses. (Psalm 107: 28, NIV)

It was Christmas break, and our family was taking a ski trip to Utah. Everything went according to plan getting to our condo, but as soon as we got there the snow began to fall. The night before we went out on the slopes, we got six fresh inches of snow and it was as smooth as butter. That morning we walked out of our condo, the snow was still dumping down, and we just could not even wait to get out on the slopes. Our first few runs were so great, nothing went wrong and it was some of the smoothest rides of our lives. As the day went on our legs began to get really tired, and runs started to get harder.

On one of the last runs of the day, I saw a tree run that had not even been skied over. It was tempting but I knew the danger that came with it, so of course I took the chance and went. The second I hit that mashed-potato-feeling snow, I knew I was in trouble. I hit the snow and was stuck like a nail in a board. For the first ten minutes, I tried to fight the battle on my own, but then I realized I needed help. I called out to my dad who was always somewhere near, and he took the long journey to help me.

Just as I called to my earthly father, every day we can and should look to our heavenly Father for help. As I struggled to get out of the snow, I realized that I could not do it on my own. I remembered that I had my father there to help me, and all I had to do was ask. If we are stuck in life, all we have to do is call to our heavenly Father and He will deliver us from things much worse than just a large mountain of snow.

This experience reminds me of my spiritual life, it shows me so many lessons in one. The ultimate lesson is something that every day people need to be reminded of. Life is hard, but life doesn't have to be as hard as we make it. With the help our heavenly Father gives us, life is easy as pie. The thing I like most about my heavenly Father is that no matter what we have done in our life, no matter how dumb of a mistake, Jesus will always be there to help us and teach us and just love us. Just like how like in my story, I was stuck and there was nothing I could do about it. Until I called out for help, I was stuck with nothing to do. After I called out and received help, I looked back and saw that without that help it was still possible, but it's much easier when you just take that time to talk to God and tell Him what you need.

— Hudson Sutton, Class of 2016

Answered Prayers
To Know

Therefore I tell you, whatever you ask for in prayer, believe that you have received it, and it will be yours. (Mark 11:24, NIV)

This past summer I had a once-in-a-lifetime experience: a mission trip to Tanzania, Africa. It all started in the month of January, 2014, four months before the plane would leave. I was running around frantically trying to find another $2000 I would need for my trip. As the weeks and months went on, I was making a good amount of money for the trip, but what I thought was enough turned out to be only about $500. As the time began to draw near, my biggest prayer was answered. My grandma was a big help and donated the remaining amount for both my brother and I. The trip was right around the corner, and I was both super excited and super nervous. I had never been on a mission trip out of the country, and I didn't know what to expect. Fortunately, I had some great friends and family to inform me what things would be like.

The trip was finally here, we went through all the travel to several different places, driving to Washington D.C., then we flew to Turkey, and eventually flew to Tanzania. When we got to Tanzania, I was in for a huge culture shock. The next few days were hard work, but so much fun. The trip went super well, and overall, is the best trip I have ever been on.

The major thing I learned on the trip was that God is always listening. We need to realize that just because we pray doesn't mean it will always be answered. Being patient and trusting in God is the best thing we can do. My experiences in Africa, and going through the process of reaching Africa, were one of the best ways of me knowing and understanding who God is.

— Hudson Sutton, Class of 2016

Loving All Gods Creations
To Love

Love each other as I have loved you. (John 15:12, NIV.)

To love one another can be a very challenging thing. Though, if you think about it, loving one another isn't all that difficult, some people just make it that way. You don't always have to love everyone to the fullest extent of the word; but everyone has value, and you should never forget that. Everyone's story is different; some people have been through a lot. But that doesn't mean you get to treat them any different from the way you yourself would like to be treated.

There are several ways that you can express and show love to everyone. Some ways are simpler and easier, just flashing a simple smile at someone could brighten their day a whole lot. Or even if someone looks like they are having a rough day, you could go up to them and have a small chat. Just ask them how they are doing, or if they want to talk that you are here for them. Small things just like that, things only take five or six minutes of your time could make someone's entire week.

When I was little I lived in Southern California. In Southern California there are a lot of homeless people. A lot being an understatement. I would always look out of my window in the car and see them sitting there, holding signs and what not. Since I was only five or six at the time I couldn't read all that well. All I really knew about them is that my mom would always lock the doors when we would pull up at a stop sign near one of them. She would look at them with such pity on her face, but she would never do much more than that, neither would anyone else, really. One day when we were leaving Target I saw one of those many homeless people. It was a woman in her mid-thirties. Which was kind of a rare occurrence. She was very dirty and looked hungry. My mom had just gotten a massive amount of groceries. I was sitting in my car seat, eating a box of the thin Oreos.

When we stopped at the red light, I looked at the poor lady sitting on the concrete and did the unthinkable. I rolled down my window, which I was surprised me, because usually it would have been locked. As my mom whiplashed her neck backwards to scold me, she saw I was holding a bag full of my favorite cookies. I called the lady over to me and handed her the bag through the window. With my mom utterly silent, and me smiling wildly at the lady, I knew I had done the right thing. The lady thanked me, and I rolled up the window.

There are several ways that you can express and show love to all of God's creations. It doesn't have to be in a big elaborate way. You could be five or eighty-two, but you are never too old or too young to show God's love to everyone and everything. God will love you no matter what. So there is no reason that you should not do the same.

— Jada Taylor, Class of 2018

God's Bigger, Better Plan
To Know

"For I know the plans I have for you," declares the Lord, "plans to prosper you and not to harm you, plans to give you hope and a future." (Jeremiah 29:11, NIV)

I grew to know God when I moved to America. I'm from Wurtzburg, Germany, and neither of my parents cared about God. My parents were both in the military, and so we never really went to church. Then one day they split. My oldest sister lived in America at the time and started going with this guy who treated her like his daughter. This was a full-grown man who my mom didn't know. So my mom, in a fury, gathered up some cash, got her passport, and went to America to take my sister back to Germany.

The next day this man came to see my older sister, but instead found the much bigger, intimidating mother. She told him to leave and never come back. Around this time, my grandmother had started going to church so, while my mom was on leave, she was constantly asking her to come to church with her. With my mom refusing every time, my Grandmother decided to finally give up. Finally, one Sabbath morning, my mother decided to go to church. While there, we ran into the man who had been seeing my sister. He made some small talk and left church.

Later that day at home, my grandmother said, "You know Tim is still single."

This confused my mom because he was married when we first met him. Sometime later my mother was resigned from the military and started going to church with my grandmother. She got to know Tim.

It got to the point where my younger sister said, "Can I call him daddy?"

My mother snapped, "No!!!" However, after some time dating, they finally got married and my sister was able to call him daddy. You may be asking how this led to me getting to know God.

Years later, when I had grown and was able to understand more, I was having some problems with my step-father when I realized that it all happened for a reason. It didn't *just* happen. Jeremiah 29:11 says "'For I know the plans I have for you,' declares the Lord, 'plans to prosper you and not to harm you, plans to give you hope and a future.'" And so every day I get up with the hope that God has a plan for my day.

— Chase Teague, Class of 2017

Panic Mode
To Serve

Why would you ever complain, O Jacob, or, whine, Israel, saying, "GOD has lost track of me. He doesn't care what happens to me"? Don't you know anything? Haven't you been listening? GOD doesn't come and go. God lasts. He's Creator of all you can see or imagine. He doesn't get tired out, doesn't pause to catch his breath. And he knows everything, inside and out. He energizes those who get tired, gives fresh strength to dropouts. For even young people tire and drop out, young folk in their prime stumble and fall. But those who wait upon GOD get fresh strength. They spread their wings and soar like eagles, They run and don't get tired, they walk and don't lag behind. (Isaiah 40:27–31, The Message)

Some of you know I am the queen of "do it myself," "just muscle through and get it done." Those of you who do not know me, I am a typical Type A personality. Try harder, push further, work faster; whatever it takes to complete a task.

With a recent personnel upheaval in the GCA business office I have been in panic mode. How will I make sure the department continues to run smoothly and efficiently? How will I staff to meet the demands? How will I divide the workload?

God reminded me today, in two situations, He is the muscle I need.

Since 2004 apparently the IRS has not recognized my tax returns. I did not know this until December 2013, when a friendly, helpful IRS agent called my office phone. She notified me of the issue, and how to proceed. I was not worried because I had proof of filings and had paid the appropriate taxes. However, the situation did make Christmas a bit like receiving a lump of coal as a gift.

Several months ago I hired a tax attorney in Atlanta because the taxes, penalties and interest were escalating. Panic mode set in. The attorney scheduled an appointment in June with an IRS agent and had a good meeting. She understood the situation but did not have the authority to abate any charges. I was not sure of the plan moving forward but knew the attorney was working on the situation. He called me this morning and had scheduled a spur of the moment appointment today to meet with the IRS again, in a second attempt to resolve the tax issues.

When you make an appointment there is no way to specify a particular agent. It is whoever is available when your name is called. When the agent called my case, it was the original agent from the meeting four months ago—which rarely happens according to my attorney. Today she had a partial magic wand, and the amount is now significantly reduced. The attorney and I are still hopeful to further resolve the outstanding balance.

Second story:
I went to Kroger this afternoon. I was in a hurry and dashed in and out. I stopped by my house to unload before returning to work. As I was heading to the office, I realized my purse was not in the car. Panic mode. I went back and searched the house but could not locate my purse. I had the sinking realization it was probably sitting abandoned in the grocery cart at the Kroger parking lot. Cash, Credit cards. Personal information. Imagine the anxiety I was experiencing.

I called Kroger and asked if anyone had turned in a purse? Yes. Is it brown? Yes. Leather? Yes. I am on my way. I went to customer service to claim my lifeline that had been turned in by a mom and her two children. Everything was still there. My wallet, my checkbook, my day planner. I do not think anything was disturbed. I was relieved to have my belongings, appreciative of the good Samaritan and grateful for the guardian angel taking control.

So why have I been in panic mode? When will I learn to lean on God? He has a plan but I keep getting in the way of His guidance. He showed me in two BIG ways today how He is in control. I am a very slow learner but I know God will continue to be patient. I must turn my burdens over to the One who handles all the panic mode situations.

— Deborah Theus, Treasurer

Claire
To Love

Are not two sparrows sold for a penny? Yet not one of them will fall to the ground outside your Father's care.
(Matthew 10:29, NIV)

Claire is a 14-year-old chocolate Labrador. She was a Christmas gift to Molly, my middle daughter, during a challenging time for our family. Molly and Claire are best friends and have weathered tough times together. Last Friday Claire decided she was bored, and life outside her fenced backyard was intriguing. She chose to explore beyond her confines and take a walkabout.

When I return from work, Claire always greets me at the fence with a hearty tail wag, but not this particular day. I was suspicious but thought she may be in her dog house. She is not keen on loud noises and during the day there was work going on behind the fence line. It was plausible she was hiding, but I did not have a good feeling. I walked into the yard, then the shed, and peeked in her crate. No Claire. I walked all around the yard. No Claire. I immediately got in my car and started looking for her. Around faculty circle, out in the fields, the woods, behind the dorms, down Industry Lane, out to the GCA entrance, even beyond the railroad tracks. No Claire.

At this point people were wondering what I was doing driving around calling "Claire," "Claire," "where are you?" "Come here, Claire."

When I was behind the girls' dorm, Dean Janet walked over and asked what was going on? I explained the situation, and she called out to a couple off-campus dogs that sometimes roam this area. Claire and these dogs are friends and occasionally visit through her fence. Sure enough, here comes Bella, then Ranger and even Lucky, a rare visitor to campus. I was hopeful, but no Claire.

Word spread of the frantic lady in the green Suburban cruising campus and the surrounding area. The Nesmith family joined the search, even taking their minivan to the air strip. The Jenkins' family rode their 4-wheeler through all the adjacent woods.

In the evening, Dr. Gerard roamed around on a Gator and searched for over an hour even though it was sprinkling. Countless people called, yelled, and whistled. Those who knew of the situation were praying.

It was time for me to make the dreaded phone call to Molly, who is a senior attending Southern Adventist University (SAU), that Claire had been missing for several hours. I reached out to Sarah, my youngest daughter, also attending SAU to make sure they were together. It was a heart-wrenching call. They were on the way to Vespers but immediately changed their plans and headed home. That one-hour journey was miserable for all three of us.

As soon as the girls arrived home, I briefed them on all the areas that had been searched. Molly was convinced Claire would only go in one particular direction. She and Sarah struck out the way Molly sensed was correct, flashlights and headlamps leading the way. They explored at least an hour with no success. The sprinkles were now rain, and Molly was hoarse from calling out to Claire. It was time to quit for the night. Molly was so sad thinking about Claire out in the rain, cold, hungry and potentially injured.

During the same time Molly and Sarah were searching, a group of students went to the Gerards' house for Afterglow. Before their time around the campfire ended, there was a time of prayer and Claire's safety was a subject of the prayers. Afterglow concluded and the students dispersed about the same time Molly and Sarah finished their search.

On their return to the dorm, a group of senior girls asked Dean Janet if they could go outside and look for Claire. They searched the tree line behind the dorm, but as that soon seemed fruitless, they stopped and prayed again. After prayer they walked toward the maintenance building where the buses were parked. This is an area several people previously searched, including me. It was completely dark outside but there was a light this group followed, that led them.

I was home with Molly and Sarah when I received a call from Dr. Gerard, "A group of girls think they have Claire at the maintenance building."

We jumped in the car and went to pick her up. When we arrived, it was very difficult to see because there were no lights. All Molly could see was Bella and Ranger. She was heartbroken because it was not Claire.

The girls said, "No, down there."

Someone shone a flashlight into a pit and, yes, indeed, it was Claire. She had fallen in the five-foot-deep, concrete pit used for bus maintenance. Watching Molly jump down to retrieve her companion was truly joyous. It was astounding to watch Molly leap out of the pit and hoist Claire up in her arms at the same time.

After approximately six hours of adventure, Claire was finally home. She was thirsty and hungry, but so happy to see Molly. It's amazing that the God of the universe should care about the details of our lives. But even more amazing that He cares about His creatures. And we are still puzzling over the light the girls followed to the maintenance building.

— Deborah Theus, Treasurer

Hurting God
To Love

> *For I am convinced that neither death nor life, neither angels nor demons, neither the present nor the future, nor any powers, neither height nor depth, nor anything else in all creation, will be able to separate us from the love of God that is in Christ Jesus our Lord. (Romans 8:38–39, NIV)*

We were dancing and jumping and running and having a blast. I loved to do cartwheels (even if they weren't particularly graceful) and jump off the couches when my dad played music. My brother and I would just go. I was about eleven, and he was two. As all little siblings do, he would follow in my footsteps as I jumped and ran. I was either oblivious to this or didn't really care. I was just going. I did a cartwheel, and I felt my foot hit something. That something was my brother's face.

All of a sudden he was crying and screaming and BAM! Mom was there. I got yelled at, there was blood, and the music still played loudly in the background. My parents took him to the hospital the next day, and it was discovered that I had broken his nose. He went around with a black and blue face for a while. Today, nine years later, he's fine. But I did learn something from the whole experience.

My brother is a very showy, passionate person. If he's mad, you know it—and if he's happy, you know it. He expresses himself very loudly with his words and actions. Almost every time I see him he gives me a giant hug and tells me that he loves me. Amazingly, when I broke his nose, my parents gave me more of a hard time about it than he did. He may have been a little upset about it, but the next day he was back to telling me how much he loved me.

We hurt God more than we can possibly understand. Seeing sin is painful and angering to God. It goes against everything He is. When we sin, it's kind of like kicking God in the face. We may not mean it that way, but that's how it is. Our sins nailed God to a cross. But even though we hurt God over and over and over again, He doesn't stop loving us. When I hurt my brother, he didn't stop loving me. He forgave me because he loved me before I hurt him, because we are family. It is the same with God. He will always love us the same, because God's love, true love, does not change. He will always, ALWAYS, love us no less than before. Nothing can separate us from God's love, not even our sins, because we are His family, and He loved us before we hurt Him.

— Rosee Thompson, Class of 2015

Golf, and God's Peace
To Serve

In peace I will both lie down and sleep; For You alone, O Lord, make me dwell in safety. (Psalm 4:8, ESV)

The summer of 2008 was the summer that my sisters and I were enrolled for golf lessons. We would go to our local golf course every Thursday, and practice alongside ten other kids.

Sometime during the beginning of fall, near the end of lessons, my third grade best friend (who shall be known as John) joined us for a lesson of golf after having spent the day with us. We went to the driving range, and started hitting golf ball after golf ball, as the course instructed, down the range. After finishing my basket, I walked over to John to see if he was finished. When he wasn't, I wasn't in a big hurry, so I started talking to him. As we were talking, though, he kept teeing up his ball. I didn't expect him to swing, so it took me as a complete surprise when I heard the clink of the ball being hit down the range, and only a second later felt a sharp pain in my temple. Luckily, the immediate bleeding needed only seven stitches, but even so, I was scared. It was the first time that I have had a moment where I thought there was an actual possibility of dying while I was sleeping. I suppose that the ER nurses thought so as well, because I was admitted into the ICU of the Children's Hospital at Orlando for overnight watch. This was not at all comforting, and I felt as if the staff were agreeing that I might die. The thought of death, especially when shared by others, is a frightening thought for a 9-year-old kid. I had to turn to somebody for comfort, so I turned to God. He kept me calm as I went through the day that I was in the hospital.

God cares enough to comfort anyone who asks for it in their time of trial. If you have challenges in your life, or are scared of some upcoming event, you can always turn to Him. He will take care of you, so you can lie down and sleep, for He lets you lie down in safety.

— Caleb Tol, Class of 2018

Finding Rest
To Love

Come to me, all who labor and are heavy laden, and I will give you rest. (Matthew 11:28, ESV).

This caught both of our attention in the sense that we all have those huge problems that we are constantly attempting to fix, but we never seem to find the solution. Our world may seem to be crumbling around us; we feel overwhelmed and alone. In an attempt to simplify this verse, we will put it into two concepts.

Come unto me. Those who come to Christ, come as sinners to a full, suitable, able, and willing Savior; venture their souls upon Him, and trust in Him for righteousness, life, and salvation, which they are encouraged to do, by this kind invitation, which shows His willingness to save, and His readiness to give relief to distressed minds. The people invited, are not "all" the individuals of mankind, but **all who labor and are heavy laden.**

I will give you rest. What we will find when we come to Him will be: spiritual rest, peace of conscience, ease of mind, tranquility of soul, pardoning grace, and a view of free justification by the righteousness of Christ.

Every day we must come to Him and find rest, and what better day than the Sabbath, which was made for man to rest and find peace.

— Mark Torsney, Instrumental Music Director

The Love of a Father
To Love

My shelter, my mighty fortress, my God, I place all my trust in You. For He will rescue you from the snares set by your enemies who entrap you and from deadly plagues. (Psalm 91:2–3 VOICE)

I don't remember a lot of things that have happened in my life. But one thing I do clearly remember is meeting the man who would one day become very special to me. Because of previous circumstances, I was born and raised by a single mother with the support of a very loving family. I never questioned why I never got to see my father while all my other friends spent quality time with theirs. I just continued to live my life as the five-year-old girl I was. Not long after, my mother decided that it was time to change all this.

After their relationship had begun, came the day my mother finally decided it was time for me to meet the man who would soon become my stepfather. We drove to the K-mart in Beaverton, Oregon, for this event. (I still don't know why K-mart, I'm assuming they wanted to distract me with toys if things got out of hand.) Considering the fact that we lived in Walla Walla, Washington, this itself seemed odd to me. I remember that I didn't like him; he smiled too much.

Soon after, we made our big move to Atlanta, Georgia. The first few years were rough. I refused to let him be the father figure that he wanted to be to me. I turned away any acts of love and kindness. Over time my heart softened and our relationship strengthened. Sometimes like I did my stepfather, we turn away from God. As our heavenly Father, He wishes to love and protect us. Psalm 91:2–3 (VOICE) say, "He will say to the Eternal, "My shelter, my mighty fortress, my God, I place all my trust in You. For He will rescue you from the snares set by your enemies who entrap you and from deadly plagues.".". Once I let my wall fall down, I earned a loving father in its place. The same can happen to you if you let God be the loving Father He wants to be in your life.

— Jeanette Toscano, Class of 2015

Lost
To Know

Call upon Me in the day of trouble; I shall rescue you, and you will honor Me. (Psalm 50:15, NASB)

Ever since I was young I've loved riding bikes. My mom and dad would always tell me not to ride on the road unless they were out there watching me. By nature, I was born with a rebellious spirit in me, so whenever my parents weren't around or just weren't looking, I'd go out and hit the roads with my bike all alone. I'd always be just fine, and I would come back home in one piece.

Every day I would go out farther and farther exploring the surroundings of the block that my house was on. One day my parents went out on a walk just to get some exercise, and I thought it was the perfect opportunity to go for a bike ride, in the opposite direction of course. So I hopped on my bike, and I sped off tearing up the asphalt with my tires. I was out riding for about twenty minutes, and I was having fun feeling the wind hitting me and enjoying nature when I realized that I was lost. I turned around to go home, but I didn't know which way home was. I biked off in one direction trying to find my way home, but all I did was just get even more lost.

As a little boy this was one of the scariest things in my life. I broke down crying. I got off my bike and took it to the side of the road and sat down with my head in my hands. I wasn't sitting there long till I noticed that it was starting to get dark, which just increased my fear. I got a back on my bike and started to try and find my way back home again. It was hopeless. I had no idea where I was. I got off my bike again and knelt down on the hard ground and prayed for God to help me. Right as I was saying Amen I heard someone yelling. I waited a couple seconds then I heard it again, it was my dad coming to find me. I hopped on my bike and rode faster than I ever rode before. As I turned the corner I saw my dad, and not too far behind him was my house. Turns out I wasn't that far from safety. I just had to ask for some help, and it was given to me.

— Elijah Toulouse, Class of 2016

The Blame Game
To Know

Surely God does not reject one who is blameless or strengthen the hands of evildoers. (Job 8:20, NIV)

The verse above has a special meaning to me as a missionary kid. Living in the jungles of South America, my family assisted in humanitarian aid, mostly in the forms of medical care and occasionally giving things out. My dad would sometimes volunteer at the local hospital to maintain his medical license. One time he asked me to go with him. After we arrived, we both went inside and sat down in an examination room and my dad started viewing patients. It soon came to my attention, as we were seeing them, that most had been injured a while ago and should have come sooner, sooner being at least a week ago.

One guy had ripped a shoulder muscle six weeks before he showed up. I guess he thought it would heal on its own, or maybe he thought that the local witch doctors could fix it. The people viewed the hospital as a last resort. They try the local remedies: putting leaves on boils, drinking concoctions, pouring gasoline on infections then lighting it, etc.; then, if it didn't work, they would go to the hospital. This gave the hospital a bad name since, by the time they get there, they are usually too far gone if the problem was life, and end up dying there. So if you die at the hospital, then it's the hospital's fault, not the witch doctor's. God gets blamed because they died seeking help from the right place when they died.

Sometimes I think we do this to God. We do something bad then we get the penalties of our actions so we turn to God for help. But God does not remove consequences most of the time. If I rob someone or steal something, He forgives us but we still have to deal with the repercussions. If nothing happened afterwards, we would not think twice about doing things we shouldn't do. Then when God has us deal with the penalties, we blame Him because we prayed for them to simply go away, and they did not. If you find yourself in a situation that you put yourself in, then God is not the one responsible. However, if we call on Him, He can help lead us out of our situation.

— Brandon VanFossen, Class of 2017

The Roommate
To Know

Surely God is my salvation; I will trust and not be afraid. The Lord, the Lord himself, is my strength and my defense; he has become my salvation. (Isaiah 12:2, NIV)

Deciding to come to GCA was a big step for both my family and me. I was scared about whom I was going to room with, and how we would get along. I wondered if the person would like me or if we were going to become best friends by the end of the year. Settling into my room first, I had a nice hello speech prepared to break the ice for when she came. When she did come, I chickened out and just let the adults do the talking.

Later on it was just my roommate and me talking. I found out that she is from Bermuda, where my family is from. We stared talking about the pink beaches, the clear blue water, and how much we missed our family over there. After a while I realized I had nothing to worry about. As it says in Matthew 7:7 (NIV), "Ask, and it will be given to you, seek, and you will find; knock and the door will be opened to you."

I didn't have to be afraid. God had my back and answered my prayers. We just have to ask and believe that He will fulfill. Trust in God. We can only see a little bit down the road, but God can see down every curve.

— Simone Vaughn, Class of 2019

Blocking our Connection
To Know

If we confess our sins, he is faithful and just to forgive us our sins and to cleanse us from all unrighteousness. (1 John 1:9, KJV)

When I was about seven years old, I had a hard time coming when my parents called. My parents thought I was ignoring them to be disobedient. A few months later we went to the doctor for a checkup. I passed all the tests with the exception of the hearing test. The doctor looked into my ears and saw something crammed inside. A few painful moments later he extracted a craft bead from either ear. Apparently, I had stuck a craft bead in either ear and forgot about them and they had gotten wedged in my ear canals.

The craft bead can be compared to sin. Sometimes we choose to block our connection with God resulting in us traveling down the wrong path. We might choose to ignore God because there is something else that we think is more important than spending time with Him. God is more important than anything we could possible do. He is the only one that can help us get rid of sin. If we ask Him, He will help us take sin out of our lives, but we have to be willing. The Bible says, "If we confess our sins, he is faithful and just to forgive us our sins and to cleanse us from all unrighteousness.

Personally, I get caught up in all the worldly things that I forget to spend time with God. Even sometimes I choose not to just because I think that the alternative option is better. You have to be willing to put aside the distractions and ask God to help you get closer with Him.

— Tim Verduzco, Class of 2016

God's Strength in our Weakness
To Know

But he said to me, "My grace is sufficient for you, for my power is made perfect in weakness." Therefore I will boast all the more gladly of my weaknesses, so that the power of Christ may rest upon me. For the sake of Christ, then, I am content with weaknesses, insults, hardships, persecutions, and calamities. For when I am weak, then I am strong. (2 Corinthians 12:9–10, ESV)

When Paul was preaching to the Corinthians, he told them a story about a thorn in his flesh. He stated that this thorn was put there to keep him from becoming conceited so that he would not boast. Paul begged God to take the thorn away because it was bothering him, but God refused. He told Paul that His grace was all that he needed, and His power and strength becomes perfect in weakness. Paul was then proud of the thorn in his side. It reminded him that even through hardships, insults, and weaknesses, in God he has strength.

Overcoming human weakness is not an easy task. It is definitely not something we can hope to do on our own. We need to seek to know the character of God, and His love, so that He may work in us to overcome weakness. If we work to know Him, and fall wholeheartedly into Him, we will be able to grow stronger. In striving to see Him and trusting fully in Him, we don't have to fear weakness. We can depend on God and on His strength. Every weakness and struggle that we face presents an opportunity for God to work in our lives. We can take pride in all of our weaknesses, because if we know God and allow Him to cleanse us, He will give us strength.

If we go about each day, and just spend time getting to know God, we can overcome weakness. Paul felt weak, but when he fully relied on God and realized His grace was sufficient, the feeling of weakness was released from him. If we know God and His grace, it will work in us every day so that we may conquer our weaknesses. His power will rest upon us and He will give us strength.

— Tori Waegele, Class of 2018

Love Parents
To Love

My son, hear the instruction of thy father, and forsake not the law of thy mother; for they shall be an ornament of grace unto thy head, and chains about thy neck. (Proverbs 1:8-9, KJV)

Everyone has their love, and their loves are from many different places: friends, classmates, or family. I think the best love is from our parents, because they give us a warm home. Many parents abandon their child. But if you have a good family, and your family cares for and loves you, do you give the same love back to your parents? Do you help your mom buy vegetables and cook? Mothers cook almost every day from the time we you are born. Fathers always work hard to make money to take care of the family. Do you ask you dad for spending money, but never give him money? In China we stress filial piety is the first love in our life, to love your parents. Yesterday was Mother's Day. Call your mom and say, "I love you."

Power, position, money, many things are important for you. They all build on life. Your parents give you a healthy life, so then you can pursue those things. Maybe you are the most important in your parent's life. Don't lie, don't be stubborn, listen what they told you, learn how they pay for your things, understand they work hard. I am thankful for the beautiful life that my parents have given me.

— Aimee Wang, Class of 2016

Afraid of …
To Love

I praise you for I am fearfully and wonderfully made, wonderful are your works: my soul knows it very well. (Psalm 139:14, ESV)

This summer I went back to China and, knowing that almost every one of my classmates in America could swim very well, I decided to learn how to swim.

The first day I came to the swimming pool, my teacher told me I needed to adapt to the water. Because I was afraid of water, even hearing the sound of a waterfall was scary, I tightly grasped my teacher's arm and started to go in the swimming pool. Feet first, then legs, then upper body.

When my neck could feel the water, I said to myself "NO!" and struggled hard, but my teacher didn't let me came out. I was scared and thought I would die. ... 1 minute ... 2 minutes ... 5 minutes passed ... I was still alive! I had survived my first class. Day by day, every day I overcame difficulties, and every day was better than the last day. Finally, I knew how to swim and I think that's interesting now.

Psalm 139:14 says I'm fearfully and wonderfully made—God did the wonderful work on me, He helped me to overcome difficulties. My soul knows it very well.

God helped me to overcome my difficulties in my swimming class—but not just in my swimming class—He was helping me with everything in my past life. He created me and let me be the special and wonderful person I am to Him today.

— Aimee Wang, Class of 2016

Near the Light
To Know

You, LORD, keep my lamp burning; my God turns my darkness into light. (Psalm 18:28, NIV)

When I was a child, I couldn't sleep by myself. Either I would sleep with my grandparents or my parents, because I was scared of the dark, which means I can't sleep by myself at night. When I was child, I remember a stormy night. I was sleeping by myself, and I heard something broken near the windows. After the lightning there was a black shadow next to my window that looked just like a monster. I found out later that shadow was the tree's shadow, and the broken sounds were also from the tree, but after that night I can't sleep by myself anymore.

After that happened, I slept with my grandparents until middle school, I started trying to sleep by myself, but no matter how hard I tried, I just couldn't stop running to my parents' room in the middle of the night, and I have to keep the light on when I'm sleeping. I always felt something is staring at me in the dark. I sleep with the light on, trying to avoid the feeling, but whenever someone turns off the light, even if I'm sleeping, I will wake up. I just can't sleep without lights, I won't feel safe with the lights off.

Just like I am, some people are scared of the darkness in their lives. They are always trying to find light in their life to keep them safe. I think that light is God, He saved us from the dark, but the dark is always around us. We have to stay with Him. If not, one day we will fall into that dark.

— Jiajie Wang, Class of 2016

My Cousin
To Know

The Lord your God is with you, the Mighty Warrior who saves. He will take great delight in you; in his love he will no longer rebuke you, but will rejoice over you with singing.
(Zephaniah 3:17, NIV)

When I was seven I lost my dear cousin. I couldn't realize that at the time, because I was too young. I knew nothing about death, only that he left and wouldn't come back anymore. I still remember that the day before he died, he came to my house and taught me my math homework because I had a final test that day. He was teaching me, and he was really good at math. He always helped me with my classes. He was such a nice person to me and with all the people around him. I saw Jesus in him. I wish I could tell him about myself, about how much I love him, and about how much I miss him. I didn't realized how much he did for me until he left me. I was always rude to him. If I could go back to the past, I would change everything.

People often do this. They always realize something when it's already too late. My cousin used to tell me, "Don't put your emotions on your works or on others." I think he was right. I always put too much emotion on things. That's why I always get mad over some small things with the people close to me, or the people around me. I loved my cousin, I saw Jesus in him.

— Jiajie Wang, Class of 2016

To Know God Will Be There for You
To Serve

For I know the plans I have for you," declares the Lord, "plans to prosper you and not to harm you, plans to give you hope and a future. (Jeremiah 29:11, NIV)

Sometimes in life I tend to doubt God. I can't see what's in my future and that scares me. Sometimes I am not patient. I get upset because of what God hasn't done, instead of focusing on what He has already done for me.

A year ago I was unsure of what school I wanted to go too. My best friend was going to a really nice school, and he wanted me to be his roommate. I really wanted to go by this point, so I constantly begged my parents, but they kept reminding me about how expensive the school was. When I went to academy days I wanted to go even more, but deep down I knew it would never work. I did not see all the things God was lining up for me and I focused my energy on doubting His power.

Summer came and I was miserable. My parents told me to stop asking them about academy, so I finally knew what to do. I started asking God about it. I told Him how I felt and how much academy meant to me. Surprisingly it worked, putting my full trust in God actually paid off. God actually had a plan, and He knew the plan before I even asked. He was just waiting for me to come to Him. A few days later, God gave my parents the idea to call and ask about the cost. After they did, God kept working miracle after miracle financially. Not long after that I was accepted into the academy.

God has a plan for our lives and He wants to do amazing thing with our future. We must accept the fact that God has everything under control.

— Jonathan Wendt, Class of 2017

Standing up for Jesus
To Serve

Therefore take up the whole armor of God, that you may be able to withstand in the evil day, and having done all, to stand firm. (Ephesians 6:13, ESV)

When I was in the fifth grade, I was asked to preach a sermon on the second coming of Jesus. At first, I was so scared to stand in front of a church as a ten-year-old and preach to a congregation of 300 people. I prepared, and the day finally came for me to preach on finishing the work for God. I was worried about saying the right things, but I forgot the real purpose. That purpose was to preach for God. I cried in the bathroom prior to the sermon, and my uncle told me that this was the work of God. I needed to share this message regardless of my age. At the end of the sermon, I can say without a doubt people were blessed by the message I had shared from God. I was the messenger. God used me to touch the lives of people that needed a blessing of His Word.

In times when we are afraid, in doubt or uncertain of what the result will be of what we are trying to accomplish, we need to put our full trust in God. God will take any distraction away to focus in on what we need. If we desire to do service for God, He will use us in ways we can't fathom. We shouldn't be afraid to take a stand for what we believe. As Christians God can use us no matter what we do. If we put our faith in God and share His word with the lost, we can take a stand for Jesus.

The text for today tells us to take up the whole armor of God. I believe that means to avoid temptations and sin and that is possible through God's armor, while taking a stand for Him. With God by our side, anything is possible. We can withstand evil. Satan tempts us into doing things that are wrong and unjust. He doesn't want us to do what is right, but if we take up this armor, we can stand for God and share His word with people that need seeking.

Prayer: "Dear Lord, Help me to put my trust in you today by putting on your armor. Help me avoid Satan's lies and temptations so that I may take a stand for you." Amen.

— Sam West, Class of 2016

Witnessing for God Through Service
To Serve

Go therefore and make disciples of all the nations, baptizing them in the name of the Father and of the Son and of the Holy Spirit, teaching them to observe all things that I have commanded you; and lo, I am with you always, even to the end of the age.
(Matthew 28:19–20, NKJV)

When I was in the eighth grade I went to Manchester, New Hampshire, to go on a summer canvassing job. I had never thought of going to New Hampshire. I had never even been that far north in America. I have lived in Georgia all my life, and not once did I consider giving up my entire summer to go work in a strange place. Doing God's work in a place I had never been before really made me feel uncomfortable, and I had no idea what to expect.

Touching people's lives through literature blessed me in ways you can't imagine. I had no idea what kind of people God would show me behind those doors. God put me to the test that summer, and I touched as many lives as I could through the literature I put in their hands. Books such as *The Great Controversy*, *Peace above the Storm*, and *Steps to Christ* were put into the hands of people who did not know God.

If we put our full trust in God, He promises to take care of us. Sometimes I felt down and upset while on the trip. When I wasn't able to sell a book to someone, I had to continue on. Some days I didn't make any money. But the money didn't matter, as long as I was preparing souls to enter into the kingdom of heaven.

We cannot serve God if we are not connected to God. We have to be right with God so that He can lead us to prepare people for His Kingdom. We cannot do it alone, but with God all things are possible. Serve Him today. Invite the Lord into your life so that others may see Him through you. Nothing is too big for God, put Him to the test today. Trust me, you won't be disappointed.

Prayer: Dear God, please use me as a witness for you so that I may serve others. Help me to trust you no matter what comes my way. In Jesus name, Amen.

— Sam West, Class of 2016

The Stairs
To Love

Thou wilt shew me the path of life: in thy presence is fullness of joy; at thy right hand there are pleasures for evermore.
(Psalm 16:11, KJV)

When I was little I wanted to hang out with my sisters all the time. I was the youngest, so they didn't want to hang out with me. Sometimes they did, but most of the time they didn't. They went upstairs once, and I wanted to follow them so I did. The only problem is that their rooms are upstairs and I could walk, but not upstairs, not without help. I tried to go upstairs anyway, and I fell and started cry.

My mother heard me and came to see why I was crying. She came and was going to take me away from the stairs, but I was stubborn and didn't want to go (to the living room and play). I wanted to go to upstairs and play with my sisters, so I tried again. When I tried again, my mom helped me by putting my hand on the railing. As any mother would do, she followed me upstairs!

When I think of how my mother followed me to make sure I didn't get hurt again, I think of Jesus, how He never forces us to do something (just like my mom didn't make me go to the living room). Instead God is always there to take our hand, (when we are willing to give it to Him) so He can lead us away from danger, He always loves us no matter what mistakes we make! I love how Jesus never criticizes us!

Here is the cool part about Him—He is always there for us to hang on to when we need help the most and feel as though we can't stand up and face it alone (when we technically can't). The cool part is that we are never alone, God is always there with us, and we never have to be afraid to ask for help.

One of my favorite verses that help me remember that God is there, is Matthew 14:31 (KJV) when Peter took his eyes off of Jesus and he fell: "O thou of little faith, wherefore didst thou doubt?" God might ask us that question over and over again but He is always willing to help us get our faith stronger in Him.

One other verse says, "Thou hast enlarged my steps under me, that my feet did not slip." (Ps. 18:36, KJV) These verses remind me that God is always there to help me get back up on my feet all the time! The verse from this morning is also the same. It reminds me that God is the leader of my path, and I would have it no other way.

— Kori Wilkens, Class of 2019

To Know God Will Never Leave Us
To Love

And behold, I am with you always, to the end of the age.
(Matthew 28:20, ESV)

June 14, 2015, was the day my life changed forever. It was just like any other day. My brothers and I were planning to go watch a movie. Everyone went except my brother Joel. We all went to the movie and had a lot of fun. When we got home, we didn't know were Joel was. The light was on in our basement and my friend, Andrew, and I went to go turn it off.

That's where we found him. He was hanging from the ceiling. He had hung himself while we had been gone. I didn't know how to react because no one saw this coming. My parents were devastated, and there was no reason why he did it, nothing to tell us why. I prayed and I prayed all the time after that. I couldn't get through my day without praying. Praying was a reminder to me that God was helping me get through this.

When Jesus says, behold I am with you always, He means it. Jesus will stay with us through the good and bad. There is never a time in our life that He isn't trying to help us. When Jesus says to the end of the age He means that also. Time is nothing to Him and He will be with us forever. Jesus loves us so much and He wants us to lean on Him when we are going through hard times.

We can apply this to our life in so many ways. Just like God was there for me when my brother decided to commit suicide, so God will be with us any time that we are hurting. Whether it's a loss of a loved one or if one day we just fall on our face. There is no limit to God's love. God helped, and is still helping me to this day to get over this loss. God gives us hope so we will always know that we have hope to see those people again. Jesus is coming back and I know I will see Joel again in heaven.

— Alec Williams, Class of 2016

God Can Use You Anywhere
To Serve

For I know the plans I have for you, declares the Lord, plans for welfare and not for evil, to give you a future and a hope. (Jeremiah 29:11, ESV)

When I first came to Georgia-Cumberland Academy, I hated it. I did not want to be here, and I did not enjoy it at all. I did not know anyone besides my older brother, which was not a good thing. I figured that I would get whatever reputation he had left, and no one would actually know me before deciding if they liked me or not. But God had a different plan in mind. I had slowly been drifting away from God during the past four years that I attended public school. God knew that He could use me here at GCA, even if I did not like it here. Throughout that year God slowly started to bring me back to Him. He was forming a plan that I would help Him try to get to people back home.

As I started to listen more in church and religion class, I started to understand God more and want a relationship with Him. He was showing me how I could serve Him anywhere. As my faith grew stronger, my friends back home started to notice a change in me. They started to ask me questions about God, questions that they had because they are atheist and were questioning their belief. I would answer what I could, and what I could not I told them to look up in the Bible. They just laughed and said they did not have time, so they did not. God kept using me throughout the year to show people that even if you might not know it, God already has a plan for you. One day God will reveal the plan to you and He will use you, if you let Him.

— Alec Williams, Class of 2016

Don't Know God?
To Know

This is eternal life that they may know you, the only true God, and Jesus Christ whom you have sent. (John 17:3, ESV)

I have always been the person that goes to a Christian school, vespers, and church because that's what my parents expected. I've been in Christian schools almost all my life, and I've enjoyed them. The spiritual aspect wasn't solid, and I didn't really try to improve my relationship with God. When I came to Georgia-Cumberland Academy it all changed for the best. I remember my first worship services at GCA had a powerful impact on my life. I didn't really know God until I was in my sophomore year. I remember sitting in church and hearing the music, and it was so touching along with the church service.

Do you have a friend that doesn't know God? What should you do when you have a friend that doesn't know God? It says in the Bible, "And He said to them, 'Go into all the world and preach the gospel to every creature'" (Mark 16:15, NKJV). Everyone should be open to sharing the Word of God. Jesus was born into this world to save us from our sins. Jesus wants everyone to know about Him, and He wants us to love Him. He loves us more than we could ever imagine. We should share the word so that everyone will know God.

Now that I know God, I want to thrive to build my relationship with Him. I'm very thankful because my parents are the main reason why I know God today. We should allow everyone to get to know God. Try inviting your friend to come to church and learn about who God is and what He has done for us. God loves to see us share the gospel.

— Cole Williams, Class of 2016

Personal Devotion
To Love

I call on the Lord in my distress, and He answers me.
(Psalm 120:1, NIV)

My best friends and I decided to go on a camping trip this past summer. We had been planning on going on a camping trip all summer, and we finally were going on our weekend trip. The campsite was five miles away from a public road, and it was on top of the ridge with only one campsite. After we got up the long gravel road, we walked a quarter of a mile to the campsite. After dinner and a long evening of jokes, we decided to go to bed.

That night one of my friends woke us up because of a noise he heard in the distance. The noise got louder and it was coming closer. My friend decided to scream really loud to scare whatever was coming our way. We laid there in our tent in fear. We then realized that we had encountered a black bear. The bear then started walking right next to the tent. We prayed for God to protect us. After a couple minutes that felt like hours, the bear decided to walk away. All night we laid there in fear, praying to God for protection while the bear circled our tent for the rest of the night.

In Exodus, the story about the crossing of the red sea can be related to praying to God when you are scared. The children of Israel escaped from Egypt, and were pursued by the Egyptians. The Egyptians were trying to capture the people. Moses said, "Do not be afraid, stand still, and see the salvation of the Lord." God protected the people and split the sea so that the people could escape from Pharaoh.

Whenever we find ourselves in a situation where we are scared or worried, call upon the Lord for guidance. He will be there for us and never leave us. We most pray to Him, and pray about the situation. As in the Bible the children of Israel prayed to God for guidance and He was there for them.

— Cole Williams, Class of 2016

On Your Own
To Love

"No weapon formed against you shall prosper, and every tongue which rises against you in judgment you shall condemn. This is the heritage of the servants of the Lord, and their righteousness is from me," says the Lord. (Isaiah 54:17, NKJV)

Constantly he struggles with despair and unacceptance. He is alone in his room with no help on earth. Even though he has had friends to talk to, it is not always enough. That is because some things in life you just have to figure out on your own. The sad part is that it's never easy. This terrible feeling is not necessarily just a feeling, but Satan trying to keep you as far away as God and happiness as possible. Yet in all of the dark places in his head, there is a small light constantly reminding him that nothing can break down his self-esteem. He's not aware of this voice telling him this but he'll soon figure it out.

All the time Satan tries to ruin our self-esteem. He always gets us in our feelings, making us unaware of what God has given us. This brings us back to Isaiah 54:17, which is that absolutely no weapon formed against us can prosper. We fail to realize that so many times when we are alone, that God is bigger than any weapon that Satan has made to destroy us.

Feeling alone is a terrible thing. I think we teens experience it the most, more than anyone. I use this verse whenever I'm feeling lonely or angry, especially angry. This verse always reminds me that people and Satan are irrelevant when they try to bring you down. Because God's weapon is far greater than any other.

— Jordan Williams, Class of 2016

His Love
To Love

You are precious to me, and I have given you a special place of honor. I love you. That's why I am willing to trade others, to give up whole nations, to save your life. (Isaiah 43:4, ERV)

Most views of self-image growing up aren't the best. Everyone in their life has that doubt, wondering whether or not they're attractive enough, or maybe if anyone loves them, and my favorite, being embarrassed of their flaws. I struggled with self-esteem and with learning about God's love, and now that I'm a teenager, it's gotten much worst. Low self-esteem is a thinking disorder in which an individual views him/herself as inadequate, unlovable, and/or incompetent.

Once formed, this negative view permeates every thought, producing false assumptions and progressive self-defeating behavior. Over seventy percent of girls ages fifteen to seventeen avoid normal daily activities, such as attending school, when they feel bad about their looks. More than forty percent of boys in middle school and high school regularly exercise with only the goal of increasing muscle mass. Seventy-five percent of girls with low self-esteem reported engaging in negative activities like cutting, bullying, smoking, drinking, or disordered eating.

To love God, you have to learn how to love yourself. God doesn't make junk. Okay you maybe have some flaws, but who doesn't? Everyone sins and He knows that, that's why Jesus died on the cross for our sins. I want you to know that if no one else thinks you're special, God does. When you don't see any point in living anymore or even think along those lines, please don't give up. God loves you, I promise. Do you sometimes feel worthless? Or, at times, have you been slighted or treated as though you were of little value? How much does God care for us? And how much does He value us?

Just one look at the cross will tell you how valuable you are to God!

— Makaya Williams, Class of 2018

Opening Our Hearts
To Love

I will not leave you as orphans; I will come to you.
(John 14:18, NIV)

A few years ago a middle-aged couple, whose kids were grown, opened up their big, empty hearts to three little boys. The boys had never had a stable home and didn't have a family that loved them. The youngest couldn't remember having a mother that held him and gave him hugs and kisses.

When the couple heard about these three boys and met them, something clicked. Their first thought was that they were too old to start over and raise three young boys. Their second thought was grandparents raise their grandkids all the time. The couple was very active and loved outdoor activities. They are very committed to their church and are leaders of a church youth group.

The couple had to overcome many challenges in order to obtain custody of the boys. They prayed every night for God's guidance. It took several long months of countless meetings and phone calls, but finally the boys got to come live with them. They knew that if it were God's will, everything would work out.

The boys now call them Mom and Dad, and I call them my three little brothers. They now are my next-door neighbors. When I met the boys, I knew that we were going to be very close. After a few months, they started looking up to me as their big sister. I taught the oldest one how to play basketball and he taught me how to wake surf. I love playing Dumb Luck with them, and watching the Bronco games together. At night, I thank God for my wonderful neighbors who opened up their heart and home to these precious boys. The point of this story is if we are open to believe God's promises, He will take care of defenseless children and He will provide people to take care of defenseless children.

— Olivia Williams, Class of 2017

Justice or Just Us
To Know

Does God pervert justice? Does the Almighty pervert what is right? (Job 8:3, NIV)

BAM! Invading with their many weapons of mass destruction, aliens try to conquer the world. The world watches as the armada of spaceships fly overhead. In the distance they see a speck zooming from the east. Is it more ships ready to conquer the world? No! Here come the superheroes! Superhero #1 flies right up the fray. Chunks of foreign metal fall to the ground as they punch their way to the Mothership. Superhero #2 is not far behind. Using their supernatural strength, they grab a ship and swing it around destroying massive ships left and right. BOOM! Superhero #3 jumps from falling ship to falling ship and races to the Mothership. Many other heroes deal with the aliens on the ground. The Mothership starts to tilt. It glows hot and CRACK! The ship breaks apart. A moaning-scream sounds through the ranks of invaders. Defeated, the armada turns back to their home planet. A cheer rises up. The heroes has once again saved the day and delivered justice to the world!

Today with the rise of comic books and movies, we have seen many superheroes and villains rise and fall. The evolution of these fictional characters fascinate us. We see how each individual achieves or fail to achieve, their justice or vengeance. Such as, Hero A's family was killed. Consequently, Hero A turns into Avenger to achieve vengeance. Avenger goes and finds the killer of their family and brings them to justice. But is that really justice? Today we often confuse justice with vengeance. When we feel slighted, we want to slight back. It is only fair right? However, is this the way God feels?

In the Bible God tells us to never take our own revenge. It says that vengeance is God's and that He will repay all the trespasses against us. He tells us to leave our revenge, our justice in His hands. And yet as much as we should, we delight in taking our own revenge. We count up the slights and the wrongs that this person or that person has done to us and revel in the thought of repaying each and every one of them. And yet we feel angry when we see those people that hurt us, despised us, forgiven by God. Emotions well up inside us as we see the haters, the scoffers, the unbelievers come to Christ.

We ask God, "Why did you forgive them? Did You not see what they did to me? Do You not care enough about me to punish them?" We quake with anger at this offense, at this mocking, at this injustice to us. Even so we forget that God does the exact same thing for us. God is justice and He is mercy. He will repay the ones who do not come to Him for all the things that they did to His people. Vengeance is the Lord's and He will do what is best for everyone. Justice will come one day. We just have to wait.

— Ashlee-Rose Wilson, Class of 2019

God Gave Us His Word
To Know

Jesus answered, "It is written: 'Man does not live on bread alone, but on every word that comes from the mouth of God.'"
(Matthew 4:4, NIV)

When I graduated from kindergarten, one of the gifts I opened up was a small picture frame with the verse Jeremiah 29:11 (NIV) written on the bottom. It said, "'For I know the plans I have for you,' declares the Lord, 'plans to prosper you and not to harm you, plans to give you hope and a future.'"

I had no idea that this verse was meant specifically for me, so I put the picture frame up on my shelf and ignored it for a few years. After all, I was in kindergarten.

Almost exactly eight years later, I had my eighth grade graduation. While getting ready to open gifts, I received a small stand with a Bible verse on it from the pastor of our church. The verse was Jeremiah 29:11 again.

That summer was very, very difficult for me. My parents wanted to send me to a Christian high school, but the nearest school was an hour away. We knew a lot about GCA, but my family didn't want to send me to the dorm, so the best option was to move there. Unfortunately for us, it would take a lot of work. That included cleaning up the entire house, and moving things into storage. After that was all done, we had to wait for views on our house, and, as humans, it is hard to be patient. After someone finally made up their mind to buy the house, it was our turn to go on a house hunt. We looked for a while, and we finally picked a large house right on the road to GCA. Let's just say, we ended up moving into our new house the day before my school started. It was very stressful for all of us.

One night after a couple had seen our house, and didn't like it, I realized that the verse had been following me around. After looking at the small picture frame, I finally understood. God had plans for me, and no matter how much worldly issues tended to get in the way, He would always be there to guide me, and protect me. He tells me personally that He will make sure that nothing will hurt me when I am in His hands.

Before I figured out what my favorite Bible verse is, people used to ask me. I used to sit there and state some saying off the top of my mind, but now I know. We all have some verse or text that is special to us, we just have to figure it out. Remember, whatever it is, God sends them our way so that we can get to know Him more and understand Him better. That is why God gave us the Bible in the first place, to know and understand Him.

— Isabelle Woods, Class of 2019

I Am Right Here
To Know

You will seek me and find me when you seek me with all your heart. (Jeremiah 29:13, NIV)

It was my senior year, and I had just gotten through playing an intense game of ping pong with my friends. Walking to chapel we were laughing and talking about what had happened. I took my seat in the chapel and began scanning the crowd for my girlfriend's black puffy jacket and maroon hat. There she was (or so I thought) sitting two seats in front of me. I called her name … no response, so I did it again this time louder … no response. This time more puzzled, I did it once more but even louder. There was nothing but giggling beside me. As I slowly turned my head to look to my left I see her. Sitting right next to me with a smiling face and shaking her head.

We do this God all the time. We call out for Him when we think we need to. Then when He doesn't show up, we get mad and discouraged. Instead of getting mad at God for not being where we think He should be, we should stop and look to our left and right for Him. God promises us in Jeremiah 29:13 (NIV), "You will seek me and find me when you seek me with all your heart." We need to stop telling God how and where to be, and open our hearts to find him.

— Campbell Wurl, Class of 2015

Servant
To Know

I can do all things through Christ who strengthens me. (Philippians 4:13, NKJV)

Make me, oh Lord, be Thy humble servant
Help me, Lord, not be a burden.
Make me serve You wholeheartedly
And let me shine as brightly.
My voice not be as bold

And my heart not so cold.
Make me speak Your Word above all else
And make my words as swift as winter's airs.
Then let me hold Your righteous right hand
Help me show You as the latest brand.
Show me Your Word is true
And give me even the slightest clue.

Hold me strong so I do not fall
Catch me as if I am a baseball.
Help me be as strong as a pillar
And let me pierce their hearts like a driller.
Then let me spread Your Word and glory
And give You the best story.

— Kapila Zulu, Class of 2017

Knowing God
To Know

This is what the Lord says: "Let not the wise boast of their wisdom or the strong boast of their strength or the rich boast of their riches, but let the one who boasts boast about this: that they have the understanding to know me, that I am the Lord, who exercises kindness, justice and righteousness on earth, for in these I delight," declares the Lord. (Jeremiah 9:23–24, NIV)

When I was at my old school, Alpharetta High School, I always asked myself why my parents were so forceful and tried to control everything I did. I hated life and couldn't accept the fact that I couldn't make my own decisions as a growing teenager. My parents would always force me to go to church and the times I actually told them I didn't want to go, they would always get mad at me.

When I came to GCA I found out that it's not only my parents who saw things in this light, but it appeared to be all Christians who thought like this. I thought to myself that if God wanted us to have the freedom of choice, is it up to us to decide if we were ready or wanted to go to church.

Months went by and I still thought like this. There were moments when I was at church that it just got so boring and dull, I just slept. On my way home I wondered if it was all because most of the sermons where directed at the older audience than towards what we teenagers could relate to. Maybe if they did that, it would be more appealing to us.

I was sure this was the issue and that it was just because how uninteresting some pastors could get, but in the mix of all that I understood why we were asked to go to church. I think when we leave GCA, none of us have much of an excuse and can't say we didn't learn about God, because GCA has given us all the tools we need. At the end of it all, it will be pretty hard to say we don't know God.

— Kapila Zulu, Class of 2017

Everything Happens for a Reason
To Serve

For I know the plans I have for you, declares the Lord. Plans to prosper you and not to harm you. Plans to give you hope and a future. (Jeremiah 29:11, NIV)

It all began one night when my parents were talking in the kitchen. They called me over and told me that my dad had applied for a job in America. This was very exciting for me because I always wanted to live in a different part of the world. He got the job but he had to leave earlier than the rest of us because he travels a lot. My mum couldn't get her papers sorted out early enough for all of us to move, so my brother and I would've been home alone a lot and we were only in the eighth grade.

All throughout eighth and ninth grade, whenever he called, I always asked my dad when we would move with him. I was now in the tenth grade and my mum's papers still hadn't been finalized. I decided that I didn't want to go anymore because I was losing hope and I realized that I would miss my friends too much. The papers were finalized, and my brother and I left about two or three months earlier than my mum. I told my dad that if I didn't like it after three months I would leave, and he said that was fine. But after three months were up, I told him that I didn't like it, but he "claimed" not to remember what I told him, and so I had to stay.

I hated it for the first year, and I just wanted to go back home to Zambia. I asked God so many times why He brought me here and why He's keeping me here, because all I wanted to do was leave. Towards the end of the school year, some lady from my church told us about GCA. I was interested and decided to check it out. It seemed fine and I knew I would get the hang of it, because I had already been to a boarding school for two years. I took the tests I needed to, and I got in.

GCA has made me know God more and desire to have a relationship with Him. I realized then that this was His plan for me the entire time. God knows that this is the place that I'll have the best chance of making it to heaven, and I know it too. That's when I thought of this verse and how important it is. It applies to our lives so much. God knows everything, and He does everything for a reason. Sometimes we wish we knew what that reason was, but that's not for us to worry about because the more we focus on what we don't know, and look for answers to questions that we can't answer, the further we drift away from God. The more we focus on the things that we do know about Him, the closer we get to Him and learn to trust Him more.

—Tidale Zulu, Class of 2017

To Love the Way God Would Love
To Love

Love is patient and kind; love does not envy or boast; it is not arrogant or rude. It does not insist on its own way; it is not irritable or resentful; it does not rejoice at wrongdoing, but rejoices with the truth. Love bears all things, believes all things, hopes all things, endures all things. Love never ends.
(1 Corinthians 13:4–8a, ESV)

Growing up in my household has been tough, not all the time, but a good portion of it. My parents seemed like they were fighting every other night and it was a nonstop thing happening in our home. Some nights I would cry because my mom was slowly turning into a tiny bit of a drunk and my dad seemed to not care about my mom. Some nights that was true and some nights that wasn't. Don't get me wrong, I love my parents and I know they love me. Through that one thing—love—our family is held together, and love can only be described through the above verse.

This verse, in my mind, is God describing love to humans and what love is really supposed to be like, and the verse starts like this: "Love is patient love is kind; love does not envy or boast." This part of the verse describes love as kind. Love will not be mean to others and will be kind. It will also never be jealous of other people and what they have, because you love them and you won't think negative thoughts toward others. The next part of the verse says, "It does not rejoice at wrongdoing, but rejoices with the truth." Love does not feed off of evil and nor will it ever, but instead it always feeds off of what is right and true. The last part of the verse says, "Love NEVER ends." This is the most important part of the verse. Because it basically says that once we love something through God we will never stop loving it, and we can love the way God would love.

— Anonymous

God Is There for You
To Love

When I look beside me, I see that there is no one to help me, no one is to protect me. No one cares for me. (Psalm 142:4, GNT)

My week was going terribly. I was so stressed out, and I felt that there was no one to talk to. I felt completely abandoned by God. I kept getting in trouble with my parents that week. It seemed like the yelling and punishments had no rest. Each day would start out fine as if nothing had ever happened the day before, but twenty or thirty minutes later my mom and I would get into an argument. She would get furious with the tiniest bit of something. I remember that week we were at the grocery store and we were walking back to the car. I was carrying a bag with bread and a bag with eggs. The bread bag was under the eggs, my mom told me to move it so the bread wouldn't get squashed.

I began to joke around with her and kept walking saying, "What? I can't hear you," and telling her the bread wouldn't get smooshed. She got frustrated and began to get me in trouble, over a joke. It was terrible. I literally got in trouble for absolutely everything. I couldn't breathe without getting in trouble. I felt like everything was my fault, and that my parents expected me to be the perfect child. I had no one, and especially God wasn't with me.

The more I prayed it felt like the worse it got. That week I spoke about it to my grandpa and he really helped me understand what I did wrong and what my parents' point of view was. He understood they were exaggerating it more than what it should have been, and that they could have taken it in a better way. One of my really good friends also so helped me understand and gave me advice. They told me that my parents were most likely stressed out that week. I realized that they were and that the smallest things I did would stress them out more. I then understood what I had to fix. I felt God once again through my grandpa and my friend. I had opened my eyes and understood what I was blinding myself from. God was there the whole time and I just didn't realize it. God is there for you no matter what, in the toughest times He will always be there. Even if you don't feel Him, trust me He is always there taking care of you.

"The Lord himself will lead you and be with you. He will not fail you or abandon you, so do not lose courage or be afraid" (Deut. 31:8, GNT).

— Anonymous

Bibliography

White, Ellen G. *Steps to Christ*. Nampa, ID: Pacific Press Publishing Association, 2003

Swanberg, Dennis. *Man Does Not Live by Sports Alone*. New York, NY: Simon and Schuster, 2006

White, Ellen G. *Humble Hero*. Nampa, ID: Pacific Press Publishing Association, 2008)

White, Ellen G. *Acts of the Apostles*. Nampa, ID: Pacific Press Publishing Association, 2002)

White, Ellen G. *Selected Messages*, Vol. 1. Hagerstown, MD: Review and Herald Publishing Association, 2007

Fellman, Eric. *Moody Monthly*. Chicago, IL: Moody Publishers, Moody Bible Institute, January 1986

We invite you to view the complete
selection of titles we publish at:

www.TEACHServices.com

Scan with your mobile
device to go directly
to our website.

Please write or email us your praises, reactions, or
thoughts about this or any other book we publish at:

TEACH Services, Inc.
P U B L I S H I N G
www.TEACHServices.com • (800) 367-1844

P.O. Box 954
Ringgold, GA 30736

info@TEACHServices.com

TEACH Services, Inc., titles may be purchased in bulk for
educational, business, fund-raising, or sales promotional use.
For information, please e-mail:

BulkSales@TEACHServices.com

Finally, if you are interested in seeing
your own book in print, please contact us at

publishing@TEACHServices.com

We would be happy to review your manuscript for free.

www.ingramcontent.com/pod-product-compliance
Lightning Source LLC
Chambersburg PA
CBHW051035160426
43193CB00010B/951